The Integration
Of Faith and Learning

The Integration Of Faith and Learning

A Worldview Approach

Robert A. Harris

Cascade Books
A division of *Wipf & Stock Publishers*
199 West 8th Avenue, Suite 3 • Eugene OR 97401

The Integration of Faith and Learning
A Worldview Approach

Copyright © 2004 Robert A. Harris

Cascade Books
A division of Wipf and Stock Publishers
199 W. 8th Avenue, Suite 3
Eugene, OR 97401

ISBN: 1-59244-671-X

Publication Date: May, 2004

www.wipfandstock.com

cv1

Table of Contents

Introduction

Overview. This book was written to give you (the Christian college student) both the background of ideas and the practical tools needed to develop your skills for integrating Christian knowledge with the knowledge you will gain during your years of higher education. While you probably recognize that few of your professors at a public university will share the Christian faith, you also need to be aware how your professors' worldviews shape what is presented to you as fact. Even if you attend a Christian college or university, you will most likely be using textbooks written from secular worldviews.

Early chapters provide a clarifying discussion of the way knowledge claims work in the academy, and how claims, interpretations, and provable facts are often confused. Several chapters compare and evaluate the current, contrasting knowledge frameworks (philosophical naturalism, postmodernism, and Christianity), presenting the Christian worldview as the most complete, rational, and accurate representation of all reality. Chapters on "Joining Faith and Learning" and "A Taxonomy for Worldview Integration" provide you with tools, examples, and situations that will enable you to work out the practical aspects of integration in various situations.

Outline. Chapter 1 sets up the background for integrating faith and learning by stressing the nature of knowledge itself. A major source of the apparent conflict between Christian knowledge and some of the knowledge claims promoted in many universities is that the knowledge comes from different theories about what counts as knowledge.

Chapter 2 argues that integrating faith and learning is crucial for the Christian student and scholar. Christian knowledge must not be compartmentalized but must be connected to all other knowledge to produce the most comprehensive and reasonable view of all existence.

Chapter 3 discusses the impact of an individual's worldview and theory of knowledge on how each person sees and interprets reality. Worldviews can even affect the way we process information, causing us to apply biased standards and subjective interpretations, and one's theory of knowledge influences which ideas are accepted as true and which are rejected as false.

Chapter 4 shows that personal political commitments, the politics of power, and social factors all influence which ideas are promoted and which are neglected or even marginalized. Whether in individual departments or entire scholarly communities, many factors other than the pure pursuit of truth are involved in the advancement of knowledge claims.

Chapter 5 discusses the foundational, untestable beliefs that underlie everyone's view of reality and how they influence our experience and thinking. Many in the academy exclude God at the outset as a philosophical preference, and this exclusion impacts their processing of information and truth claims. On the other hand, including God as part of one's basic beliefs is actually more rational and provides the basis for a better explanation of reality.

Chapter 6 provides a more detailed look at scientific naturalism and what its core beliefs and assumptions are. Included in the discussion are the limitations of this view for explaining the complete picture of reality, the value of genuine science, and the problems created by equating science and materialist metaphysics.

Chapter 7 lays out the basic beliefs and practices of postmodernism, offering a brief history of its origins and its complications. Examples of postmodernist thought are presented to show their hostility to Christian truth. Also discussed is how postmodernism has created its appeal by rebelling against the excesses of scientism and by producing ideas that seem plausible on the surface.

Chapter 8 discusses the generally accepted Christian worldview. Biblical authority is stressed, together with the caution that life is a process of understanding God's word. The chapter compares the Christian worldview to those of naturalism and postmodernism along several dimensions.

Chapter 9 offers several criteria for evaluating worldviews, and then examines naturalism, postmodernism, and Christianity in light of these criteria. The chapter also discusses how to think about knowledge claims, how to analyze claims for fallacies, and how to differentiate between reasonable exposition and ideological dogma.

Chapter 10 defines the beginning practical steps to integration and how to put your learning and faith together in meaningful ways. Included is a discussion of the two-way street of learning: Faith informs learning and learning informs faith.

Chapter 11 provides a paradigm that you can use to make specific connections between your faith and the subject matter of your studies. The tools provided allow you to discover where the knowledge claims have originated, what is behind them, and how to separate out the truth.

Chapter 12 encourages you to become the best scholar you can. We need a Christian intelligentsia to take its place in the marketplace of ideas and to speak powerfully for the truth.

Acknowledgements. Many people helped to make this book a reality. Thanks to David Root, my editor at Cascade, for his helpful ideas and suggestions; and to Jim Tedrick, general manager at Wipf and Stock. I appreciate the feedback and enthusiasm of readers of the manuscript, including Brett Peterson, Patrick Rist, Gary Ramm, Paul Gould, Abby Nye, David Mitchell, and A. S. A. Jones. Thanks to my agent, Les Stobbe, for his encouragement. I am especially grateful to Phil Robinette for the many conversations we've had about this book and its content and his constant support for the project. And my special gratitude goes to my wife Rita, who literally made this book possible by allowing me the time (and book buying) I needed to research, read, and write.

2 | 10

Chapter 1
Backgrounds to Integration

The word integration means to form or blend into a whole, to unite. The human intellect naturally seeks to find the unity that is behind diversity and, in fact, coherence is an important mark of rationality. In conceptual integration, one's theological beliefs are blended and unified with propositions judged to be justifiably believed as true from other sources into a coherent, intellectually satisfying world view. One of the goals or results of integration is to maintain or increase both the conceptual relevance of and epistemological justification for Christian theism.
> — J. P. Moreland[1]

Faith is exercised in light of all that we know and believe to be true. Consequently, what we believe intellectually is extremely important.
> — Michael L. Peterson[2]

1.1 An Overview of the Integration of Faith and Learning

The integration of faith and learning is not a strange, quaint, or unusual process, nor even one that is unique to Christianity. The integration of learning (or knowledge) is an activity performed by everyone who understands the need for a coherent worldview, by everyone who knows that believing conflicting claims is not reasonable. Some Eastern philosophies hold that believing two or more contradictory things is acceptable, but most of us want to understand the world of knowledge and the world itself as a rational and coherent whole. To do so, we must incorporate or integrate new knowledge of any kind into the structure of our current knowledge. Further, if we understand "faith" in the broadest way, as the set of basic beliefs, preferences, and presuppositions that guide our lives, then everyone—religious or not—practices the integration of faith and learning, too. We all want our beliefs about reality to be consistent with all that we learn and experience.

Integrating Knowledge. Every time we learn something, we engage in the process of integrating knowledge, for integration is the process of connecting knowledge with knowledge—connecting facts, ideas, and other information together in a way that unifies them. Every time we encounter a new claim about knowledge, we work on integrating it into our overall knowledge. Knowing what we already do, how does the new claim fit in? Integration, then, is the process of fitting new knowledge in with existing knowledge, a process of coherence making, done naturally, every day whenever new information or knowledge claims are presented to us. Since every person's store of existing knowledge is unique and individual, so is the process of integration.

The two essential requirements for successful integration are consistency and coherence. You probably recognize these as two skills involved in any critical thinking activity.

- *Consistency.* The new knowledge must be consistent with what we already know. There must not be a conflict between the claims. Contradictory ideas cannot both be true in the same way. If there is a conflict, either the new knowledge claim must be adjusted, reinterpreted, or rejected, or what is already known must be adjusted, reinterpreted, or rejected.
- *Coherence.* One's entire set of knowledge must fit together into a unified whole. Our overall view of reality must make sense as a more or less harmonious, interrelated set of ideas. Our view of reality comes not only from facts we learn but through observation, experience, reason, interpretation, and even basic assumptions about the world, ourselves, and others.

Significantly, then, for every thoughtful person claims about new knowledge are not accepted immediately and as presented, but are first tested against current knowledge and against beliefs about, for example, what is possible, what is likely, and what is compatible with one's other knowledge. When someone tells you a story that seems hard to believe, you may conclude that it is a "tall tale" rather than a description of fact. This conclusion is the result of your automatic integrative process. The story fails the consistency test by making claims beyond what you know or believe to be true or possible.

Types of Integration. Our efforts to bring harmony and consistency to our whole stock of knowledge include several activities.

- *Connecting knowledge with knowledge.* As already mentioned, here a new knowledge claim is brought into play with currently held knowledge to see how everything fits. The new claim may be accepted, rejected, adjusted, or "put on the shelf" until later when sense can be made of it (that is, when it can be successfully integrated). And sometimes, current knowledge must be adjusted in light of the new.

- *Connecting knowledge from one area with knowledge in another area.* Discoveries or theories from one area of learning can influence our thinking in another area. The findings about brain chemistry, for example, may influence theories in psychology about human behavior and motivation. New discoveries in history may change the way political scientists view the actions of past governments.

- *Connecting knowledge with one's larger beliefs about the world.* In the process of finding coherence, we bring to bear our beliefs about how rational the world is, what is possible to exist, what human nature is like, and so forth.

- *Connecting knowledge with one's basic presuppositions and values.* Sorting out how one's basic beliefs fit in with one's personal experience is the integrative process of finding meaning in life. When, in addition to asking, "What is it?" or "What happened?" you ask, "What does it all mean?" then you are working on this integrative issue. Discovering the What of life gives us knowledge, while discovering the So What of life gives us wisdom.

Integrating Faith and Learning. Christians perform the same kinds of integrative tasks as those described above, with the crucial addition of Christian knowledge, based on Biblical authority, as both a part and the ultimate test of all other knowledge. When we look for consistency and coherence in our knowledge, we do so within a Biblical framework. Christian faith is both a type of knowledge (a set of truth propositions) and a worldview (an interpretive framework for creating understanding and making sense of all reality). The assumptions behind the integration of faith and learning are these:

- *All truth is God's truth.* Christian knowledge (Biblical teaching, belief in God, human nature as fallen but redeemable, etc.) should not be considered a separate realm of truth or reality, but as a vital and clarifying part of the whole of reality. Christian knowledge must be part of the entire integrative database.
- *There is no conflict between God's truth and other truth.* Conflicts arise when true meets false, or more commonly, when there are incompatible interpretations, presuppositions, preferences, and worldviews. The most common work in the faith and learning area is that of integrating apparently conflicting interpretations rather than apparently conflicting facts.
- *Secular learning is incomplete and often distorted.* The worldview of philosophical naturalism, which limits all reality to the material world, is inadequate to explain all of existence because of its truncated coverage. The worldview of postmodernism is defeated by its basis in relativism and its abandonment of transcendent meanings. Only the Christian worldview supplies a complete, objective, and rational explanation for all of existence.
- *Christian integration is based on a "Biblical framework of reality."*[3] This framework functions as an objective measure of all knowledge claims, a touchstone against

which all claims to truth are tested. Biblical authority is the starting point. The clear implication here is the crucial importance of good hermeneutics—the skillful and accurate interpretation of the Biblical text.

- *Truth is the most important goal of learning.* The goal of integrating faith and learning is the development of a coherent, unified system of understanding, a full knowledge and harmony of all truth. Truth must take precedence over politics, ideology, and wishful thinking.

Intentionality Needed. The integration of faith and learning is such an important topic largely because, even though it is talked about extensively, too little of it seems to occur. The bias in the academy and in the larger culture against Christian truth and Biblical authority has had the effect of disconnecting Christian knowledge from other knowledge, even in the minds of some Christians. The positioning of worldviews like naturalism and postmodernism as the only way to understand the world presents further challenges because of the bias they inject into the arena of learning. For these reasons, integration must be undertaken with deliberateness. Christians must be intentional about making the connections between their faith and the knowledge claims they encounter and careful to keep the Biblical framework in the foreground as the structuring principle of truth.

In sum, successful integration of faith and learning depends on a thorough, accurate, and carefully thought through understanding of the Bible, together with a good understanding of how academic knowledge claims are made and the worldviews underlying those claims. Skillful interpretation in both areas is a key factor.

1.2 The Search for True Knowledge

When Pilate asked Jesus, perhaps sarcastically, "What is truth?" he asked one of the most important questions anyone can entertain. And during the two thousand years since he asked it, the question has become enormously more important. As you will discover in the chapters that follow, how this question is answered, who has the cultural authority to define its meaning, and what the criteria are for an acceptable answer—these and their related issues are fundamental to shaping culture, science, civilization, and even religious faith. As individuals, what we know—or think we know—to be true shapes our outlook, our goals, our behavior, and our happiness. The ideas a society considers to be true (as well as those it considers to be false) influence the society's views about justice, morality, the value of human life, and so on. A society's implied answers to the question, "What is truth?" are written into nearly every law that governs our behavior.

If you are attending a university (or thinking about it), no doubt a major reason for doing so is to gain knowledge that you will be able to use, not only in a career but in filling out your awareness of the world, helping you to make better decisions, and improving your philosophy of life. And, as a Christian, you want your learning to help you to grow closer to God and to bring you a better understanding of his ways and his world. That's what higher education or higher learning is all about. But here we already have a problem. It is impossible even to think about integrating faith and learning until we understand what learning really is. What does learning consist of? Just how did this stuff called "knowledge" that is to be learned come to be in the first place? What is the relationship between learning and knowledge and truth? Only after we ask and appropriately answer questions like these can the process of integration proceed wisely and effectively.

Some people have an understanding of education that goes something like this. "Truth, well that's facts instead of just opinions or wrong information. And lots of facts make up knowledge. So if you memorize many facts—which is what we call learning—then you have a bunch of knowledge and that's education." The equation is seamless, it seems: Truth = facts = knowledge = learning = education. Using this view, integrating faith and learning will be a process of figuring out how this learning fits in with one's faith, or more commonly, how one's faith fits in with this new knowledge. What's wrong with that?

The short answer, which we will explore at length later on, is that knowledge consists of much more than facts. Something has to be done with facts in order to produce knowledge. "Let the facts speak for themselves" is one of the fallacies of an uninformed view of knowledge. Every fact, in other words, is interpreted through a person. Even whether something is or is not a fact belongs to the realm of interpretation. Knowledge involves meaning, a relationship to facts, and thus meaning lies outside of facts. An old joke will clarify this point.

> A man trained a flea to jump whenever a bell was rung. The man wanted to see how deeply the flea was conditioned, so he began to pull the legs off the flea one at a time. Each time, however, the flea still jumped when the bell was rung. Finally, the man pulled the last leg off the flea. He rang the bell repeatedly, but the flea didn't move. The man concluded, "When all of the legs are pulled off a flea, it can no longer hear."[4]

Of course, this is a joke because no one would actually make such a conclusion, but the story vividly points out that knowledge is often the result of much more than a collection of objective facts tied with a bow. Knowledge is usually the result of facts subjected to analysis, inference, and interpretation, influenced by assumptions, presuppositions, theoretical concerns and methodological constraints—and even philosophical preferences.

In their classic work, *How to Read a Book*, Mortimer Adler and Charles Van Doren remark on the sometimes problematic nature of facts in their "Third Stage of Analytical Reading":

> You cannot read for information intelligently without determining what significance is, or should be, attached to the facts presented. Facts seldom come to us without some interpretation, explicit or implied. This is especially true if you are reading digests of information that necessarily select the facts according to some evaluation of their significance, some principle of interpretation.[5]

Adler and Van Doren later make the point that while facts that do indeed reflect reality cannot change, other facts "are to some extent conventional" in the sense that "propositions that are considered to be facts in one epoch are no longer considered to be facts in another."[6] Because we are fallible as discoverers and interpreters, sometimes what we thought was knowledge turns out to have been wrong. We thought we knew something, but now we know better. What we thought was knowledge was really only a wrong belief.

1.3 Knowledge Versus Belief

If you have ever taken a speech class or read very much in the opinion pages of the newspaper, you'll be aware that some writers and speakers "win" their arguments, or at least score debating points, by carefully defining their terms in ways that favor their point of view. If, for example, "mental processes" are defined as "thoughts of which we are aware and can understand," why then, there is, by definition, no such thing as unconscious mental processes. That may be an extreme example (the example, in fact, commits the fallacy of begging the question), but you can see that the definition of a word can influence the outcome of an argument.

For our interest in integration, it is important to understand how some relevant words are defined, and by whom, lest we unknowingly meet a Humpty Dumpty:

> "When I use a word," Humpty Dumpty said in rather a scornful tone, "it means just what I choose it to mean—neither more nor less."
> "The question is," said Alice, "whether you *can* make words mean different things."
> "The question is," said Humpty Dumpty, "which is to be master—that's all."[7]

In order to avoid confusion, then, let's define three important words: truth, knowledge, and belief. These will be working definitions and we will be talking about these ideas more in later chapters as well.

Truth we will define as a correct account of reality, what really *is* the case, or the way things *really* are. As Christians we believe that some truths are absolute and unchanging ("God created the heavens and the earth"), while other truths can change ("The temperature is 71 degrees" may be true right now, but not true this evening). When Jesus says, "You shall know the truth," he doesn't mean that he will tell us a fairy tale just to make us happy and unafraid of death. As we will see later on, truth is not limited to what is known, what can be proved by experiment, or what people agree is true. It is what really is, and as time goes on and we learn more, we may need to refine what we think is true to align more closely with what really is true. Truth is out there, whether or not we have a correct apprehension of it right now. We reject the idea that all truth is relative.

Knowledge, for our purposes, is awareness of the truth, of course, but also learning, understanding, the significance of the facts. Personal knowledge is often first-hand experience or knowledge based on the results of an experiment. But most knowledge is not personal knowledge.

While the nature of knowledge is one of the crucial debates of our contemporary world, we will concur here with the standard definition offered in traditional philosophy, that knowledge is "properly justified true belief." This is an important definition for what it says about the relationship between knowledge and belief. Knowledge, in other words, is *a form of belief.*

Belief we will define as a conviction that something is true, based on evidence, trust, reason, or authority, rather than personal experience. It is usually thought of as less conclusive or not quite as strong as knowledge.

These definitions are important for at least two reasons. First, it may not always be clear whether a particular idea in your head (that you have just learned, say) is a piece of knowledge or "just" a belief. A given piece of information may move back and forth. What began as a belief (a reasoned conclusion, let's say) became knowledge through some experimental verification. Or what was thought to be knowledge (as we saw in the previous section) turns out upon further investigation to be merely a wrong belief.

Second, if knowledge is "awareness of the truth" and truth is "a correct account of reality," then some knowledge (such as God's working in the world) can be derived from revelation or other non-experimental sources. Not all knowledge of "the way things really are" can be established through the scientific method. Thus, what may at first be categorized as a belief by our definition actually turns out to be knowledge. (See Chapter 3 for an extended discussion about the nature of knowledge.)

Moreover, in Christendom, some (but not all) of our beliefs are based on faith (or trust). Even though they may be fully reasonable and consistent with all our other beliefs and knowledge, these beliefs derive directly from our personal relationship with Christ and our trust in him. And much of what Christians believe (from Scripture, reason, experience, and so on) is actually knowledge.

I have belabored these definitions for a reason. In the academy, some scholars are fond of emphasizing the difference between knowledge (which is what they believe to be the case) and religious belief (which is what they believe to be personal, subjective, and usually false ideas). I hope you can see that the situation is more complex than that. Much of what is presented as knowledge, (both inside the academy and out) might actually be more accurately described as belief because it can be described as a conviction based on trust or authority. No one can do every experiment personally or think through the implications of every event or set of data. Scholars must trust each other and rely on the reports and conclusions their colleagues present in publications, both inside and outside their own field of specialization.

Similarly, what these scholars depreciate as mere belief is truly knowledge; it just happens to be knowledge outside their narrow definition of knowledge. As we will see in Chapter 5, those most insistent on distinguishing knowledge from belief are the scientific naturalists, who in theory allow only empirically verifiable data to be knowledge. But their definition of knowledge is much too constrained to cover what is and can be actually known, and besides, not even they actually follow it in practice.

1.4 Christian Belief

If you attend a secular university, then, you will most likely be confronted with the attitude that you are faced with a body of new *knowledge,* and you should not allow your mere *belief* (that is, personal, subjective, and probably false ideas) to interfere with it. The sooner you can either rid yourself of those silly ideas or compartmentalize them so that they do not interfere with real knowledge, the better off you'll be.

The implication seems to be that we Christians know, somehow, that what we only *believe* is not really true, but we believe it anyway because it "works for us," or because it gives us emotional comfort. You'll recall that Karl Marx called religion "the opiate of the people," and many others have called it a crutch. It may have psychological benefit, like the sound of a waterfall, but it has no truth content. We could argue, of course, that our detractors *prefer* to believe that about us and about Christianity because it gives them comfort not to have to confront the claims of the faith seriously. As long as they can keep us in a little irrational box, they feel safe. At any rate, there is often a smirk of condescension behind their use of the word *belief.*

My view, on the other hand, is that no one — no Christian, anyway — wants to believe something that is not true. We want to see the world as it really is and to know ourselves as we really are. For every thinking human being, Christian and non-Christian, truth should be the highest goal and have the highest value in our lives. We must be willing to follow the evidence wherever it leads. Self delusion is rightly criticized by nearly everyone. Who wants to live a lie, to be motivated by false ideas? That would be tragic, indeed.

My position, then, is that we not argue about the difference between knowledge and belief as they are tossed around in conversation, but that we focus on the nature and the problem of knowledge itself. What is presented as sturdy knowledge isn't always so. Moreover, Christianity contains a large body of knowledge relevant to the contemporary world, and this knowledge needs to be advanced to the forefront of the cultural and worldview battles now raging. In a word then, don't become confused or swayed by definitions of these words that imply that Christianity is less real or less true than whatever is being presented to you as an alternative.

1.5 Integration and Critical Thinking

Before you attempt to integrate your faith and your learning, then, you must train yourself not to accept knowledge *as found*, but to be skeptical of each claim, to examine it and analyze the process through which it passed on its way to the pedestal. Take a proactive, challenging attitude toward knowledge claims. This process is the essence of critical thinking. Education is not about memorization; it is about learning how to think. You must learn to engage knowledge actively, demanding justification for it, looking into the process of its construction to see what underlying assumptions it is built upon, and how reasonable was the process of inference that led to it. Knowledge that passes the test—let's call it true and worthy knowledge—should be welcomed, while the rest should be sifted to separate the good parts from the rest. Even the knowledge you deem to be probably untrue, overgeneralized, or slanted should be learned, for there is value even in wrong or bad ideas. (And, of course, you will probably be tested on them.)

Not everything you will be taught in the academy is truth in its deepest sense. I'm by far not the first person to point out that some academics are fond of blurring the distinction between what is really true or actually known and what they just think is right, or wish to believe, or hope is true. Academics are human beings, with the usual variety of human passions, wishes, interests, and agendas. Most are truth seekers, I believe, but sometimes the current state of knowledge leads to wrong conclusions. I recall sitting in a physical anthropology class as an undergraduate in the late 1960s and listening to the professor declaim rather emotionally about the impossibility of continental drift. The supposed fit of the continents was poor and there was no decent evidence for supposing that there had been some sort of Pangea, a single continent in the past. Today, the idea of continental drift is widely accepted, of course, and we all know that changes occur in scientific understanding of the world. The point of interest, though, is the emotional fervor that this particular professor had for the view then current. This fervor is not uncommon. Even realizing that scholarly trends and conclusions are subject to change, many academics are firmly convinced about the current model and resist criticism of it, even to the point of lashing out angrily if the model is questioned.

In some cases, professors prefer to find and teach conclusions that conform to strongly held ideological commitments, even at the expense of a more objective interpretation of evidence. Some literary critics, for example, see every novel, play, or short story in terms of who is being victimized. "Read until you find the victim" is an often quoted watchword. *Hamlet*? It's about the victimization of Ophelia. *Jane Eyre*? It's about Jane's victimization by rigid social hierarchies. And so on.

A first principle for integrating faith and learning, therefore, is to *be cautious, even a little skeptical, about information*. Do not assume that what you read in a textbook or hear in a lecture consists of a series of unimpeachable facts or unarguable conclusions. Learn how to think. Examine and test the information you consume. As Paul says, "Examine everything carefully; hold fast to that which is good" (1 Thessalonians 5:21). Test the source of the information. Remember that there are other reasons for making knowledge claims than the desire to share pure truth with the world.

One of my favorite proverbs is, "The central work of life is interpretation." Most of our lives are spent thinking about what something means, where something leads, what conclusion can be drawn. Think about learning this way, as a problem-solving process. You are the knowledge detective, and it is up to you to gather huge amounts of ideas, details, claims, and scraps of evidence; then you must work with them actively, thinking hard, to put them all together into a coherent whole to determine "what it all means."

1.6 Integration as an Ongoing Process

A second principle of integration is that *you don't have to make a decision to accept or reject every piece of knowledge presented to you*. If you don't have time to examine or process the information presented to you, just remember it without putting a "believe this" or "don't believe this" tag on it. Keep it in mind, but, especially if it appears to conflict with Scripture, don't swallow it without checking it out first.

For example, suppose your professor says, "Well, regardless of the religion or philosophy he or she follows, theist or atheist, everyone is in some way a determinist, so that no one ultimately believes in free will." Instead of believing this statement to be true, and instead of rejecting it as false, you can simply file it away, remembering, "The professor says that. . . ." You may not have the knowledge yet to decide about this issue, or the tools even to think about it intelligently, and that's okay. In the meantime, just file it away. I hereby give you permission to say, "I don't know yet," when asked about an issue you have not yet thought through. You don't have to have an opinion on everything.

How old do you think the earth is? Is it several thousand years as those who follow some calculations based on Biblical genealogies claim, or is it several billion, as those claim who rely on radiometric dating and geological uniformitarianism? Or is it somewhere in between? Have you seen a list of assumptions for these dating methods? Have you studied how the dates are determined? How old is the earth? You don't have to commit to an answer.

Another of my favorite proverbs is, "The more you know, the better you can see." People who have little knowledge often find learning difficult because knowledge builds on knowledge. The more you know, the more analogies you can construct, the easier it is to compare the new information with information you already have and therefore make sense of it. When you are first learning a new subject, you often do not have the storehouse of previous knowledge that will enable you to assess the new learning adequately. And even when you do gain a lot of similar or otherwise relevant knowledge, you need to have the time and thinking skills to process the new material before you can integrate it into your personal world of the known. In other words, you need not alter your view of reality immediately after every new knowledge claim is presented to you.

The proverb applies to Biblical knowledge as well. At this point in your life, you may not have the deep and wise understanding of all Scripture that you will eventually need to integrate fully your Christian faith and the learning you are gaining from your formal education. Eighteenth-century writer Samuel Johnson once noted that just the New Testament requires a lifetime of study to understand and digest fully. The more Biblical knowledge you gain, the clearer the picture of God's message will become for you and the more easily you will see the interconnections of all knowledge.

In other words, don't be in a rush to judgment: A third principle of integration is that *the process of integration will require the rest of your life.* And as J. P. Moreland reminds us, the integration process is both a personal and a social one, involving individual Bible reading, study, and thinking, together with discussions, reading, and working with others in the Christian community to come to the best understanding of each issue:

> To be engaged in the task of integration is to embark on a journey that is at once exciting and difficult. Integration is no easy task and it is a life-long project that should occur within an individual believer's life and among the various members of the Christian community working together.[8]

We are especially blessed to live in a time when there are many books, articles, and Web sites that address integration issues, and the Christian community as a whole is becoming much more worldview aware and is developing great resources to aid in the integration process.

The longer you live, the more you will learn—about the world, about knowledge, and about God. You'll be able to think better, integrate old learning more substantially and new learning more quickly. As you learn more about the world, you develop that circumspection, that understanding, that wisdom that lets you see things whole, that all truth *is* God's truth. Only time and lots of thoughtful, prayerful learning can accomplish this. You can see from this, by the way, the value of learning as a crucial tool in the life of every Christian.

Reading this book, then, is only a beginning. After you read it, don't be concerned if you feel that you don't have all the answers or can't make all the connections you want to. The goal of this book is to open the door to The Big Picture, to steer you in the right direction. You won't be at the end of your journey right away.

1.7 Integration and the Educated Christian

Traditionally, the philosophical attacks on Christianity often took the form of perceived conflicts between the world as it is and the claims of faith. For example, a common challenge to the existence of God was the problem of evil. Why would a good God allow evil in the world? Or even, How could God exist in a world that has evil? Many of the answers, from the Fall, to free will, to the power of God to bring good out of evil, made use of theological knowledge and philosophical arguments. The attacks were met with reasons and arguments and Scriptural truths.

Today, the attack is much more insidious, taking place not by argument and rebuttal but by redefining what knowledge is (surprise—Christian faith is not knowledge, but only belief, where knowledge equals truth and belief equals wishful thinking). As a result, there is no need to attack Christianity directly (though a few people are now proclaiming how harmful all religion is), because Christianity is rendered by definition virtually irrelevant in the marketplace of ideas. Charles Darwin recognized the effectiveness of this sort of technique as far back as 1873, when he wrote:

> I have lately read Morely's *Life of Voltaire* and he insists strongly that direct attacks on Christianity (even when written with the wonderful force and vigor of Voltaire) produce little permanent effect: real good seems only to follow the slow and silent side attacks.[9]

Claiming that Christian faith is merely private, subjective, weakly grounded or even false belief renders it of little importance to the non-Christian world. By insisting that faith is a private, subjective matter, the attackers hope to marginalize

Christianity into irrelevance, to push it to the outer regions of significance until it falls off the edge into an effective nonexistence. Rather than a body of coherent, propositional truths about the nature of mankind and the world, it is now just religious emotion, fine for those who like that sort of thing. You are welcome to your own emotions, for who can argue with feelings? Just don't let them get in the way of anything serious, like ideas.

And such attacks do more than immunize the non-Christian world from the faith. They also can be harmful to new Christians, who may accept them as accurate descriptions of the faith, agree to be marginalized, wrapped up in an inner cocoon. A number of Christian students come to the university with a rather weakly grounded and untested faith, to face the criticism and scorn of a highly intelligent community that encourages them to put off their childish ways. Unless Christians can be equipped to understand both the strength and truth of their faith and its connection to the world of knowledge, there is the possibility that it will be lost or rendered ineffective.

Such attacks can be met only by thoughtful, well educated Christians who understand the methods being used and who can fight for their rights to promote a better basis for knowledge than the alternatives currently promoted by our adversaries. To be blunt, I'm asking you to become something of an intellectual. One of the biggest mistakes Christendom made in the whole history of the faith occurred when too many believers began to yield the intellectual arena to the secularists. Consider the faith-and-reason debate. Instead of arguing the truth, that faith is the foundation for reason, that faith of some sort is necessary before any rational conclusions can be drawn, too many Christian leaders yielded to their critics and said, in effect, "Well, you can have reason and we will have faith."

What the world needs today is a Christian intelligentsia. We need deeply learned and fully integrated Christian philosophers, intellectuals, scientists, historians, novelists, journalists, good thinkers of every kind. Ideas are fought with ideas. If no one brings to bear the powerful thinking needed to combat error, then error will lie back, grow fat, and rule the world. We need Christians who can outthink the secularists (the philosophical naturalists and the postmodernists). There are many gaping holes in their worldviews and in their methodologies, and we need Christians to drive a truck through those holes, honking the horn.

The secularists would love it if you were to become an anti-intellectual, dismissing the "tainted knowledge" and "false claims" rampant in the academy. You could feed their prejudices and render yourself unable to fight the fight in the marketplace of ideas. On the other hand, they will hate it if you learn their ideas, test them against the truth, and expose their unwarranted assumptions and conclusions. This is the new evangelism, where a lost but educated world has swallowed a host of questionable knowledge that has persuaded it of the irrelevance or even falsity of Christian faith. The primary goal of this book is to help you negotiate this world in a way that will not only preserve but strengthen your faith, as you acquire the tools for bringing learning and faith into a coherent system of knowledge. But the secondary goal is to equip you to take this good news to your friends and to the lost, who do not understand that they are every day presented with conclusions derived from worldviews hostile to Christianity, and that these conclusions are designed to be incompatible with faith. It will be your task to show that, however incompatible some knowledge claims are with the Christian faith, the fact remains that real knowledge is compatible.

1.8 Implications for Integration

Faith and learning *can* be integrated, and neither faith nor learning should be considered a separate or independent arena of life. One's faith commitment, whether to Christianity or philosophical materialism or some other metaphysical framework, inevitably affects one's understanding of the world and the knowledge in it. The Christian who holds faith apart from learning will thereby be engaging the realm of knowledge on the basis of some other metaphysic, not on no metaphysic. Christian presuppositions have been so long exiled from intellectual life that, as Nicholas Wolterstorff notes, "Many . . . Christians scarcely see the world as Christians. Our indigenous patterns of thought are not those of Christianity but those induced by the modern scientific world view."[10] And this worldview is permeated by its own philosophy and presuppositions. Therefore, do not believe those who say that their practice of knowledge acquisition and evaluation is fully objective and metaphysically neutral. As we will see in more detail later on, that is not the case. Even what a "fact" is depends in part on one's beliefs and preconceptions. But more than that, learning is about gaining understanding, and that means finding meaning in the sea of facts. And all interpretation is to some extent based on one's deepest beliefs, one's faith.

It follows, too, that in order to integrate faith and learning well, both must be taken seriously. There is much to learn about both. Lots of reading and hard thinking must take place to bring these arenas together, partly because so many people are interested in claiming that the two are incompatible or separate realms. Take your faith seriously. Learn about it and find its strength and robustness. Christianity is not just a feeling. In fact, it's more than just the path to God (though, of course, that's its most important aspect). It really is the truth in the sense of being an accurate and meaningful account of the world, the only truly rational and comprehensive account of everything. And take your learning seriously. Learn to discern the true from the false, the fact from the claim, and take charge of worthy knowledge that it might be turned to the service of God.

Summary

This chapter sets up the background for integrating faith and learning by stressing that a crucial aspect of integration involves the nature of knowledge itself. In philosophical terms, a major source of the apparent conflict between Christian knowledge and some of the knowledge promoted in many universities is that the knowledge comes from competing epistemes (different theories about what constitutes knowledge). It is more important than ever for Christians to become highly educated and to understand how the arena of learning actually works and to recognize the nature and source of various knowledge claims. Only in this way can we always be "ready to make a defense to everyone who asks you to give an account for the hope that is in you . . ." (1 Peter 3:15).

Questions for Thought and Discussion

1. To this point in your education, what strategies have you pursued to connect (or integrate) what you learn academically with your Christian faith? How effective have these strategies been?

2. The wholeness of Christian faith includes personal relationship with Christ, agreement with theological propositions, emotional experience, faith commitments, reasoned argument, and intellectual aspects. Of these, this book will be stressing the cognitive (intellectual, thinking) aspects of Christianity, as the Christian worldview is developed in philosophical terms. Some have argued that in American Protestantism especially the life of the mind and the life of faith have been too far apart. How would you respond to this? To this point, how has your own faith been expressed? Of the components listed above, which ones have had greater expression and which less? What are your feelings about exploring the intellectual side of Christian commitment?

3. The widespread impact of hoaxes, urban legends, and tabloid newspapers has probably already made you somewhat skeptical about knowledge claims. And your education so far has likely already helped to make you a critical thinker. At this point, how do you apply your own attitude toward new knowledge claims to the academic material (textbooks, lectures, etc.) you encounter?

4. Has this chapter encouraged you to dedicate your mind to the service of the faith? What role do you see for a Christian intelligentsia in the world?

---

[1] J. P. Moreland, "Philosophical Apologetics, the Church, and Contemporary Culture," *Premise* 3:4 (April 29, 1996), p. 6. Retrieved from http://capo.org/premise/96/april/p960406.html.

[2] Michael L. Peterson, *With All Your Mind: A Christian Philosophy of Education* (Notre Dame: University of Notre Dame, 2001), p. 49.

[3] Sidney Greidanus, "The Use of the Bible in Christian Scholarship," *Christian Scholar's Review* 11:2 (March 1982), pp. 138-147, reprinted in *Discipleship and the Disciplines: Enhancing Faith-Learning Integration*, Coalition for Christian Colleges and Universities, 1996, Unit 4, p. 20.

[4] I do not recall the source of this joke, which I repeat from memory. For another version (and possible source) see Schuyler W. Huck and Howard M. Sandler, *Rival Hypotheses: Alternative Interpretations of Data Based Conclusions* (New York: Harper & Row, 1979), p.xiii.

[5] Mortimer Adler and Charles Van Doren, *How to Read a Book* (rev. ed., New York: MJF Books, 1972), p. 165.

[6] Ibid., p. 186.

[7] From Chapter 6 of Lewis Carroll's *Through the Looking Glass*. Quoted in Peter Heath, ed., *The Philosopher's Alice* (New York: St. Martins, 1974), p. 193.

[8] J. P. Moreland, p. 6.

[9] Quoted in Gertrude Himmelfarb, *Darwin and the Darwinian Revolution*. New York: W. W. Norton, 1962, p. 387.

[10] "Book summary notes on Nicholas Wolterstorff, *Reason Within the Bounds of Religion*, 2nd ed. (Grand Rapids: Eerdmans, 1984)," in *Discipleship and the Disciplines: Enhancing Faith-Learning Integration*, Coalition for Christian Colleges and Universities, 1996, Unit 2, page 36.

Chapter 2
Why Integrate Faith and Learning?

The Christian mind must be dynamic, flexible, and able to expand and develop as we clarify and correct our knowledge of truth. It must be able to withstand the temptation of gradually acquiescing to what we know to be un-Biblical and anti-Christian. We must not become accomplices in the secular enterprise which wittingly or unwittingly robs God of His rightful place at the core and foundation of all knowledge. . . .
  — Kenneth O. Gangel[1]

A Christian university must be a living revelation of the stewardship of the Truth. Those who comprise the Christian university must know their position in Christ, and their position in the world, specifically the world of academia.
  — Lynn Marie Kohm[2]

2.1 Is Integration Really Necessary?

One view of the issue surrounding faith and learning is that there really is no issue at all. Because "all truth is God's truth," there is no need to integrate anything: you cannot integrate something that is already a whole or a unity, and everything—faith and all knowledge—is already one. The Bible, the natural world, the events of history, all speak of God and his ways.

Now, in the previous chapter, we have already begun to see that the issue is more complicated than that, owing to the varying definitions of knowledge and truth now present both in the academy and in society at large (and because all human apprehension of truth is partial and constantly unfolding). As we will see in more detail later on, while it is indeed correct to say that "all truth is God's truth," we still must ask Pilate's question, "What is truth?" or perhaps more to the point, "But just which truth or what meaning of truth do you have in mind?" Identifying true knowledge and separating it from questionable interpretations imposed on it by hostile world-views is certainly desirable and is one necessary step in the process of integration.

A little thought will also make it clear that theological knowledge (such as belief in God's sovereignty) on the one hand and non-theological academic knowledge (such as the various theories of human personality) on the other hand need to be brought together in some coherent manner in order for the learner to have a unified understanding. This is the heart of integration. Integration involves the development of inter-connections, relationships, and mutual clarifications between Christian truth and academic content. We might call integra-tion the construction—or discovery—of the wholeness and coherence of all knowledge, specifically of the knowledge about human nature and human destiny. How the fall of mankind relates to the number of electrons in an oxygen atom is not what we are talking about. What is at issue is the rela-tionship, the unification, between what Scripture tells us about the meaning and purpose of life, our origin, the image of God in us, and the knowledge obtained by research, thinking, dis-covery, and study of the natural world and the human person. And what does this unified understanding tell us about how we should live? Clearly, then, integration is essential for a sta-ble and coherent view of the world as well as for living a life of wise choices. It is not a process that takes place automati-cally as a result of the unity of truth.

2.2 Why Not Follow the "Two Realms" View?

Another way to approach the issue of integration is some-times called the "two realms" view. Those who advocate this view say that the challenge of integration resides in the diffi-culty of being both religious and academic, that Christian stu-dents and professors have "dual identities." Many of these people see their faith and their role as scholars as distinct, though in some way connected. They see themselves as scholars who also happen to be Christians, who learn and teach much as their secular counterparts do.

Where theology and scholarship do encounter one another, these professors and philosophers tend to minimize the conflict presented by the scholarship coming out of the secular world views. They adopt what is called the compatibilist view of integration because they see faith and their academic discipline as compatible or perhaps complementary with each other, without the need for resolving conflicts.[3] These scholars often seek points of overlap or harmony as a means of providing a dialogue between the two areas of their lives. And, in fact, this technique is often a useful part of the integration process.

My difficulty with the two realms view and with limiting integration to compatibilism is that, as I mentioned in the previous chapter, it often accepts too readily the content of each academic discipline *as found*, taking for granted the validity of the controlling epistemology of the academic discipline or at least accepting the discipline's knowledge claims as objective, empirical, and without metaphysical, value-based preferences or interpretations. The assumptions underlying the methodology of each academic discipline are often invisible because they are taken for granted as the accepted foundations for the extension of the discipline's knowledge. Yet it is just these assumptions that Christian scholars need to identify and assess, in order to determine what philosophy (worldview, metaphysics) directs the discipline's activity.

Another objection to the "two realms" view is that it has outlived its reason for existence. This view—going back at least as far as Tertullian—in its modern incarnation is a holdover from nineteenth century pietism, when evangelicals felt threatened by the rise of knowledge claims from Darwin, Marx, and Freud and the general rise of modernist, secularist learning. That is, some Christians felt that learning itself was a threat to their faith (hence the rise of anti-intellectualism among some Christians at that time), and their response was to hold faith apart from learning to keep their faith safe. They were not prepared to respond to the onslaught of anti-Christian claims coming from the educated world. So learning was rejected and faith was faith for its own sake. One should believe simply by an act of will. This may be where the idea of "blind faith" came from.

At any rate, that reason is no longer operative. The Christian faith and the Christian worldview not only can stand their ground quite well in the intellectual arena, but they provide a better, more comprehensive, and more rational picture of reality than their competitors. It has long been time for Christians to stop being defensive about their beliefs and to proceed with confidence into the marketplace of ideas.

An argument similar to the "two realms" view has been adopted from some scholars in the natural sciences who wish to prevent a competing metaphysics from interfering with their own. These scholars say that "science and religion don't answer the same question." This argument gives us a clue about how the secularists often present the conflict. They assert that to bring theological ideas into scientific questions is to make a "category mistake." Arguers along these lines often cleverly cite obvious disconnects between science (or technology) and religion. Theology really doesn't have a lot to say about which antifreeze works best, they say. Or, a Christian worldview won't help you solve matrix equations. In its technical aspects, science indeed addresses different questions from religion, but science long ago expanded the claims of its domain well beyond technology. Today, science and religion do indeed answer the same questions, for science now offers explanations about our origin, our destiny, the meaning of life, and so on. As Edward Davis says,

> For many in the modern world, science itself wears the mantle of religion: it provides a creation myth, reveals our true nature as actualized genes, proclaims the promise of salvation, gives us every good and perfect gift, offers eschatological hope, and functions as the ultimate arbiter of truth.[4]

Any discipline that answers metaphysical questions such as those regarding human nature or the purpose and destiny of life should have its claims subjected to challenge and argument by Christians who have competing answers. Whenever the meaning of knowledge becomes an issue, it is a false claim that Christianity and the academic disciplines are in different domains. Christians are called to be a light in shaping their culture by offering better explanations and by presenting the Truth to a confused world. The danger of adopting the "two realms" view is that it will compartmentalize the faith and leave a secular metaphysics on the throne unchallenged. Compartmentalization is marginalization. It is putting the lamp under the bed.

2.3 Integration Produces Confidence in Learning

When I was a public university freshman (during those riotous days of war protesting and tear gas), most of my professors viewed faith and learning as incompatible. Faith to them was a quaint holdover from a pre-scientific world, an obstacle to the modern world of secular learning. They made it clear that the sooner their students understood this, the better. A few professors even took it upon themselves to try to "liberate" us from our faith, and took frequent shots at religious ideas and commitments. Others patronizingly allowed that personal faith commitments were all right, "Whatever works for you," provided that those commitments did not interfere with *real* knowledge — the knowledge proclaimed by their disciplines.

These attitudes and practices continue today. Christian faith, labeled "belief," is put in tension with scholarly pronouncements, labeled "knowledge," with the implication being that knowledge (awareness of what is really true) is always preferable to belief. When the two conflict, the belief is almost by definition wrong.

It's no surprise, then, that many Christian students have developed some fear of learning. Before they left for college, they were warned by well-meaning friends, "Don't get so much education that you lose your faith." This fear is not without a grain of truth. Many devout Christians, especially if they go to public universities and graduate schools, find their faith successfully undermined, weakened, and sometimes destroyed as they continue to drink unquestioningly at the fountain of secular learning. If learning is hostile to faith, if there is an inevitable conflict between the two, then be careful not to allow too much of this troublesome thing into your head.

But this view is exaggerated and distorted. The conflict is not between faith and learning. The conflict is between faith and some parts of learning—interpretations and ideas shaped by worldviews and assumptions that are ultimately incompatible with Christian knowledge.

In fact, another way to think about the problem is to say the conflict is between two faiths. According to Michael Keas and Kerry Magruder, "No one is without faith commitments, regardless of common claims to religious or worldview neutrality by scientists and other scholars. All reasoning involves faith commitments embodied in one's first principles, and reciprocally, all faith involves reason."[5] Everyone must take for granted many assumptions and presuppositions—take them on faith, if you will—in order to live and work in the world (which, we assume on faith, is actually out there). Thus, they conclude, "In short, it is not a matter of whether faith will inform reason, but rather which faith will inform reason."[6] The faith may be in God or in naturalism or postmodernism or Marx or oneself or science, but it is a faith nevertheless.

If you learn to divide the truth, to separate out the genuine knowledge, to integrate that knowledge with your understanding of God's word and God's world, then learning will be an ally of faith, and the more you learn, the deeper your faith will become. Let me toss in just one example. You may be grateful when, after you cut your finger, you soon stop bleeding. Your blood clots. That by itself is reason to be thankful to God for his wonderful design. But did you ever wonder how this works? Why does your blood clot? Why does it stop clotting? That is, once your blood starts to clot, what keeps it from clotting all the way through your body? The answer is that there are about twenty different proteins interacting in a highly complex cascade, some of them promoting clotting in the right place and some inhibiting it in the wrong place. Once you read the details of blood clotting (which takes Michael Behe about twenty pages to explain) I think you'll have a much greater appreciation for this system and God's sovereignty than before.[7]

If someone should ask you to sum up this book in one sentence, here it is: The process of integrating faith and learning allows faith to support and clarify learning, and at the same time allows learning to support and clarify faith. Engaging in the process of integration will increase your confidence in the learning process and make you eager to learn more, as you continue to develop strategies to combine faith and knowledge. The better you are able to use your growing knowledge of the faith to understand how knowledge works, the better educated you can become. And the more education you get, the more solidly grounded your faith will become. If you read this book in the way I intend it, you will finish it by committing yourself to getting at least a Ph.D.

2.4 Secular Learning Is Incomplete

The academy is at war today. Two great philosophical systems are going at it tooth and claw, and in many ways they have nearly opposite views of reality. The first goes by several names, including philosophical materialism and scientific naturalism, and more recently, modernism, to set it against the second system, postmodernism. (Ideally, the battle should be threefold, with the worldview of Christianity as the third combatant.) Generally speaking, the natural sciences are in the camp of the modernists, while the humanities are in the camp of the postmodernists, and the social sciences are in the middle of things. These worldviews will be discussed in more detail in Chapters 6 and 7.

The point I want to make here, though, is that, as widely different as these two approaches to knowledge are, they share one outlook in common. Both reject the validity of theological claims. Technically, both systems would say they are "anti-metaphysical," and claim that metaphysical statements (such as, "God is wise") are unintelligible and meaningless. However, as we will see later, both systems are themselves grounded in metaphysical assumptions, so that to say they reject metaphysics would be incorrect, strictly speaking.

Because both of these worldviews reject transcendence, the objective reality of good and evil, the existence of the soul, and so on, they lack completeness and fail to explain the fullness of life and experience. Most people are looking for meaning and purpose in their lives, but how will they find them when they are surrounded by worldviews that tell them there is no such thing as moral truth, that all judgments of value are meaningless or at best personal preferences, and that the entire realm of spiritual striving and belief is merely irrational emotionalism? These worldviews proclaim that the values and ideas we hold most dear—love, goodness, truth, beauty, honor, righteousness, compassion—are either outside the realm of truth because they are impossible to verify experimentally (scientific naturalism's view) or else they are merely personal descriptions of subjective experience (postmodernism's view).

Any worldview that denigrates as unintelligible all those ideals and aspirations that give life its highest meaning seems to provide a shrunken and inadequate picture of reality. For the most reasonable understanding of everything (the unity of truth), we need a worldview that is more complete and that embodies a better organizing principle than either of these, one that allows for reality, objectivity—and yes, absoluteness—in every part of our life and experience, not just the mechanical, physical parts. For a worldview to say, "We can't explain much," is one thing, but to claim, "We can't explain much, but what we explain is all there is," is quite another. The discerning Christian is tempted to quote Prince Hamlet to the holders of these small worldviews, when he says, "There are more things in heaven and earth, Horatio, than are dreamt of in your philosophy."

2.5 The Christian Worldview as a Clarifier

Unlike the two worldviews described above, the Christian worldview does not narrow and distort knowledge, but expands and clarifies it, explaining aspects of experience that cannot be accounted for adequately by postmodern or naturalistic models. Because the two views currently battling for domination in the academy are not likely to disappear anytime soon, it is up to you to develop the ability to integrate what you learn as processed through these models with what you know to be a better understanding of the nature of knowledge and reality.

The process of integration should not be seen, then, as a method of rejecting knowledge, but as an activity of clarifying, filtering, and correcting misinterpretation. Or better, integration provides a touchstone for testing the claims about knowledge that you will encounter during your educational career, and for the rest of your life. Chapters 10 and 11 offer practical advice to help you with this process.

It is sometimes said that the goal of Christian education is to add a Christian perspective to a discipline and to the subject matter. By now you will be able to predict my objection to this position. Even though it is convenient to speak of "a Christian perspective" when discussing events or ideas, strictly speaking, such a phrase is misleading. A perspective is often taken to mean a partial view or angle, an opinion or a few additional ideas added to a basic set of facts or events. Christianity is not just a viewpoint from which to observe and comment on the knowledge and events of the world. As a worldview, it is instead a way of seeing the world. In philosophical terms, it provides a more comprehensive and rational epistemology, a theory of knowledge that explains the world rather than comments upon it.

I have emphasized this seemingly small point in order to rebut the idea, sometimes expressed, that Christianity is somehow just an extra, an added bonus, to be attached to the scholarship of the academic world. Christian knowledge is more than an alternative commentary; it provides a standard of truth for taking an objective look at all knowledge claims, for assessing and critiquing them.

In a word, then, we are not talking about knowledge enhanced by belief. We are talking about an alternative theory of knowledge. That is the point to remember because that is the point most commonly denied by those in the academy who would prefer to keep Christian epistemology on the periphery of respectability.

2.6 A Commitment to the Unity of Truth

Indeed, Christianity actually has a more encompassing view of truth than the two other worldviews described above. For the Christian, truth includes the knowledge gained by empirical investigation, by reason, and by revelation. Thus, the faith is in a unique position to unify knowledge and see the wholeness of the world. The grounding in Biblical authority provides a solid foundation for assessing and understanding everything, from the creation to the strivings of our hearts. There is neither an indulgence in subjectivity, nor a restricting of the name of truth to only part of the realm of true things.

As a result, truth in all its variety—from how computers are made, to why we sneeze, to the purpose of life itself—can be for the Christian a constant resource for serving God and working well in his kingdom. Christian truth should relate intimately to the rest of the world of truth, just as every kind of knowledge can be harnessed for kingdom building. In a word, faith and learning should be interconnected, each supporting the other in the believer's walk.

Because we recognize that knowledge of the truth is knowledge about God and his universe, the pursuit of truth is in some sense the pursuit of God, who reveals himself through the creation (including us, his children).[8] Whatever the truth is, we want to know it, because it tells us about God, the author of truth. (Surprisingly enough, we will learn that for some people, even in the academy, ideological or philosophical commitments are more important than the pursuit of truth.) There is no place, then, for anti-intellectualism in Christian learning or life. The wisdom of the world, the scientific method, problem solving skills, developments in technology, all have much value and truth we can learn from and use. The truth may be mixed with philosophy and interpretation that are hostile to faith, but the core that is indeed truth is valuable nevertheless.

2.7 What Happens Without Integration?

If, after college or university, you are like most graduates, you will be working with information for the rest of your life. If you do not learn as an undergraduate how to integrate new knowledge claims, new conclusions about the nature of humanity and the natural world, new theories of interpretation and scholarship, with your Christian faith, then you may never develop that skill. A common result of the failure to integrate faith and learning is a split between the two, and a division between faith and mind. In other words, faith becomes compartmentalized and therefore intellectually irrelevant. Faith serves only emotional needs. New knowledge, instead of strengthening faith, is perceived as a constant threat, so it is either rejected or isolated away from the faith-in-a-box.

Another possible result of the lack of integration is an awkward syncretism, where faith is somehow held simultaneously with purported knowledge and inferences—and whole worldviews—hostile to it. An attempt is made to accept secular knowledge as found and to attach faith to it in some compatible manner. A common result of this tape-and-glue approach is that the secular learning gradually weakens faith, either making faith little more than emotional commitment or eventually destroying it altogether. It is sad to see the number of formerly committed Christians who lose their faith in graduate school as they allow the worldview of their chosen disciplines to overwhelm their faith and erase it almost completely.

A further consequence of integrative failure is a lower quality of life. Accepting one of the hostile worldviews will result not just in wrong belief about plants or a wrong idea about history. Ideas have consequences for life and behavior. Contemporary culture is built on the worldviews we are discussing. If you examine films, music videos, magazines, song lyrics, even political arguments, you will see values derived from scientific naturalism, postmodernism, and the Judeo-Christian heritage, all scrambled together and competing for dominance. Integration is not just for the sake of having a neat, sensible philosophy. Life is built on our deepest philosophical commitments. For example, to come to believe that "random molecules are all there is" will have a definite influence on personal behavior, as well as belief about the possibility of transcendent hope and the meaning of life itself. Moral formation is connected to knowledge and to one's view of the world. You may have heard the saying, "If you teach people that they are merely animals, don't be surprised when they begin to act like them."

Perhaps the most tragic effect that results when integration does not take place is the failure of that Christian to be a light. We are called to be a transformative voice both in culture and in the intellectual arena, to offer a better view of the world, life, and humanity. The Bible doesn't call it the "good news" for nothing.[9] The world needs a superior understanding of things. It needs the truth, and that truth can be presented only by those who know how to challenge the wrong ideas that now dominate civilization.

2.8 What Are the Results of Integration?

Successful integration is a powerful way to strengthen your faith and bring you to a greater love of learning. Once you understand how knowledge and learning and faith really work, you will begin to discern how the world really works. You will understand both truth and error more clearly and feel the beginnings of wisdom stirring in your soul. You will see that everything truly does fit together in God's world, and you'll see how trustworthy his word is as a test for the values and practices of a narcissistic modern world.

The Christian worldview as a test of knowledge claims will enable you to separate out false and harmful doctrines presented in the guise of truth, to protect yourself from the ideologies and agendas of those who would misuse learning for political purposes. Rather than being whipsawed by the winds of relativism, you will stand firm on the anchor of truth. You will gain confidence that your pursuit of real truth is on the right track and that you are not being deceived by specious claims.

An active, capable integration of faith and learning does much more than provide a solid grounding in truth, enabling you to resist the culture's inevitable move toward extremes. While faith informs learning and provides the basis of truth by which all knowledge can be assessed, learning itself can contribute mightily to faith. You can strengthen your faith by strengthening your mind. Learning in the various disciplines will allow you to elaborate and extend your faith by expanding your understanding of the world. Understanding of God and God's world can be improved, clarified, and enhanced by learning more about the world. Learn how the same DNA expresses itself as an eye or toenail, learn about human nature and behavior in history and the social sciences, and discover the possible lives (with their choices and the consequences of those choices) of characters in literature. You will be able to see how your studies contribute to the Christian worldview.

Oxford University professor Alister McGrath reminds us that integration includes making the connections between faith and living, driving us to a uniquely Christian way of thinking and acting. It is a process of making the faith relevant to everyday activity and to our everyday encounters with the world, in whatever profession we choose. He says,

> But what if we were able to look ahead to a day when we would have financiers who knew as much about the Christian faith as they did about economic theory? And more than that: not simply that they knew about both, but were able to relate them, and bring them together in such a way that we could talk about "evangelical economic theory"? You can extend this list as long as you please. My point is simply that we need to make connections with what is going on in the real world, and allow the gospel to bear on the issues that are facing those who live and work in our complex modern culture. We cannot allow the gospel to be squeezed out of that culture because it is seen to be of no relevance on account of our failure to make those connections in the first place.[10]

Integration, then, goes beyond the intellectual and spiritual benefit of a satisfying and coherent worldview. It is practical. It is life changing, helping to direct your activity and professional work. And it goes beyond the personal. Integration is evangelistic. It can be world changing.

Successful integration will allow you to live in the world and still not be of the world. Your learning will help you grow wiser, more compassionate, and you can move forward rather than backward, reascending to values that have been lost or muted. And you will discover that your faith really is the truth and worthy of your deepest intellectual commitment.

Summary

Integration is crucial for the Christian scholar. Faith and learning must engage in continuous interaction. Christian faith provides a necessary foundation and method for dividing the truth and freeing the mind from the ideologies that often accompany learning in the academy. Learning provides greater knowledge of God's world, work, and person, as well as knowledge of the creatures he sent his son to save. Integrating faith and learning produces the most comprehensive and reasonable view of all existence. The educated Christian can become a powerful witness in the world, demonstrating the power of unified, coherent and faithful knowledge.

Questions for Thought and Discussion

1. Discuss the strengths and weaknesses of the "two realms" view of integration.

2. Compatibilism is a common type of integration. Have you used this approach in your learning so far, and if so, what are some successful examples? That is, what specific academic knowledge have you found compatible or even supportive of your faith?

3. Explain the difference between Christianity as a perspective on knowledge and Christianity as a worldview to be integrated with knowledge or knowledge claims.

4. In what ways does it now appear to you that the integrative process can strengthen your faith? Are there ways you think that the process might challenge your faith?

---

[1] Kenneth O. Gangel, "Integrating Faith and Learning: Principles and Process." *Bibliotheca Sacra*, April-June, 1978, p. 104; retrieved online at <http://www.ici.edu/journals/bibsac/7584/78b1.htm>.

[2] Lynne Marie Kohm, "What is a Christian University? or How to Achieve Preeminence as a Graduate Institution," p. 21; retrieved online at <http://www.regent.edu/admin/cids/christianuniv.pdf>.

[3] See, for example, William Hasker, "Faith-Learning Integration: An Overview," *Christian Scholars Review* XXI:3 (March 1992), pp. 231-248; retrieved online at <http://www.gospelcom.net/cccu/journals/csr/hasker.html>.

[4] Edward B. Davis, "Some Comments on the Course, 'Introduction to Christianity and Science,'" retrieved online at <http://www.messiah.edu/hpages/facstaff/davis/course.html>.

[5] Micheal Keas and Kerry Magruder, "Unified Studies Natural Science F-2002 Packet," Oklahoma Baptist University, 2002, p. 21. Retrieved from http://www.okbu.edu/academics/natsci/us/311/pack.pdf.

[6] Ibid., p. 24.

[7] See Michael Behe, *Darwin's Black Box: The Biochemical Challenge to Evolution* (New York: Free Press, 1996), pp. 77-97.

[8] Romans 1:20: "For since the creation of the world His invisible attributes, His eternal power and divine nature, have been clearly seen, being understood through what has been made, so that they are without excuse" (NASB-U).

[9] For just a few references to the good news, see Acts 8:12, Acts 13:32, and Romans 10:15.

[10] Alister McGrath, "The Christian Scholar in the 21st Century," Christian Leadership Ministries. Retrieved from http://www.clm.org/real/ri0002/mcgrath.html.

Chapter 3
Where Does Knowledge Come From?

Without any censorship, in the West fashionable trends of thought and ideas are carefully separated from those which are not fashionable; nothing is forbidden, but what is not fashionable will hardly ever find its way into periodicals or books or be heard in colleges. Legally your researchers are free, but they are conditioned by the fashion of the day.
— *Alexander Solzhenitsyn[1]*

The agnostics rule America, quite regardless of the popular piety to which politicians pay lip service, because their metaphysics (i.e., scientific naturalism) rules the universities, and the universities control the social definition of knowledge.
— *Phillip Johnson[2]*

3.1 What is Knowledge?

If someone were to ask you why you have come to college, you might include among your reasons preparing for a career, learning how to think, developing your life's philosophy, or getting a clearer view of yourself and the world. Importantly, all of these answers include the need for a sturdy knowledge base, so one reason to come to college is to gain knowledge. That's not only a worthy but also an essential goal. People are fond of repeating the dictum, "Knowledge is power." We all believe that knowledge is the key to understanding the past and present and for equipping us for the future. But just what is knowledge?

In the Western philosophical tradition, knowledge is connected to truth. Knowledge is the awareness of some true thing (a fact or idea), with the truth of the thing supported by reasons or evidence. Knowledge, in other words, is a belief that we have good reason to think is true ("justified true be-lief"). In theory, what is presented to us as knowledge (in the classroom or textbook) should be the product of a calm, objec-tive, rational examination of all available evidence. Knowledge should always be reliable, trustworthy. But things are not so simple as that.

The study of the nature of knowledge is known as episte-mology. It can get fascinatingly deep, as when we ask, "Can we truly know that other minds really exist?" (If you can find time in your studies, I recommend that you take a course or read a couple of books on epistemology. You'll find the subject enlightening.) For our purposes, though, we will stick to some more practical questions about knowledge:

- What can be known?
- What kinds of knowledge are there?
- How can you know something?
- Where does knowledge come from?

If you think about these questions for a minute, you will see that the answers are not easy or obvious. The crucial point, though, is that there is more than one answer to each of these questions. And which answers are true depend on your worldview. Many arguments revolve around fundamental disagreements about the answers to one or more of these ques-tions.

3.2 Whose Epistemology?

A first challenge in the realm of knowledge is that these questions are often answered differently by different people. In fact, there are many epistemologies. There are differences even in the Western philosophical tradition. For example, the epistemology attached to scientific naturalism rules out any knowledge not arising from the physical world, from experi-ments and observations. On the other hand, the epistemology of Christianity includes knowledge derived from Biblical au-thority. The epistemology of rationalism includes knowledge derived from reason apart from empirical observation.

Moreover, now that the Western philosophical tradition has come under the stress of postmodernism, additional epistemes have gained prominence. Postmodern epistemology generally holds that "knowledge" (note the quotation marks) is an unstable, subjective, socially created idea, whose claims are really only relativistic statements of opinion. To postmodernists, the difference between real knowledge and a mere knowledge claim is only a matter of semantic quibbling. And some individuals have epistemologies that include believing as knowledge whatever they "feel" is true at the moment. Truth for them might be defined as emotional resonance rather than some actual matter of fact.

It follows, then, that in order for you to understand what claims to knowledge are being made, you must have some idea of "where they are coming from," so to speak. What is the underlying episteme behind the information you are being presented with? Does the information (or knowledge) source believe that truth exists or that reason is a valid source of knowledge or that only observation of physical data can produce knowledge? Does the source believe that any subjective view of causes and events is as good as any other?

You can see the problem. If you have one epistemology (from the Christian worldview) and the professor or the author of the textbook has another (from naturalism or postmodernism), then you must evaluate the offered knowledge in light of that fact, and perhaps judge some of the claims as limited, open to question, or even possibly untrue.

For example, suppose you read this statement: "Since there is no such thing as divine revelation, all claims to divine revelation are either hallucinations, self-deceptions, or lies." From an epistemology that rules out all non-naturalistic explanations of events as sources of knowledge, that statement would be acceptable, even true. But from an epistemology that includes the divine as a source of knowledge and experience, it is false.

Or, suppose you read the following: "Since no text has any stable or definite meaning, but is subject to an infinite number of interpretations, the meaning of 'love your neighbor as yourself' means that, since you love your own body, you should love your neighbor's body also." An epistemology that posits an infinite number of interpretations for every statement and that grants at least some status to every interpretation, will logically (if that's the right word) lead to the acceptability of this statement. But in an epistemology that includes a more rational hermeneutic (theory of interpretation), such a meaning for this Biblical passage is ridiculous. (Do note, by the way, that some postmodernist literary theorists agree that, even though there are infinite interpretations for a text, some interpretations are better than others even though no single interpretation should be privileged over every other.)

Here are some questions about knowledge produced by the differing views of its nature:

Is knowledge discovered or constructed? The postmodernists say that knowledge is not something objective "out there" waiting for us to discover, but instead it is an agreed-upon idea or set of statements created by consensus among its producers. In other words, scientists do not make discoveries. They come to agreement about claims about making discoveries. This view is called constructivism, that knowledge is socially constructed. As we will see later in Chapters 4 and 7, this claim, while wildly exaggerated, does contain a kernel of truth if we understand knowledge not as objective truth but as a communal claim to truth.

Is knowledge limited to what is empirically verifiable? The advocates of scientific naturalism claim that only experimentally demonstrable events constitute knowledge. Knowledge claims coming from reason or philosophy or metaphysics or religion are false, even unintelligible statements and therefore cannot be knowledge. Those with a larger worldview, however, assert that even apart from any scientific proof, we can know, for example, that it is wrong to torture babies.[3] And I know that in the past I have been the friend of (had a relationship with) say, my aunt and uncle, though they are no longer alive to confirm it. I can't prove it, but I know it is true. Christians believe that the Bible is a source of knowledge, especially about things that we cannot see or test directly. Knowledge of what is good, of human nature, of the reason for our spiritual feelings—all of this is important knowledge not derivable from scientific experiment.

What is the role of reason in connection with knowledge? Is it important for knowledge to be rational? Can reason produce knowledge? Can reason be relied upon to distinguish true knowledge from false? Postmodernists often claim that reason and logic are tools of oppression and should be rejected or redefined. But Christians believe that when God says, "Come, let us reason together" (Isaiah 1:18), he is implying that he gave us rational minds for productive use.

Does truth really matter in the creation of "knowledge"? Are there values higher than truth? Is ideological purity or the exercise of power or the achievement of success more important than an undesired truth? Unfortunately, this issue is at the crux of too much teaching these days.

Postmodernists like to put words like *truth, knowledge,* and *facts* in quotation marks (sometimes called sneer quotes because they sneer at the words they surround) to call attention to their belief that what is referred to by these words does not exist in any objective form. Your truth and my truth may both be "true," but neither is true in any absolute way. To the postmodernist, "truth claims are only fictions."[4] The frightening implication of this position is, as Gene Edward Veith, Jr. says, "Those who do not believe in truth are more likely, I believe, to lie."[5]

And this fear is not without foundation. In his article in *The American Journal of Sociology*, "The Ten Commandments of Writing," sociologist Gary Alan Fine offers some standard advice, such as "revise brutally," "develop your own style," "use humor," and so forth.[6] Then, he adds one more piece of advice for the writers of sociology, "Lie sometimes."[7] He continues:

> There are places for "fact," and places for fiction. . . . Sometimes creative fictionalizing helps the author create a good story without harm to the thrust of the argument—indeed, helping it. Those of us who study personal experience stories or life histories (our own or others) know that we should not trust them as facts, although they can be trusted as narrative. So it is with our sociological storytelling. Such stories are effective in encouraging the recall of the ideas behind the stories. Narratives are more effective than abstracted statistical information in promoting memory. . . .[8]

Telling lies helps the argument. Make up things to help prove your point. Fine concludes, "I am arguing for the possibility of a sociology that is not so tied to principles of efficiency, conciseness, rationality, and knowledge at the expense of poetic language, joy, emotion, and insight. . . .⁹ A sociology that is "not so tied to . . . knowledge"? Perhaps Fine does not view knowledge as involving any kind of stable truth, placing him in the postmodern camp. His use of quotation marks around the word *fact* seems to confirm this. Only those old-fashioned modernists think there is such a thing as a genuine fact. And yet, for those of us who still believe there is a difference between what is true and what is not, what actually happened and what did not, how are we to respond to the kind of scholarship Fine recommends?

We as Christians would not regard making up things as a legitimate means to "prove your point." We recognize the difference between a fictional story (such as a novel or a parable) that conveys moral or philosophical truth and a fictional story presented to us *as if it were literally true*. To us, "creative fictionalizing" and factual knowledge are not the same thing. We would consider it highly important to know if the author of the article we are reading or the lecture we are hearing shares the view that "poetic language, joy, emotion, and insight" are more important than a correct picture of reality. The question of "whose episteme?" then, is an important one to answer as we read, hear, and learn.

When you read or listen to others, then, see if you can discover what theory of knowledge lies behind the ideas they are presenting. Chapters 6, 7, and 8 will help you understand more clearly the three main competing worldviews and their associated epistemes.

At the same time, however, you should realize that while many professors are indeed rather squarely in either the modernist or the postmodernist camp, other professors and most students are epistemological eclectics, combining a mixture of modern, postmodern, and even leftover Judeo-Christian ideas about knowledge. Talking to someone with such a smorgasbord epistemology can be challenging because many people can hold several conflicting or incompatible views at the same time. "Yes," they may tell you, "all morality is relative and personal, but if someone steals my car, that is *wrong*."

At any rate, you will benefit from identifying the epistemological foundations for the knowledge claims you hear. Beliefs about what possibly can or cannot be true (or whether there is such a thing as truth) will obviously shape the ideas you encounter. Seek out the reasons or evidence behind knowledge claims and be careful about accepting such claims simply on the basis of a confident pronouncement, sweeping statements that "everyone knows this," and the like. Be especially cautious if knowledge claims are made with ideological vehemence. See Chapter 9 for more information.

3.3 The Impact of Worldview on Knowledge

As we have just seen, the idea that objective truth is the highest goal of learning, while still often given lip service, is not always pursued. We should not, however, see examples like those above as evidence for some kind of conspiracy against goodness or truth. Many of those who insist on promoting as true what is objectively false are well intentioned, even idealistic. They want the world to become a better place, believing that it is now troubled and in need of remediation along the lines that harmonize with their worldview. Idealistic worldviews can exert a powerful influence on one's view of knowledge and on the nature and the role of truth in the production of knowledge. Worldviews often generate preferred truths — that is, ideas which, if true, would support the worldview of the person. There is a strong desire to believe some things, to want with emotional fervor for them to be true, and a similar desire to want ideas opposing the worldview to be false. Christians are often accused of this kind of belief, but it applies to nearly everyone, including professors and other scholars. Awareness of this fact will enable you to sort out evidence and knowledge claims more intelligently.

In his classic book, *Hoaxes*, Curtis MacDougall, notes that "in politics as in everything else, people believe what they want to believe and disbelieve what does not square with preconceived ideas."[10] This knowledge processing is actually a normal part of developing a stable view of the world. Where it becomes a problem is at the point where we cease to consider that we may be wrong or that new evidence may be right, in spite of its implications for our position, or when we choose to believe something because it flatters our ego. Phillip Johnson puts it bluntly: "The painful truth is that we are naturally inclined to believe what we want to believe, and we may adopt some fashionable intellectual scheme because it allows us to feel superior to other people. . . ."[11]

The influence of one's worldview to block disconfirming evidence has been pointed out as an issue for critical thinking and problem solving. Two phenomena have been observed in the way many people gather and process information.

Confirmation bias. Those who have developed a hypothesis or arrived at a conclusion have a strong tendency to seek further information that confirms their position. An important rule of hypothesis testing and problem solving is to seek all kinds of information, including information that may conflict with the conclusion in question. For example, if an investigator is working on the cause of an aircraft accident, the hypothesis (or tentative conclusion) may arise that the crash was caused by pilot error. A good investigator will continue to look for other kinds of evidence as well, however, including any evidence that might show mechanical failure, weather-related problems, or even a bomb.

The difficulty arises in areas where people have a strong desire to believe a certain conclusion, where worldview, politics, or other considerations make one conclusion strongly preferable. In such cases, there is a tendency to seek only information that supports the preferred conclusion and to ignore all other information. There is no attempt to seek disconfirming evidence.

A good example of confirmation bias is the story of the peppered moth. In the 1950s, Bernard Kettlewell set out to prove the operation of natural selection by studying the two varieties of peppered moth. Before the industrial revolution, most moths had been light colored, while after the revolution most moths in sooty, industrialized Birmingham were dark colored. Kettlewell argued that the pollution-darkened tree trunks eliminated the advantage of camouflage that the light moths had enjoyed, and that the dark moths now were more similar to the tree trunk colors, giving them a selection advantage when predators (birds) arrived for a meal. Kettlewell concluded that this change in proportion between light and dark moths did indeed show natural selection in action.

However, Kettlewell did not look for evidence that might have called his conclusions into question. When other scientists looked beyond the two areas studied by Kettlewell, they discovered that in some places, dark moths far outnumbered light ones, even though the tree bark nearby was light colored.[12] Perhaps more revealing, Kettlewell "changed his methodology in mid-course" when he was not getting the results he wanted, according to Judith Hooper.[13] The impression we get, she says, is that "when he got data he didn't like he often altered his experimental design."[14] As a result, he "always seemed to find what he expected would be true."[15] Finding an example of natural selection in action, then, was not a question to be answered for Kettlewell, but an agenda to be fulfilled. Such an attitude lends itself easily to confirmation bias.

Evaluation bias. In addition to the confirmation bias, which can cause investigators to ignore conflicting evidence, another bias can cause conflicting evidence to be rejected unfairly even when it does appear. Those who hold certain conclusions that support their worldview often welcome with little scrutiny further evidence that supports those conclusions, but evidence which conflicts with those conclusions is subjected to extremely critical and skeptical assessment. In other words, a double standard for the acceptability of evidence is applied. A greater degree of proof is required of evidence that conflicts with preconceived ideas or pet theories. Sometimes the level of proof required is so high that virtually no piece of conflicting evidence is allowed to stand.[16]

The Kettlewell study of peppered moths serves as a good example of evaluation bias also. The conclusions were welcomed unquestioningly by those eager to have proof of the mechanism of evolution. The story became a standard one in many biology textbooks. As Hooper says,

By the 1960s it had conquered all the textbooks, influencing the minds of four decades of biology students. It is the slam dunk of natural selection, the paradigmatic story that converts high school and college students to Darwin, the thundering left hook to the jaw of creationism.[17]

In subsequent years, however, a number of studies showed that Kettlewell's work was deeply flawed, containing more than a dozen problems that rendered his results meaningless.[18] For example, Kettlewell released and observed the moths during the day, when in nature they are night fliers. He placed them on tree trunks when they do not normally rest there.[19] He argued that the camouflage colors helped natural selection, when the moths in fact do not rest on color-matching spots of trees, but prefer the underside of branches.[20] Alison Motluk notes that "the list of Kettlewell's scientific shortcomings is fairly long," and asks, "How did all these flaws pass peer review? Why was this study accepted as gospel before it was replicated? Why did so few people go back and read the original papers before passing the story on?"[21]

Kettlewell's results were welcomed not only by evolutionists, but by the writers of science textbooks, some of whom even today continue to repeat it and reprint the staged photographs of moths on tree trunks (using dead or sleepy moths placed manually).[22] Motluk concludes, "The idea that the fittest survive became more than just a scientific theory—it had huge social implications as well. Many of the experts whose duty it was to cast a critical eye over the work seemed to want so badly for it to be true that they overlooked its glaring deficiencies."[23]

In a review of Judith Hooper's book *Of Moths and Men* about Kettlewell's work, Rita Hoots says that

> Hooper shows how the scientists inadvertently sought to confirm their beliefs in natural selection rather than actually testing the hypothesis, changing methods when results did not agree with the selection hypothesis. As Hooper ably demonstrates, our understanding is molded by subjective as well as objective factors; self-interest, personality, contrast-

ing worldviews, and human foibles influence the construction of scientific tests and the interpretation of evidence.[24]

Notice the phrases above: "wanted so badly for it to be true," and "inadvertently sought to confirm their beliefs." These are the conditions under which evaluation bias most easily influences the assessment of claims. Always remember that there is often a lot more at stake than merely whether an idea or claim is true. The stability and credibility of an entire worldview may be on the line. Of course, no worldview will rise or fall on the basis of the truth or falsehood of a single experiment, but every battle is viewed as important by some in the academy. You have certainly heard of the culture wars. The battle metaphor is apt. Especially now that Marx and Freud have been so thoroughly discredited, some see only Darwin as left to hold the fort of materialism. The battle therefore has descended to trench warfare. Not a single inch of ground may be yielded to the hated creationists or their allies, lest God be allowed into the world.

Chapter 5 contains additional material on worldview and the influence it plays in the way we view knowledge, argument, and evidence.

3.4 The Issue of Authority

Observers of the battle between naturalism and postmodernism sometimes remark that a principal crux of the conflict seems to be the role of authority. In fact, some have surmised that the ever-increasing claims of science to answer all the questions of life in naturalistic terms, together with the continuous rise in deference to the voice of science in every arena, have led to the rebellion against authority that we see among the postmodernists. If science, as many insist, provides the only authoritative voice about the world and what is truth, then those who are outside of science need either to submit to its pronouncements, become scientists themselves, or deny the power of authority. (As we will see, the Christian worldview provides another answer by disagreeing with the premise that science alone is the source of truth.) Many disciplines traditionally outside the sciences have attempted to remake themselves on a scientific model in order to join the voice of authority claimed by science. But others, especially in the humanities, have taken the position that authority itself is a problem.

The Christian worldview agrees with that of naturalism (or modernism) in recognizing the necessary and useful role of authority in the aggregation and transmission of knowledge. Many people make discoveries and share that knowledge with others, thus building civilization's stock of knowledge. (Think about the fact that most great civilizations are located within fifty miles of the ocean or a river. Trade in goods, inventions, and especially ideas makes civilizations rise and grow. Cultures tend to be highly eclectic: They adopt the best ideas from each other.) Thus, neither Christians nor naturalists find reliance on authority problematic in itself.

If you think about it for a minute, you'll discover that most of what you know is based on authority. If you read that eating too many transfatty acids in your food is bad for you, you probably believe it. That belief is based on your trust in the medical authority reporting the discovery. If you've never visited the Eiffel Tower but still believe that it really exists, you do so based on authority. If you point to a photograph as evidence, you are still relying on an authority, attesting that the photograph is genuine and has not been somehow faked.

No one can personally do every experiment, check every fact, or test every claim. We rely on the reports of others whom we deem reliable for nearly everything we know. There is nothing wrong with that. When someone asks us how we know something, we are likely to make an appeal to authority. "I read it in the paper," or "It was on the news," we say. Legitimate, even necessary, appeals to authority are based on our trust in the sources of the information. We do not believe just any claim or any source; we accept the word of those we believe have the knowledge or expertise to offer us true and accurate information.

Sometimes authorities with equally respectable credentials disagree with each other. Many battles are fought in the courtrooms and in the media by pitting authorities against each other. In the courtroom, attorneys often play a numbers and prestige game. The side with the largest number of the most famous experts is expected to sway the jury in its favor. If the matter is highly technical, the jury might be tempted to rely on the number and reputation of the experts rather than on the details or even the reasonableness of their testimony.

However, the authoritative voice can be abused. Sometimes authorities are wrong. An incorrect claim may come from wrong or missing evidence, an incorrect interpretation of the evidence, or even bias—some kind of political or philosophical agenda. Some authorities make claims to facts when they are merely offering opinions. Indeed, the logical fallacy of the appeal to prestige occurs when authorities urge belief for a claim (especially when the claim is controversial or open to question) simply on the basis of their authority. (The only exception to this would be an Authority who has absolute knowledge and whose claims are absolutely trustworthy.)

Especially in the last fifty years or so, the doctrine of scientism has become pervasive. Scientism is the claim that only science is the source of truth. All other claims to truth are just meaningless babble. A few people have wondered whether this exclusive claim to have knowledge might not be the source of postmodern rebellion: If the only voice of authority (science) marginalizes the ideas coming from the humanities (the origin of postmodern thought), then authority itself must be rejected. Whether or not that is true, many observers believe that one result of this "science is all" dogma has been the attempt to make every other discipline as science-like as possible. The social sciences have over the years come to rely increasingly on statistics, experiments, and studies that use, as closely as possible, the scientific method, in order to show their empirical value. Another result has been the attempt on the part of some to exploit the aura of science by claiming that their ideas are scientific rather than merely interpretive or philosophical. In the words of law professor Phillip Johnson:

> The very fact that science speaks so authoritatively in our culture tempts ideologues and worldview promoters to claim the authority of science as validating claims that in fact are not testable by experiment, and that may go far beyond the available evidence. In a word, the scientific method can

be counterfeited, and the counterfeit may be certified as genuine by the most prestigious authorities in our culture.[25]

Thus, while the Christian worldview assents to the role of authority in presenting knowledge, our worldview parts company with naturalistic views in some of the claims to knowledge, claims which are illegitimately made in the name of science. And we clearly disagree with the general claim that science is the only authoritative source of genuine knowledge.

A final problem of authority facing the university today is that authority based on knowledge has given way, at least to some extent, to authority based on power. Some ideas (and some prospective faculty members) are excluded from the academy while others are entrenched monopolistically through acts of pure power rather than through considerations of merit. In the area of scientific naturalism, there are many stories of articles blocked from publication and careers derailed because the wrong ideas—ideas that conflicted with currently held views—were being offered.[26] In the postmodernist area, where authority is rejected altogether as a source of knowledge, power is admitted to be the remaining tool for the promotion or suppression of ideas.[27]

Authority, whether enforced by power or consensus, should be attended to and heard out, but it should not be taken as the final word on any subject. Truth is the ultimate value for Christians, and truth is not determined by a vote or by whoever has control over the dissemination of information. Learn how to think for yourself and to weigh and judge arguments and evidence. Ask how something is known, who agrees and who disagrees, where you can find out more. You will soon be able to discern when claims are being promoted merely on the basis of appeals to prestige and when there is good evidence for them.

3.5 Implications for Integration

The ideal of the university—an ideal held more widely in the past than in the present—is the pursuit of truth, undistorted by political agendas or biases of any kind, including antitheological biases. In this ideal place everyone says, "Let's sit down together and put all the evidence on the table and examine it dispassionately. Let's hear the pros and cons of this idea and see if we can determine whether or not it is true. Let's see where this leads." The problem today is that for many in the academy, worldviews that are actively hostile to Christianity shape the knowledge claims and the methodology of investigation of some faculty (and the textbooks they write). Evidence that can potentially threaten the integrity or credibility of a worldview is either rejected as untrue or irrelevant, denied ontological status, or reinterpreted in a way favorable to that worldview. No longer are those who feel threatened willing to allow the evidence to lead just anywhere, especially if that anywhere includes the direction of God.

When you listen to a lecture or read a textbook or do other assigned reading, then, strive to identify the worldview of the professor or author. By what is said directly, or by "reading between the lines," see if you can determine where the information is coming from and how its presentation has been shaped by that worldview. You can usually identify a worldview by noting the following principal aspects:

- Religious or metaphysical disposition (theist, atheist, agnostic)
- Ontological set (basic assumptions; see Chapter 5)
- Epistemology or theory of knowledge
- Axiology or source and influence of values
- Political orientation and social views

Much of your analysis will be made simpler by your knowledge, mentioned in the previous chapter, that most academics tend to share a highly secular worldview. Even though the modernists and the postmodernists are at war with each other, they tend to share a similar metaphysics and political orientation.

When I taught critical thinking, I regularly looked through the many available textbooks on that subject. I was often amused to notice that the political orientation of the authors was evident in their choice of examples. Since most of the authors were leftists, they usually chose examples from political conservatives to demonstrate logical fallacies and examples from liberals to demonstrate better thinking. Similarly, their agnostic metaphysics were evident in their discussions and examples involving God. Somehow, those irrational Christians couldn't seem to argue logically. The irony, of course, is that the author of a critical thinking textbook should, I would think anyway, strive to be objective and fair in the use of arguments and examples. To create the impression that "to be logical is to be left" or that "faith is not logical" is to create a message that is both unfair and untrue. And since many critical thinking professors are philosophers by training, they of all people should recognize the complexities of epistemology and metaphysics they seem so happy to manipulate in favor of their preferred position.

Now you know not to be shocked when you encounter statements or implications in a textbook or lecture that openly (or even subtly) conflict with your own worldview. You will no longer sit back in amazement and ask, "How can this be?" You know how it can be.

See Chapters 10 and 11 for help with the activities of integration.

Summary

An individual's definition of knowledge (what can and cannot be true, by definition) exerts a powerful influence on the way each person sees and interprets the world. Worldviews can even affect the way we process information, causing us to apply biased standards and subjective interpretations. Authority is a valuable source of knowledge, but it is subject to dangers and limitations as well. It is important to learn how to discern the epistemology behind knowledge claims because professors and textbook writers usually do not announce their view of knowledge or their worldview in general.

Questions for Thought and Discussion

1. We live in an age where rebellion and resistance to authority are rampant, especially thanks to our highly individualistic culture and the advertising industry (which likes to appeal to our selfish, rebellious hearts). What is your own feeling about authority and its role in representing or supporting knowledge claims? How much do you rely on authority in various areas of your learning? How much do you resist authority? Explore the proper role of authority in the transmission of knowledge. (Think about different kinds of authority, as well.)

2. Discuss your own experience with confirmation bias. Have you discovered it in your own thinking? Have you seen it in others? What are some effective strategies for resisting this phenomenon?

3. Construct a personal, working definition of *knowledge*, and explain (with examples) how it includes everything it should encompass and excludes everything it should omit.

4. Explain how worldview and other biases may *unintentionally* influence an honest investigator's interpretations and conclusions. Can you think of some ways to reduce unintentional bias?

---

[1] These comments come from Solzhenitsyn's address at Harvard University, long before the fall of the Soviet Union. His address is well worth reading in its entirety. Alexander Solzhenitsyn, "A World Split Apart," June 8, 1978, available at
<http://www.Columbia.edu/cu/Augustine/arch/solzhenitsyn/harvard1978.html>.

[2] Phillip E. Johnson, *Objections Sustained: Subversive Essays on Evolution, Law & Culture* (Downers Grove, Ill.: InterVarsity Press, 1998), p. 115.

[3] I am indebted to J. P. Moreland for this example. Other examples of non-empirical knowledge his lists include "fairness and kindness are virtues, hatred is a vice, what Hitler did to the Jews in World War II was immoral."

See *Love Your God with All Your Mind: The Role of Reason in the Life of the Soul* (Colorado Springs: Navpress, 1997), p. 143.

[4] Veith, Jr., Gene Edward, *Postmodern Times: A Christian Guide to Contemporary Thought and Culture* (Wheaton, Ill.: Crossway Books, 1994), p. 49.

[5] Ibid., p. 51.

[6] Gary Alan Fine, "The Ten Commandments of Writing," *The American Sociologist,* Summer 1998, 19:2, pp. 152-157.

[7] Ibid., p. 156.

[8] Ibid., p. 156.

[9] Ibid., pp. 156-157.

[10] Curtis D MacDougall, *Hoaxes* (2nd ed., New York: Dover, 1958), p. 89.

[11] Phillip Johnson, *The Wedge of Truth: Splitting the Foundations of Naturalism* (Downers Grove, Ill.: Intervarsity, 2000), p. 36.

[12] Wells, p. 144.

[13] Judith Hooper, Of Moths and Men: An Evolutionary Tale (New York: W. W. Norton, 2002), p. 254.

[14] Ibid., p. 255.

[15] Ibid., p. 256.

[16] See the discussion of this technique in Michael A. Cremo and Richard L. Thompson, *Forbidden Archeology: The Hidden History of the Human Race* (Los Angeles: Bhaktivedanta, 1998), pp. 180-184.

[17] Hooper, p. xvii.

[18] See the summary of many of these in Hooper, pp. 265-270.

[19] Wells, p. 148.

[20] Alison Motluk, "'Of Moths and Men' by Judith Hooper." *Salon.* 18 Sept. 2002; available at <http://www.salon.com/books/review/2002/09/18/hooper>.

[21] Motluk, op cit.

[22] Wells, p. 150.

[23] Motluk, op. cit.

[24] Rita Hoots, "Hooper, Judith. Of Moths and Men: An Evolutionary Tale," *Library Journal*, August 2002, p. 136.

[25] Johnson, *Wedge*, p. 37.

[26] For just a few examples, see Cremo and Thompson, op. cit, about Thomas E. Lee (pp. 346-353) and Virginia Steen-McIntyre (pp. 362-366). See also Jonathan Wells, "Catch-23," *Center for Science and Culture*, July 1, 2002, available at <http://www.discovery.org> for the experience of Michael Behe. And see the story of the suppression of an article for *Omni* by Gene Fairley in "Darwinism: A Time for Funerals," *Contrast*, March-April 1983, pp. 4-5.

[27] In Chapter 7, we will see that many postmodernists actually make much use of authority, citing with approval the writers they admire.

Chapter 4
Political and Social Influences on Knowledge

The acceptance of theories depends as much on the psychology of human beings as on the content of the theories. It is human beings who decide, individually and as a community, whether a theory indeed has explanatory power or provides understanding. This is why seemingly "extrascientific" factors such as productivity, portability, storytelling power and aesthetics matter.

> — Roald Hoffmann[1]

In theory, scientists proclaim themselves ready to follow the facts wherever they might lead. But in practice, the social mechanisms of the scientific community set limits beyond which its members in good standing cross only at their peril. When eminent authorities announce their rejection of certain categories of evidence, others hesitate to mention similar evidence out of fear of ridicule. Thus anomalous evidence gradually slides from disrepute into complete oblivion.

> — Michael Cremo and Richard Thompson[2]

4.1 The Politics of Knowledge

There is another problem with knowledge. A nutshell description might be that it involves the difference between theory and practice. Even though the knowledge source might have what appeals to us as a credible epistemology that declares the need for objective, reasoned, demonstrable proof, in practice the claims for knowledge that arise might not follow that theory adequately. The ideal of totally unbiased investigation and reasoning is a worthy one and should always be maintained. Nevertheless, we must admit that few people, ourselves included, can achieve it perfectly.

For example, as Christians, we can agree that much worthy knowledge can be derived from the epistemology of scientific naturalism, even though we believe that this worldview is too limited and even ultimately incorrect. In theory, the scientific method of observation and experiment should be a reliable source of knowledge. And in practice, it often is. However, the search for knowledge is influenced by a host of non-objective factors, including personal interests and values, beliefs about where knowledge can be found (search here instead of there), expectations, hopes, theories, politics, metaphysics, funding from grants, peer pressure, prestige, and so on. As we will see in Chapter 6, the insistent confusion between philosophical materialism and the practice of science creates many problems in knowledge and interpretation.

You probably first learned to be cautious about information and knowledge claims coming from apparently authoritative sources by watching or reading advertisements. In the process of hearing amazing claims about a product and watching the sometimes unbelievable way a product could solve all kinds of problems, you probably began to be suspicious or even skeptical. Or perhaps you believed the advertisers until you tested their product against the claims made for it. The new shampoo really didn't make attractive members of the opposite sex want to run their fingers through your hair; the new deodorant did not make you more popular than ever; the new cleanser didn't really clean your bathroom all by itself. So, it wasn't long before you realized that advertisers exaggerate, slant, distort, omit, and imply many claims that in a neutral presentation would not be so flattering to their product. The advertisers show only one side of their product, a very favorable side.

Advertisers, of course, are advocates of a particular point of view—the view that their product is wonderful and that you need it. Another way of looking at this is to say that advertisers are partisans, biased supporters of a cause, the cause of their product. In this view, advertising might be seen as a type of politicized knowledge, knowledge distorted by a political agenda or orthodoxy. In this case, the orthodoxy is that the product can do no wrong.

The most obvious kind of political partisanship, of course, is what we think of first when someone mentions politics: the social and economic ideals and goals that distinguish the left from the right, the liberals from the conservatives, in the American political process. Advocates of every viewpoint, from the far left to the far right, as well as advocates on every side of many social policies (pesticides, guns, cigarette smoking, school vouchers and so on) often present their arguments in a way that favors their own conclusions and downplays the arguments of the opposition.

Perhaps you've discovered that the news media often reflect partisan political views in their reporting. You may have learned to be cautious about the news, teaching yourself to ask what has been left out, slanted, or presented in a biased way. We live in an era of spinning—distorting facts in a way that favors a particular position. A news release from a manufacturer is likely to present a different view of a labor dispute from that of the labor union involved. You may even have seen some of the information about the liberal bias of the news media, from, say, the American Society of Newspaper Editors[3] or the Media Research Center,[4] or Bernard Goldberg's recent book.[5] Whatever your personal political viewpoint, you realize that you cannot expect news reporting to be balanced or unbiased.

If you have been at a public university for any length of time, you are also by now aware that the overwhelming majority of faculty members are leftists. One look at 1500 faculty members at 20 universities revealed that more than 91 percent had leftist political affiliations. At Cornell, the figure was 96%, at UCLA 93%, at UC Santa Barbara, 98%.[6] You will not need too many weeks of classes to learn that you cannot expect a balance in political views at the university.[7]

Clearly, then, one type of political bias that affects knowledge at the university is that of the social and economic policy preferences that distinguish our political parties. But if we return to the example of advertising for a moment, you can understand that there are other possible political biases that can distort the view of knowledge in the academy. At the heart of political bias is a preferred "truth," a desired dogma, one type of which has recently been called political correctness. At the university, certain opinions, ideas, or points of view tend to become ascendant and take over departments, areas of study, or even the entire academy. These ideas are then maintained strongly against all opposition. What is claimed to be true or genuine knowledge to be exalted and what is claimed to be false and to be ridiculed or ignored is too often subject to political and personal philosophical considerations rather than considerations of reason and evidence.

This personal bias is sometimes the case even with scientific knowledge. As Thomas Kuhn notes in his book, *The Structure of Scientific Revolutions*, theory often directs the construction of experiments and the observations that reinforce and refine the theory.[8] In fact, he argues that "in the sciences fact and theory, discovery and invention, are not categorically and permanently distinct. . . ."[9] Both research and conclusions are influenced by the reigning theory (or paradigm, as Kuhn calls it):

> [Normal science] seems an attempt to force nature into the preformed and relatively inflexible box that the paradigm supplies. No part of the aim of normal science is to call forth new sorts of phenomena; indeed those that will not fit the box are often not seen at all.[10]

Scholars and scientists are human beings, and as such they have personal beliefs and values that sometimes influence their scholarly work. The search for knowledge, while theoretically an unfettered journey down the path of truth, wherever it leads, is in practice often powerfully shaped by social and cultural considerations.

For example, many people reject Christianity not because they have examined its claims and found them unconvincing or untrue, but because Christianity includes a moral code that opposes their interest in premarital sex and extramarital sex. Belief in God makes abortion more difficult to support. A religion that stresses humility represents a sturdy challenge to the desire to follow the rampant narcissism of contemporary society. And our faith encourages us to resist the baser elements of our fallen nature, such as greed, dislike of authority, self-indulgence, and so forth. Many in the academy have particular difficulty because they see Christianity as both anti-feminist and pro-American (that is, encouraging patriotism). Christianity is therefore rejected because of a dislike for its cultural and behavioral implications, not because of its questionable truth status. In other words, for some people, knowledge claims with undesired social consequences *cannot be permitted to be true*. And anyone who holds such hated views is to be kept from grants, hiring, publication, and promotion.

Similarly, sometimes knowledge claims that harmonize with desired beliefs are still valued even though they have been demonstrated to be wrong. For example, nineteenth-century scientist Ernst Haeckel is well known for his drawings of embryos. Historian of science Charles Singer describes Haeckel as follows: "Ernst Haeckel (1834-1919) was an extreme champion of evolutionary theory. He was an excellent artist, whose imagination was prone to rule his pen and brush."[11] And biologist Jonathan Wells notes that "Haeckel's drawings are misleading in three ways: (1) they include only those classes and orders that come closest to fitting Haeckel's theory; (2) they distort the embryos they purport to show; and (3) most seriously, they entirely omit earlier stages in which vertebrate embryos look very different."[12] But Haeckel misled his readers by more than just a rigged selection or omission. Says Wells, "In some cases, Haeckel used the same woodcut to print embryos that were supposedly from different classes. In others, he doctored his drawings to make the embryos appear more alike than they really were."[13]

It is bad enough that Haeckel's work was welcomed so enthusiastically as "proof" of evolution and the theory of recapitulation even though scientists knew almost from the start that Haeckel had cheated. Wells notes that "biologists have known for over a century that Haeckel faked his drawings; vertebrate embryos never look as similar as he made them out to be."[14] The real scandal, though, is that even very recent textbooks, including ones published in 1998 and 1999, still repeat Haeckel's drawings or slightly redrawn versions, together with incorrect claims about their similarity.[15] The desire to believe an idea and to marshal support for it is sometimes so strong that even discredited support is still cited by the idea's defenders. Politics can play a powerful role in shaping one's epistemology.

The distorting influence of political concerns and the support of a desired ideology can be seen over and over again. Let's take a look at a few examples from various fields of learning to see more clearly what can happen.

In 1928, anthropologist Margaret Mead published *Coming of Age in Samoa*, which claimed that the practice of uninhibited, frequent sex by young people in that country resulted in a healthier adolescence, free from neurosis, crisis, stress, and even rape.[16] The implications were clear. The problems of modern American society result from the sexual restraints put on it by an oppressive culture. Others soon spelled out the implications that Americans should adopt sexual promiscuity as part of their psychologically healthy growth.[17] The book was welcomed enthusiastically and uncritically by those who approved of its implications. Many embraced it as a "scientific" basis for the free-love philosophy they advocated. The book became required reading for millions of college students from the 1930s through the 1970s.

Then, in 1983, the findings of the book were shown to be false. Instead of a free-sex environment, Samoa at the time of Mead's investigation was a sexually strict society, strongly emphasizing virginity before marriage both from a cultural and a religious standpoint.[18] Mead had based most of her conclusions on the "recreational lies" of just two Samoan girls who had, out of embarrassment over her frank questions, agreed with Mead's preconceptions about sexual liberty in Samoa.

It is instructive, of course, to realize that generations of students were fooled by the false views of this book and the harmful implications for Americans who adopted them. It is also instructive to realize that the conclusions of the book came largely from the preconceptions and desired outcomes of Margaret Mead, who wanted so strongly to find certain facts that she did indeed think she found them, in spite of extensive evidence to the contrary, much of it recorded in her own journals. This is a salient indication of the power of an ideology to control perception in the face of facts. And it is even more instructive to learn that many professors, who found the book's conclusions in harmony with their own philosophies, promoted it uncritically for so many years.

But also highly instructive is the reaction from academics to the exposure of Mead's poor science and wrong conclusions. Anthropologist Derek Freeman, whose book *Margaret Mead and Samoa: The Making and Unmaking of an Anthropological Myth* revealed Mead's errors, recounts the reaction in the afterword of his book *The Fateful Hoaxing of Margaret Mead*. He says that "the embarrassment of those whose beliefs had been so rudely shaken soon turned to fury. . . . Thus, from February 1983 onward, I was subjected to a highly emotional and, at times, flagrantly ad hominem campaign."[19] He then recounts the "delirium of vilification" at the American Anthropological Association meeting that year, where a vote was taken denouncing his work:

> That the members of a professional association could seek to dispose of a major scientific and scholarly issue in this undisguisedly political way, attempting to dismiss, by a show of hands, a refutation based on a cogent array of factual evidence, is a striking demonstration of the extraordinary way in which belief can come to dominate the thinking of scholars and scientists and of how a hallowed doctrine can blind its devotees to empirical reality.[20]

Even after the shock of the discovery had had time to soak in, some scholars were still calling Mead's book a "humane and liberating text" and "as timely as ever."[21] The book's message was so compatible with many professors' views and agendas that they could not simply give it up, even though its conclusions are false.

Another example of the power of the desire to believe in the support for an ideology comes in the form of the 1983 book *I, Rigoberta Menchu*, purportedly the autobiographical account of a Guatemalan peasant, revealing the oppression of indigenous peasants by greedy plantation owners and the military government. While some readers viewed the book as a Marxist diatribe, it was welcomed by the academy as an instant classic of multiculturalism, showing the heroic resistance of a progressive peasant woman against the oppressive landowners and the right-wing government of Guatemala.[22] As with *Coming of Age in Samoa*, this book also became required reading for tens of thousands of college students. In 1992, the book's heroine, Rigoberta Menchu, was even given the Nobel Peace Prize for writing the book.

Then, beginning in the late 1980s and culminating in a book in 1999, anthropologist David Stoll discovered that many of the claims in the book were false. Stoll went to Guatemala and interviewed more than 120 people connected with the book and its author. As a result of his research, he learned that the book contains many fabrications, altered facts, and distortions, all designed to further Marxist ideology and associated revolutionary ideas.[23] In Stoll's words, the book "works revolutionary paradigms into one episode after another, subtracting factual elements that contradict them."[24]

Once again, it is instructive to learn that the book's ideas are heavily slanted politically in the direction that pleases many academics. "The book has strong appeal because it stresses indigenous rights, feminism, identity politics, Marxist class analysis — virtually the entire bundle of concerns of the campus left," says John Leo.[25] No wonder it was quickly canonized and made required reading on campus. It is also instructive that the fact claims in the book are often untrue and remained unchallenged for years, possibly because they were welcome.

But, once again, what is most instructive is the reaction of the academy to the exposure of the book's defects. Anthropologist Stoll recounts: "The prestige of *I, Rigoberta Menchu* was so great that when I began to talk about my findings in 1990-1991, some of my colleagues regarded them as sacrilegious. I had put myself beyond the pale of decency."[26] One faculty member said, "Whether the book is true or not, I don't care"; another said he would continue to require the book for classes in spite of the revelations about its content, and a third said that "the strict rules of veracity" should not be imposed on a narrative from the Latin American tradition.[27] Deep emotional commitments sometimes override a strict commitment to truth. Stoll concludes that "books like *I, Rigoberta Menchu* will [continue to] be exalted because they tell many academics what they want to hear."[28]

As a final example, we can turn to the politics of feminism. In 1992, the American Association of University Women (AAUW) brought out a study, *How Schools Shortchange Girls,* purporting to show that girls were being disadvantaged in the American educational system. Girls, the study claimed, suffered from low self-esteem, widespread sexist discrimination, and generally second-class status in the classroom. The AAUW spent a substantial amount of money promoting the study, and the publicity campaign resulted in more than 1,400 news reports about it.[29]

Unfortunately, as Diane Ravitch, a former U.S. assistant secretary of education noted, "The AAUW report was just completely wrong. What was so bizarre is that it came out right at the time that girls had overtaken boys in almost every area."[30] A number of studies showed that girls were excelling in school while boys were falling behind.

What was the reaction of the AAUW to the critics who pointed to these studies showing that the AAUW's claims were untenable? In 1997, the organization's newsletter compared the critics of its position to Holocaust deniers and historical revisionists.[31] That same year, the AAUW sponsored a conference designed to teach attendees how to fight the "revisionists" and continue to insist on its erroneous claims.[32]

By 1998 the study had been thoroughly exposed as "politics dressed up as science."[33] Yet a year later, the AAUW produced another report, *Gender Gaps: Where Schools Fail Our Children,* claiming that "an alarming new gender gap" was about to "cheat girls" in the area of computer science.[34] It appears to be in the interest of some scholars to view girls as victims of discrimination or even male oppression, regardless of the large amount of evidence to the contrary.

These examples are emblematic in revealing how ideologies and political (in the sense of self-serving, partisan) considerations can affect what is exalted as true knowledge and what is condemned as false in the academy.

4.2 The Sociology of Knowledge

The sociology of knowledge is the study of how social factors shape the discovery, creation, meaning, and transmission of knowledge. It is a huge field because there are many social groupings, but for our purposes we can focus on how scholarly communities influence a discipline's knowledge. Scholarly and scientific knowledge is not developed in a vacuum but in a communal way, where the opinions of one's peers, one's institution, grant-making organizations, and other social factors play an important role. The social status (or academic standing) of the experimenter often influences how favorably a particular finding is received. And, of course, the current beliefs of the knowledge community influence the receptivity of new information. As Alexander Kohn notes,

> The attractiveness of any theory in its application to society depends on how relevant it is and how well it fits everybody's preconceptions. If the fit is good, then even if the proofs are shaky, there would be a tendency to accept the theory.[35]

Kohn gives an example from the beginning of the 20th century, where an astronomer at Mount Wilson Observatory observed what he believed were rotating spiral nebulae:

> When these results were published, they were readily accepted by the majority of astronomers because they fitted the then prevailing theoretical considerations, and also because they agreed with the data accumulated in the period 1914-1916. Moreover, some astronomers repeated van Maanen's observations and confirmed them.[36]

What is significant about this finding, though, is the response to critics. Kohn continues:

> Any criticism of van Maanen's data at that time was silenced. So, when the astronomer Kurt Lundmark wrote to Harlow Shapley of Harvard University about his doubts concerning the correctness of the data, Shapley replied . . . that one could also find flaws in Lundmark's conclusions in

his own important papers about the distances of globular clusters. Lundmark did not pursue the matter further.[37]

Thus, a single veiled threat from a powerful colleague silenced the opposition.

Scholarly communities possess many ways to exert social pressure on their members, including publication or the refusal of publication, awards, recommendations for grants, movement up or down the "pecking order," and so forth. Pressures may be especially evident when discoveries or interpretations are potentially in conflict with received conclusions. According to Michael Cremo and Richard Thompson,

> Among the social processes that discourage acceptance and reporting of anomalous evidence are ridicule and gossip, including attacks on character and accusations of incompetence. Furthermore, discoveries have almost no impact in the world of science unless they are published in standard journals. The editorial process, especially the practice of anonymous peer review, often presents an insurmountable obstacle.[38]

An interesting example of this is the way Freud's early followers employed various pressures to expand the influence of Freud's ideas and to suppress opponents. Frederick Crews writes,

> A secret committee was organized and worked between 1912 and 1926, with Freud's approval, to publicize and support his ideas, and—significantly—to attack opponents of Freud's ideas by employing "malicious gossip, exclusion from official journals, and the planting of demeaning critiques in those same journals."[39]

As we will see a bit more in Chapter 9, mockery, scorn, and ridicule are lamentably frequent weapons in the war of ideas.

The role of social values in the practice of scholarship becomes evident when we think about some of the questions that shape research. Consider how the shared values of a research community will influence the answers to these questions:

- What subjects or specific issues should research in the discipline focus on?
- What subjects or specific issues should be ignored or even suppressed?
- What is the disciplinary practitioners' process for devaluing or stigmatizing certain knowledge claims?
- What questions are worth asking and what questions are not?
- What facts are important?
- What mechanism is used to agree upon "legitimation and verification systems"[40] for those facts? (In other words, what is the process for agreeing that a proposition is indeed a fact?)

The role of social power in scholarly practice is clear when we examine some of the questions that lie behind disciplinary conclusions:

- What is the meaning of the facts discovered?
- How is the meaning of the facts determined?
- When a "fact" is the result of an interpretation or inference rather than a direct observation, who has the power to decide upon the construction?
- What social process is used to come to an agreement about facts and their meaning?
- What happens when a new fact claim is resisted by its scholarly community?
- Are some fact claims or experimental results ignored for fear of the consequences?
- What role does social, political, theoretical, or perceptual bias play in the discipline's work?

From these questions, you can discern that much more than objective criteria are involved in the practice of disciplinary research. What is known or knowable (the privileged episteme, to use a postmodern way of describing it) is influenced by social factors (as well as political, cultural, and ideological ones). Communities of study (disciplinary fields) form alliances, fight battles, and come to conclusions about knowledge that are sometimes more dependent on the power or position of the combatants than on the merits of the evidence.

Of course, the very presence of competing schools of thought within a discipline, resulting in battles over what is correct, provides a mechanism for testing ideas and shows that many conflicting interpretations are not completely suppressed. But the pressure to conform to current theoretical understandings is there. Cremo and Thompson note:

> When we speak of suppression of evidence, we are not referring to scientific conspirators carrying out a satanic plot to deceive the public. Instead, we are talking about an ongoing social process of knowledge filtration that appears quite innocuous but has a substantial cumulative effect. Certain categories of evidence simply disappear from view, in our opinion unjustifiably.[41]

Social factors are critical to the understanding of disciplinary progress because of the way they shape accepted knowledge. In most disciplines, if not all, many facts should more accurately be called conclusions or interpretations, because instead of being directly observable or deducible truths, they "resolve into (1) arguments based on further 'facts,' or (2) claims that someone has witnessed something at a particular time and place. Thus 'facts' turn out to be networks of arguments and observational claims."[42] Fact claims may be interpretations and inferences based on assumptions and other inferences. It is not always easy to differentiate between objectively observable or testable facts and fact claims based on negotiated inferences. But much of scientific knowledge is inferential, developed in a community of practitioners sharing similar interests, theoretical bases, and, often, worldviews.

A final problem in the sociology of knowledge is the ideological and theoretical homogenization of the academy. Entire departments may be Marxist or deconstructionist or evolutionist or Freudian, thus diminishing the clash of opposing ideas that supply a check and a test and a motivation for fresh thinking unsuffocated by a reigning paradigm. Where a department or discipline is ideologically committed to a particular agenda or school of thought, assumptions can become invisible and conclusions may go unchallenged. New or different ideas are rejected with scorn and, often, anger. And young practitioners know that there can be penalties for rocking the boat. Social pressure to "fit in" is often quite powerful. When a young paleontologist was asked "if he had ever observed human incisions on fossil whale bone or other mammalian bone" he said, "I stay away from anything that has to do with man. Too controversial."[43] The wrong observation or conclusion can mean that tenure will be only a dream.

Perhaps worse than pressure to conform to theoretical verities is what has been called the "ideological secularization" of the academy, "the excluding, ignoring, or bracketing out of God's truth and reality in the conduct of thought and life."[44] Historian Gertrude Himmelfarb makes this point strikingly: "Today, race, class, and gender are the holy trinity presiding over higher education in America. . . . Few people have even noticed (I've never seen any mention of the fact) that religion is missing from this trinity, as if it is no longer a defining principle of one's identity."[45] Regardless of the department or school of thought, the academic community is thoroughly secularized and often hostile to Christian faith, especially where matters of faith or theological knowledge intrude upon disciplinary concerns. There are still Christian professors at secular universities, but the influence of their Christian knowledge is kept very small.

4.3 Implications for Integration

Beginning with your undergraduate major and then continuing in graduate school, you will quickly discover that your educational experience involves much more than the transmission of disciplinary knowledge and techniques. You will certainly learn the content, together with the discipline's ideas about how information is acquired, what methods are used to process and evaluate it, and so forth. But you will also be socialized into the attitudes, values, behaviors, politics, and beliefs of those teaching you, including their theoretical and even ideological biases. Some of these values and biases will be professor specific, while others belong to the discipline itself as currently configured by its practitioner community.

The risk for the Christian is that for nearly all disciplines, philosophical materialism is viewed as an integral part of the structure of knowledge. Religion, especially Christianity, is viewed as an irrelevant, even foolish, belief with no connection to the scholarship or experiments in the subject. Christian students therefore face pressure to give up or at least suppress their faith and become genuine members of their new academic community.

Many of the great universities were founded by Christians to take students with their childhood faith to the next level and show how it integrated with knowledge, grew in sophistication and power, and really did answer the questions of the universe. Today, these same universities, now thoroughly secularized, contrast the student's incoming faith with what is presented as a more sophisticated outlook, as true knowledge, an enlightenment from the myths of childhood. This promise of apparent sophistication plays powerfully on the ego and pride for many students.

Psychologist Paul Vitz traces his own movement from nominal Christianity as a young man to atheism in college and graduate school (before regaining faith later on). The reasons for his atheism are significant, because they represent a pattern seen often at the university. He says that "the major factors involved in becoming an atheist—though I was not really aware of them at the time—were not intellectual, but social and psychological."[46] With most professors and most students professing agnosticism or at least the rejection of traditional religion, it becomes difficult to fit in or be one of the gang for those who maintain their faith. Vitz says, "Furthermore, besides escape from a dull and, according to me, socially unworthy past [his life in the Midwest], I wanted to take part, to be comfortable, in the new, glamorous secular world into which I was moving."[47]

The university attempts to present a feeling of "now you have really arrived" and to make you feel that it is now time to discard those old, parochial, and silly religious prejudices that your parents instilled in you. "What are you, a mamma's boy or girl? When are you going to grow up? No one who is educated believes *that* stuff. That's for kids." As a result, many religious students come to feel ashamed of their beliefs (usually described by professors and fellow students as "fundamentalist," whatever they are in fact). Vitz notes, "The pressure from this kind of socialization has pushed many a young person away from belief in God and all that this belief symbolizes and entails."[48]

A related social pressure, especially in graduate school, comes from the desire not just to fit in but to be accepted and approved by one's professors. To get a grant, a teaching assistantship, be invited over to the professor's house, it pays to wear the same clothes. Vitz was influenced by these factors as well:

> Another major reason for my becoming an atheist was that I desired to be accepted by the powerful and influential scientists in the field of psychology. In particular, I wanted to be accepted by my professors in graduate school. As a graduate student, I was thoroughly socialized by the specific "culture" of academic research psychology. My professors at Stanford University, however much they might disagree among themselves on psychological theory, were, as far as I could tell, united in two things: their intense career ambitions and their rejection of religion.[49]

Social pressure, the desire to fit in, youthful rebellion ("Think for yourself, and what you should think is that you don't need God"), and the fact that "in the powerful secular and neopagan world of today, it is quite inconvenient to be a serious believer,"[50] all conspire to put pressure on one's faith.

The point to be underlined here is that Christians do not lose their faith at the university because they have seen their faith demonstrated to be false, or because they have engaged in an intellectual examination of the evidence or theological ideas or the implications of belief and disbelief, only to conclude rationally that their faith is false. Many lose their faith because of factors that are "not intellectual, but social and psychological," as Vitz says.

But remember that the university of your experience is only one place in one time, one environment (sometimes called The Ivory Tower because of its detachment from the Real World), and the views and social values there are not universal. You need not buy into the myth that Christianity is simplistic, an "opiate of the masses" as Karl Marx called it, or that "no smart people are Christians." One of Christianity's great strengths is that it is understandable enough to be accessible to the simplest, yet rich and deep enough to satisfy the most intelligent and philosophical. Throughout the history of the faith, many highly intelligent people have been Christians. This fact, of course, is no argument for its truth, but it is a rebuttal of the claim that Christianity is only for the simple. A common tactic of ideologues is to irrationalize the opposition—to make opponents out to be unthinking, emotional, fools. The more knowledgeable, the more able to think and argue that you become, the harder it will be for others to charge you with folly. You may even cause some hardened hearts to soften.

Equip yourself, then, and prepare for some hostility. Remember that there is much worthy knowledge at the university and that your task is to learn to sort it out and test it. Remember also that ridicule is the weapon of those who don't have good arguments. As William Paley once noted, "Who can refute a sneer?" Are you willing to be laughed at for the sake of your faith?

Summary

Scholars are human, and their beliefs and interests are often closely tied to personal political commitments, ideology, basic beliefs and other considerations. These commitments, sometimes emotionally rather than rationally based, can influence their research and their conclusions. Similarly, scholars do not work in a vacuum, but are subject to social pressures and the influence of factors connected to the machinery of scholarship (grants, promotion, tenure, publication, etc.), all which involve working with others, who may help shape the direction of the research. As a student in this not only scholarly but social and political community, you should be aware of these forces that will be pressuring you to conform. Remember that the truth is neither established nor refuted by a vote of hands or a committee. Look for the truth.

Questions for Thought and Discussion

1. What are some of the ways that political factors can be expressed in a particular course? Think beyond partisan politics (left-right) and include politics in the sense of ideological commitments (secularism, feminism, homosexual agendas, suppression of opposing ideas, etc.).

2. What are some things you might do that would help you see around political bias in a course? (Imagine that you want to learn the subject, but that the professor provides a highly biased view of it. How can you rebalance the material to give you a more objective or at least a fuller view?)

3. Find a historical controversy in your major and learn how the battles were fought. Which idea won out and why? What factors were involved? Were there social or power factors? Were these decisive?

4. What strategy have you adopted or might you adopt for maintaining and strengthening your faith in the face of social pressure (from classmates and professors)? Do you find it "inconvenient to be a serious believer" while at the university? Why or why not?

---

[1] Roald Hoffmann, "Why Buy That Theory?" *American Scientist* 91:1 (Jan-Feb 2003), p. 11.
[2] Michael A. Cremo and Richard L. Thompson, *Forbidden Archeology: The Hidden History of the Human Race*, rev. ed., (Los Angeles: Bhaktivedanta Book Publishing, 1998), p. 33.

[3] American Society of Newspaper Editors, "ASNE Survey: Journalists Say They're Liberal," *The American Editor,* May 26, 1999; available at <http://www.asne.org/kiosk/editor/ 97.jan-feb/dennis4.htm>.

[4] The Center produces many items about media bias, including a daily briefing filled with examples. For a quick overview of some survey data, see "The Press Corps: Liberal, Liberal, Liberal." *Media Reality Check.* August 14, 2001; available at <http://www.mediaresearch.org/ realitycheck/2001/20010814.asp>.

[5] Bernard Goldberg, *Bias: A CBS Insider Exposes How the Media Distort the News* (Washington, D.C.: Regnery, 2002). Goldberg's accounts come from personal observation and, while not necessarily surprising to a news viewer, provide further evidence of the bias of the network news.

[6] Karl Zinsmeister, "The Shame of America's One-Party Campuses," *The American Enterprise,* Sept. 2002, 18-25.

[7] For discussions about the political climate and the general politicization of the campus, see one or more of the following books. Roger Kimball, *Tenured Radicals: How Politics Has Corrupted Our Higher Education* (Chicago: Ivan R. Dee, Inc., 1998): Alan Charles Kors and Harvey A. Silverglate, *The Shadow University: The Betrayal of Liberty on American Campuses,* (New York: Harper Perennial, 1999); Dinesh D'Souza, *Illiberal Educatioin: The Politics of Race and Sex on Campus* (New York: The Free Press, 1991); Charles J. Sykes, *The Hollow Men: Politics and Corruption in Higher Education* (Washington, D.C.: Regnery, 1990).

[8] Thomas Kuhn, *The Structure of Scientific Revolutions* (2nd ed., Chicago: University of Chicago Press, 1970), pp. 23-34.

[9] Ibid., p. 66.

[10] Ibid., p. 24.

[11] Charles Singer, *A History of Scientific Ideas* (1959, rpt. New York: Dorset, 1990), p. 475.

[12] Jonathan Wells, *Icons of Evolution: Science or Myth? Why Much of What We Teach About Evolution is Wrong* (Washington, D.C.: Regnery, 2000), p. 102.

[13] Ibid., p. 91.

[14] Ibid., p. 82.

[15] Ibid., pp. 103-104. And see Appendix I, page 249 for his evaluation of ten recent textbooks in relation to the use of Hackel's drawings. He gives nearly all of them a grade of F for their presentations.

[16] See the account in Derek Freeman's *The Fateful Hoaxing of Margaret Mead: A Historical Analysis of Her Samoan Research* (Boulder, Col.: Westview, 1999), pp. 175, 192 et passim.

[17] Ibid., pp. 194-195.

[18] Ibid., p. 94 et passim.

[19] Ibid., p. 208.

[20] Ibid., p. 209.

[21] Ibid., p. 210.

[22] David Stoll, *Rigoberta Menchu and the Story of All Poor Guatemalans* (Boulder: Col.: Westview, 1999), p. 5.

[23] John Leo, "Nobel Prize for Fiction?" *U. S. News & World Report*, Jan. 25, 1999, p. 17.

[24] Stoll, p. 183.

[25] Leo, p. 17.

[26] Stoll, p. 216.

[27] Leo, p. 17.

[28] Stoll, p. 247.

[29] Christina Hoff Sommers, *The War Against Boys: How Misguided Feminism Is Harming Our Young Men* (New York: Simon & Schuster, 2000), p. 21.

[30] Ibid., p. 22.

[31] Ibid., p. 35.

[32] Ibid., p. 35.

[33] Ibid., p. 41.

[34] John Leo, "Gender Wars Redux," *U. S. News & World Report*, Feb. 27, 1999, p. 24.

[35] Alexander Kohn, *False Prophets*, rev. ed. (New York: Barnes & Noble, 1988), p. 7.

[36] Kohn, p. 15.

[37] Ibid., p. 15.

[38] Cremo and Thompson, p. 362.

[39] Frederick C. Crews, *Unauthorized Freud: Doubters Confront a Legend* (New York: Viking, 1998), p. 216.

[40] Michael Kearl, "Sociology of Knowledge," retrieved Dec. 20, 2002 <http://www.trinity.edu/~mkearl/knowledge.html>.

[41] Cremo and Thompson, p. xxvi.

[42] Ibid., p. 19.

[43] Michael A. Cremo, *Forbidden Archeology's Impact*, 2nd ed. (Los Angeles: Bhaktivedanta, 2001), p. 108.

[44] Book summary notes on David Gill, *The Opening of the Christian Mind: Taking Every Thought Captive to Christ* (InterVarsity Press, 1989), in *Discipleship and the Disciplines: Enhancing Faith-Learning Integration*, Coalition for Christian Colleges and Universities, 1996. Unit 1, p. 37.

[45] Gertrude Himmelfarb, "The Christian University: A Call to Counterrevolution," in *Discipleship and the Disciplines: Enhancing Faith-Learning Integration*, Coalition for Christian Colleges and Universities, 1996. Unit 2, p. 15.

[46] Paul C. Vitz, *Faith of the Fatherless: The Psychology of Atheism* (Dallas: Spence Publishing, 1999), p. 134.

[47] Ibid., p. 134.

[48] Ibid., p. 135.

[49] Ibid., p. 135.

[50] Ibid., p. 136.

Chapter 5
Worldview Foundations

Men despise religion; they hate it and are afraid that it may be true.
— *Blaise Pascal*[1]

From what I have observed, the liberal elite proceed from a certain social and political predisposition. The predisposition tends to be an adopted orientation, not a conclusion based on evidence and argument. When you sift through the arguments, you will often find that modern-day academics and intellectuals . . . have arrived at their position not, ironically, through intellect, through open-ended, disinterested thinking and enquiry, but through disposition, sentiment, bias, and ideology. Many intellectuals are predisposed to accept certain premises and arguments — a preconceived reality. They search for facts to sustain their political position.
— *William J. Bennett*[2]

5.1 What is a Worldview?

One way to understand the idea of a worldview is to say that it's a personal theory of everything. In other words, a worldview is a comprehensive and unifying way of looking at all of life, a means of bringing coherent meaning to one's experiences, thoughts, feelings, and so on. Worldviews must be personally chosen and worked out, and they grow and develop as we learn and gain more knowledge and experience. A worldview includes values, beliefs, commitments, and attitudes, together with biases and prejudices. As we have seen so far, one's epistemology or theory of knowledge is part of one's worldview, as are one's political orientation, social views, faith, morality, and so on. To offer a metaphor for a moment, we might say that a worldview provides the loom for weaving the tapestry of understanding out of the strings of experience. Our worldview tells us what is meaningful, and indeed, what each experience in our lives means. The picture on the tapestry, which could be anything from a beautiful landscape to a chaotic splash of dark abstractions, depends on how the threads are woven.

As you can see by some of the components, part of our worldview is developed from experience, adopted attitudes, and thought and argument. However, there is a core foundation for everyone's worldview that consists of a set of necessary, adopted truths. These truths or basic ideas cannot be proven, but they must be granted in order for life and experience to be coherent. The area of philosophy concerned with what assumptions are necessary in order to make the world understandable is known as ontology.

5.2 Ontology Anyone?

Ontology is the study of the nature of reality, the task of answering the question of "What is?" A good way to approach this study is to say that at the most foundational level of knowing, we have to start by asking, "What makes the world make sense?" The answers cannot be proved or disproved. They must be assumed. For example, do other people really exist, or are they all projections of your own mind? Are you really reading this now, or just dreaming that you are reading this? Notice that you certainly have firm answers to these questions, but you cannot verify or demonstrate those answers through any objective, empirical proof.

While epistemology asks, "What is true and how do you know it?" the ontological question of "What is real?" is more foundational still. It is the most foundational question. Without it there can be no understanding, no real meaning.

Over the thousands of years of philosophy, many of these basic and necessary beliefs have been discussed and argued. The goal has always been to make our theory of reality correspond to our experience of the world. So, what kinds of assumptions are necessary? Below is a small sampling of some of the assumptions generally accepted by most people today, even though every one of them has been hotly denied at one point or another in the history of philosophy. The point to note, however, is that as "obvious" as these basics may appear, not one of them can be proved. They must be assumed as part of one's foundational principles, as givens that help make sense of our lives.

- **Truth exists**. That is, some things can be known with certainty. Truth exists whether or not we currently know it accurately.
- **The external world is real**. The world we experience is not imaginary, not a dream, not a projection of our own consciousness. If we kick a rock, that's a real rock that makes our toe hurt.
- **The external world is orderly and rational**. The world is accessible to our minds and understanding. We can form correct generalizations about it.
- **There is consistency in the processes of the world**. The reliable operations of the world allow us to use past and present information to make reasonable and often reliable predictions about the future.
- **Cause and effect are genuine relationships.** We can accurately explain certain events by saying that one caused the other. Some occurrences are not coincidental.
- **Our senses are often reliable**. What we see, hear, taste, or measure has some adequate and genuine relationship to what is out in the external world.
- **Our memories are often reliable**. We can rely on them enough to maintain the process of an argument or to remember what happened yesterday.
- **Time runs linearly and non recursively**. We do not occasionally wake up yesterday or last week.
- **Our knowledge of reality can test appearances for accuracy**. Observation is not the sole clue to reality. For example a coin viewed at an angle appears to be oval, but we know that it is really round and that the appearance is deceptive.

5.3 The Assumption of God

The assumptions above are shared in common with Christians and philosophical materialists (or scientific naturalists), and they are generally shared methodologically (that is, in actual practice) by postmodernists, even though, as we will see in Chapter 7, postmodernists deny the objective and absolute nature of knowledge, truth, and even reality.

The philosophical materialists have another basic assumption, which is that nature (the material world) is all there is. Hence, every explanation, every piece of knowledge, every kind of meaning, must come from and be reduced to a natural or material object.

As Christians, we think that such an assumption is incapable of providing the best explanation for obviously real phenomena like spiritual striving, a sense of beauty, goodness, virtue, justice, and on and on. We have another basic and necessary truth to add to the list above, and that is that God is. God's presence in the creation and in the world of our experience provides a foundation to explain all those non-physical but certainly true things we experience every day.

The point is that neither the assumption of material exclusivity nor the assumption of God's presence can be proven empirically. They are not subject to proof but are assumed as part of one's ontological set, in order to answer that question, "What makes the world make sense?" The materialists say, "Random particles in motion make the world make sense," and we say, "God makes the world make sense." We think our answer is more sensible, in part because it does not deny meaning to every non-empirical statement about the world and ourselves.

Perhaps a more important point is that, because God's presence is for us a necessary part of our ontological set, the whole idea of "proving the existence of God" is a non issue.[3] No one can or need attempt to prove the truth of any basic assumption. No one demands that we prove the existence of cause and effect or that the external world is real. This is not to say that the long history of arguments for the existence of God should be forgotten. Those arguments are useful for encouraging and building faith and especially for removing roadblocks to faith among the spiritually seeking. But proving God's existence is really not the point. We do not demand that the materialists prove that the material world is all there is. We know better. That is one of their basic assumptions and it cannot be proven. For them, it is an article of faith.

Reasonable Belief. One more point should be made in connection with the "presumption of God." The assumption of God's presence is not an irrational or unreasonable assumption. Quite the contrary, as we have said, ontological basics are adopted because we find them necessary for the world to make sense. By "make sense" we mean to appear rational, to be reasonable. Without the assumption of God, the world makes much less sense, if it makes any sense at all. (Even many agnostics admit this.) Without the inclusion of God in an ontology, non-empirical concepts like justice, mercy, beauty and so on are either unintelligible, meaningless, and irrational or else socially constructed in a localized and unstable way. The existence of God makes these concepts rational and stable, grounded in his existence, his person, and his revelation.

In his article, "Theism, Atheism, and Rationality," which discusses the argument about the rationality of belief, philosopher Alvin Plantinga explains how one's philosophical and religious (or anti-religious) commitments affect one's conclusions about what it is rational to believe:

> Obviously enough, the dispute here is ultimately ontological, or theological, or metaphysical; here we see the ontological and ultimately religious roots of epistemological discussions of rationality. What you take to be rational, at least in the sense in question, depends upon your metaphysical and religious stance. It depends upon your philosophical anthropology. Your view as to what sort of creature a human being is will determine, in whole or in part, your views as to what is rational or irrational for human beings to believe; this view will determine what you take to be natural, or normal, or healthy, with respect to belief. So the dispute as to who is rational and who is irrational here can't be settled just by attending to epistemological considerations; it is fundamentally not an epistemological dispute, but an ontological or theological dispute.[4]

By the traditional tests of truth and reasonableness (correspondence, internal consistency, and external consistency) and the measures of a worldview (which we will examine later) the assumption of God is highly rational.

Evidence for God. Nor does the assumption of God's presence mean that we have no evidence of it. You may have met an agnostic or atheist who has told you, "I've never seen a shred of evidence for the existence of God." To which, I hope you said, "I, on the other hand, see evidence for the existence of God everywhere. It's in every tree, every flower, every act of love, every striving for justice, every child's laugh." You might even add, "It's in my daily personal walk with him, too." But you probably realize that the crux of the problem is not the lack of evidence, but the worldview of the person who can see none. (Maybe you should ask sometime, "And what would constitute evidence of God for you?") What is defined as evidence or what is permitted to serve as evidence is an important question, often linked to one's worldview.

Philosopher Michael Rea notes that "in order to inquire into anything, we must already be disposed to take some things as evidence." Such a disposition "to take certain kinds of experiences and arguments to be evidence" he calls a methodological disposition, something chosen by each person as part of a larger ontological set. Rea adds, "In short, we are disposed to trust certain ways of acquiring information with respect to various topics and to distrust others; and, though sometimes our being so disposed is a result of conscious and reflective activity on our part, quite often it is not."[5] In other words, we assume, sometimes not even knowing why, that some things count as evidence and some do not. What we call or recognize as evidence can be so named only from within our chosen framework.[6] The materialist's failure to see evidence for God in the natural world or in his or her own heart is therefore a defect of the materialist framework (or methodological disposition) rather than the absence of those particular phenomena that a Christian sees as evidence. The disagreement arises over the issue of what can serve as evidence.

The Presumption of Theism. Philosopher Anthony Flew claims that questions about the existence of God "should properly begin from the presumption of atheism," putting the burden of proof on those who believe in God. His reason is that we need "to have good grounds for believing" before we can make such a claim.[7] Similarly, philosopher Michael Scriven says, "We need not have a proof that God does not exist in order to justify atheism. Atheism is obligatory in the absence of any evidence for God's existence."[8] By now you can see the flaws in these arguments.

First, the choice of theism or atheism as a starting point is a metaphysical preference, an ontological choice not subject to proof. It is a pre-theoretical commitment, based on predilection, experience, and other factors acting on the heart and mind quite before and apart from any demonstration. It is a basic assumption, not a conclusion.

Second, the claim of the absence of evidence for God is a question-begging argument (a logical fallacy) because the definition of evidence that excludes evidences for the existence of God comes from within the atheist/materialist framework. Within other frameworks, there is abundant evidence.

Third, a common sense look at the world, with all its beauty, apparent design, meaning, and vibrancy, would seem to predispose a neutral observer to presume that God exists unless good evidence for his non-existence could be brought to bear. (This is exactly Paul's point in Romans 1:20.) The fact that materialists often seem to struggle with this issue, working to explain away the design of the creation, for example, would seem to back up this claim. Even the rabid evolutionist Richard Dawkins says, "Biology is the study of complicated things that give the appearance of having been designed for a purpose."[9] DNA helix co-discoverer Francis Crick agrees: "Biologists must constantly keep in mind that what they see was not designed, but rather evolved."[10]

And fourth, there is in humanity a sense of the divine, a built-in belief and desire for worship. At least ninety-five percent of the world believes in God or a god or some sense of transcendence, as if it had been planted there by the Creator himself. This would seem to be a striking indication that something is going on that deserves attention and investigation. If there is going to be such a thing as a presumption regarding the existence of God, then, it should be the presumption of theism rather than atheism.

In sum, assuming God as a basic is perfectly legitimate and reasonable, and no proof or evidence is needed, even though there are good arguments and evidences. The evidence may be difficult for the materialist to discern, but that is our point: The Christian worldview helps us to see better because it corresponds better to the way the world really is.

5.4 The Exclusion of God

So then, the Christian worldview finds God necessary in order to explain the whole of experience in a rational and acceptable way, while the materialist/naturalist worldview finds God unnecessary, right? Well, not exactly. Far from viewing God as merely unnecessary for their project, the materialists believe that God must be actively excluded from possibility. God, for them, is not just a superfluous feature of some people's beliefs; he is an undesired and dangerous element. Acknowledgement of God would bring consequences. There would be absolutes, moral rules, guilt, sin, the need for humility and forgiveness, behavioral restraints, a whole host of awful implications.

Biologist Cedric Davern makes the point, perhaps to the surprise of those who would reconcile evolution with theism, that God does not belong: "While evolutionists have come to recognize the scope for chance in their accountings, no accommodation for God is made in modern evolutionary theory."[11]

Richard Lewontin, professor of genetics at Harvard, makes clear the primacy of a worldview that excludes God and the need to have "scientific" support for it, whatever the cost:

> We take the side of science *in spite of* the patent absurdity of some of its constructs, *in spite of* its failure to fulfill many of its extravagant promises of health and life, *in spite of* the tolerance of the scientific community for unsubstantiated just-so stories, because we have a prior commitment, a commitment to materialism. It is not that the methods and institutions of science somehow compel us to accept a material explanation of the phenomenal world, but, on the contrary,

that we are forced by our *a priori* adherence to material causes to create an apparatus of investigation and a set of concepts that produce material explanations, no matter how counterintuitive, no matter how mystifying to the uninitiated. Moreover, that materialism is absolute, for we cannot allow a Divine Foot in the door.[12]

Wherever the evidence of science leads, it cannot be permitted to lead to God, lest a Divine Foot gain entrance.

Naturalist Thomas Nagel is even more direct and blunt about the desire to exclude God:

I want atheism to be true and am made uneasy by the fact that some of the most intelligent and well-informed people I know are religious believers. . . . I hope there is no God! I don't want there to be a God. . . . My guess is that this cosmic authority problem is not a rare condition and that it is responsible for much of the scientism and reductionism of our time.[13]

As we will see in more detail below, one of the goals of some in science is the active rejection of the possibility of God.

While the explicit exclusion of God is often most clearly stated in the writings of the scientific naturalists, it appears in most of the other areas of the university as well. Turning from science (or scientism, the exaltation of science as the sole bearer of all truth) to social science, we can see a similar desire to exclude or replace God with a material explanation. Writing about the appeal of psychoanalysis for some in the early twentieth century, Frederick Crews says:

Having studied Freud's early mistakes and impostures, his faulty logic, and his unreliable case histories, we can say with confidence that psychoanalysis did not make its way in the world either by curing sick patients or by demonstrating its scientific cogency. But how did it succeed then? As [many] . . . have shown, psychoanalysis flowed into deep currents of our century's thought and mood, at least within those societies that were primed to spurn religion-based traditionalism and thus to replace priests and preachers with mind doctors. And clearly, psychoanalysis afforded powerful satisfactions to its initiates, who came to see themselves as an avant-garde with a visionary mission. Freudian therapy may or may not yield cures, but it assuredly revolutionizes the worldview of many patients.[14]

Even though Freud mocked traditional religion, his ideas offered religious attractions.[15] As psychiatrist E. Fuller Torrey notes, psychoanalytic theory provided a secular substitute religion, emphasizing sexual liberation:

> The religious appeal of Freud's theory was a particular reason for its acceptance in America in the early years of this [the 20th] century. A revolt was occurring not only against Victorian morality but against traditional Christianity as well.[16]

Those who rejected Christianity still felt those God-given spiritual strivings, and some of them turned to psychoanalysis for spiritual succor.

Similarly with postmodernism, which we will see clearly later on (Chapter 7) aggressively rejects tradition, authority, and truth (and thereby is highly antagonistic to the Supreme Authority), we can say that this worldview, too, actively excludes God. The literary theory of deconstruction is one of the prominent tools of postmodernist writers. One of the most prominent deconstructionists, J. Hillis Miller, once "revealed that his critical project sought 'to demolish beyond hope of repair the engine of Western metaphysics.'"[17] Clearly, the desire to "demolish . . . the engine of Western metaphysics" is a much more hostile position than merely the adoption of a different set of basic assumptions in one's worldview.

Postmodernists do not necessarily object to religion or theism in general, as long as the believer does not claim that his or her beliefs are true in an absolute sense. That would be intolerant, and tolerance is one of the deities of postmodern thought. Such a position means that Christianity is to be rejected. Those who believe in universal truth ("truth claims" as the postmodernists say) are attempting to impose a "totalizing viewpoint" or metanarrative on other groups, and such a position is unacceptable. In a philosophy of tolerance, it is not to be tolerated.[18] Furthermore, Christians believe that Christianity is objectively true, and not just a subjective feeling or personally designed religion. Since postmodernists view religion as an arbitrary choice among many choices, all equally "true," the Christian claim that there is one truth and that faith is subject to examination, reason, and evaluation is viewed as arrogant and hence to be opposed.[19]

Postmodernists are in favor of religion when it means merely individual experience or personal feeling. There is a great emphasis on spirituality, sometimes described as "non-religious spirituality" to separate it from traditional religions with creeds and places of worship. But any religion that claims to have implications for other people—any God that might require something of them—is unwelcome in postmodern thought.

And in feminism, for those writers who do not redefine God as a female (Goddess, God the Mother),[20] God and Christianity are rejected as oppressive and patriarchal. Feminist Jill Johnston charges that "religion in all its forms is the twin agent with the legal apparatus of governments to maintain the patriarchal orientation of society and as such to continue the repression of women by the various appeals to our 'higher natures' invoking the words and deeds of the exclusive male deity." As a result, "home, church and state are the enemies of sexual revolution."[21]

God is a problem for some people.

5.5 Keeping God Out

To give you a better idea of how deeply the materialists want to keep God out of the picture, let's look at a few specific examples.

In his book *God and the Astronomers*, Robert Jastrow committed the crime of denying the absoluteness of naturalism to answer every question by suggesting that "we cannot tell by scientific methods whether the birth of the Universe is the work of a Creator or some force outside the domain of science, or is instead the product of physical forces, that is, a part of natural law."[22] As a result, Isaac Asimov wrote a sneering review in which he criticized Jastrow for suggesting that "the

Bible has all the answers."[23] Jastrow says, "Many people, either with approval or with disapproval, depending on their views, say that I am expressing in a concealed way my own personal belief in the existence of a Creator. In a review of my latest book, Stephen Jay Gould asks, 'Do I detect a theological bottom line?'"[24] Even the faintest whiff of concession to the possibility of the existence of God is attacked immediately. Jastrow, however, says his critics are wrong. He adds that he finds evolution "plausible" but that the idea "seems as much a miracle as the Biblical account of his [man's] origin. This is why I remain an agnostic in religious matters at the present time."[25]

You'll recall mention in Chapter 3 of Judith Hooper's book *Of Moths and Men* (about Kettlewell's experiments with the peppered moth). Hooper is a secular journalist, who followed an exciting story of a ferocious debate among scientists about weaknesses in Kettlewell's experiments. The problem was, the peppered moth story was almost a deity in the pantheon of evolutionary examples. To make public the flaws in the story was almost unthinkable. Hooper tell us, "Behind the story, like a monster lurking under a five-year-old's bed, is the bogeyman of creationism. Worried friends have asked me: 'Aren't you playing into the hands of creationists?'"[26] Isn't that an interesting worry? Not, "Aren't you worried that you are wrong?" And isn't it interesting that there is a worry at all? Why wouldn't her friends comment something like, "That's amazing. You are to be congratulated for advancing truth and helping science correct its errors." The obvious worry is that she is helping, even just a tiny bit, get a Divine Foot in the door. Hooper takes pains to state further that "for the record, I am not a creationist, but to be uncritical about science is to make it into a dogma."[27]

At the end of her book, Hooper returns to this problem, having discussed at length why so many scientists have been less than excited about admitting the many problems with the peppered moth research. She says, "In the current cultural cold war, many biologists fear that anything less than a united front will play into their [the creationists'] hands. Scientists who express too many doubts run the risk of being considered traitors or turncoats."[28]

Attorney Norman Macbeth, author of *Darwin Retried*, recounts in an interview how he and a colleague examined the mathematics behind population genetics. He says:

> . . . I took this article [about the limitations of population genetics] to another professor in the biology department at Ramapo College and asked her opinion of it. She came back after several days and said, "I agree entirely that population genetics is worthless stuff, but you can't publish this. If you and Eddie publish something like this the Creationists would get hold of it and throw it in our faces and we can't have that." So here we have another example, a living example, of the basic theme in my book—that they are not revealing all the dirt under the rug in their approach to the public. There is a feeling that they ought to keep back the worst so that their public reputation would not suffer and the Creationists wouldn't get any ammunition.[29]

Macbeth was not a creationist, though he was a critic of Darwinian evolution. (He seemed to like the "hopeful monster" theory of evolution advanced by Richard Goldschmidt.)

In early 1995, science writer Richard Milton was commissioned to write an article critical of evolution for Britain's *Times Higher Education Supplement*. When he learned of the plan, Oxford University professor Richard Dawkins mounted a successful campaign to have the article suppressed. In a letter to the editor of the *Supplement*, Milton comments on one of the accusations against him, noting that

> . . . it has been said, by some scientists, that I am a secret creationist opposed to neo-Darwinism for religious reasons. I am not a creationist and my criticisms of the neo-Darwinist mechanism are purely scientific objections—as any reading of the article itself clearly shows.[30]

At the end of his letter he comments:

> If this article were about any other subject—finance, politics, the economy—I know it would be welcomed as well-written

and thought-provoking even if its claims were controversial. It is only because it is about neo-Darwinism, a subject on which some biologists feel insecure and ultrasensitive, that doubts have been raised about it.[31]

Milton was soon attacked again as a "creationist ally," by a geologist writing in the *Journal of Geoscience Education*. Milton comments:

> Let me make it unambiguously clear that I am not a creation-ist, nor do I have any religious beliefs of any kind. . . . For anyone, anywhere, to say that I am a creationist, a secret creationist, a "creationist ally," or any other such weasel-word formation, is an act of intellectual dishonesty by those who have no other answer to the scientific objections I have raised publicly.[32]

To charge someone with being a creationist is obviously a dismissive act. Richard Dawkins (known for his famous com-ment that "Darwin made it possible to be an intellectually ful-filled atheist"[33]) also called Milton "loony," "stupid," and "in need of psychiatric help."[34]

What is going on here? None of these people being criti-cized is a Christian or a creationist. Yet they were all attacked or warned to beware of helping a position that might be favor-able to a theistic view of the world. If the knowledge claims and interpretations you find at the university seem not to in-clude some that are favorable to your faith, perhaps it is be-cause they are being deliberately excluded.

5.6 Implications for Integration

At the university you will likely encounter the view that philosophical materialism is the obvious outcome of either ra-tionality or science or both. "Once you know how to reason," some will say, "you become a materialist." Or, "Once you learn about what science knows, you realize the world is meaningless and empty of God." This view arises not just from the desire to proselytize you into unbelief (which is a strong motivation among some faculty), but also from a mis-taken idea about the relationship between worldview and reason. For many people, worldview preferences precede the rational support of those preferences. That is, many people have a philosophical predilection toward some belief about the world that they then support through the assembly of arguments and evidence. Their worldview is thus pre-rational rather than the required outcome of inescapable logic. Rationalism has its limitations.

To make this idea clearer, we can look at what Aldous Huxley tells us about his own journey. Huxley was the grandson of biologist Thomas Henry Huxley, one of the earliest, earnest advocates of Darwinism and the coiner of the term *agnostic*. Grandson Aldous wrote several novels, including *Brave New World* and *Ape and Essence*. In his nonfiction book, *Ends and Means*, he recounts his reasons for becoming a materialist and for seeing the world as a meaningless place. He "took it for granted" that the world had no meaning, in part because of the prevailing "scientific picture" of the world, but also, he says, for "other, non-intellectual reasons": "I had motives for not wanting the world to have a meaning; consequently assumed that it had none, and was able without any difficulty to find satisfying reasons for this assumption."[35] Notice that he tells us that the supporting reasons were *subsequent* to the desire for a meaningless world.

Huxley then generalizes from his own experience: "Those who detect no meaning in the world generally do so because, for one reason or another, it suits their books that the world should be meaningless."[36] In other words, there is an element of self interest in preferring one worldview over another. Worldviews have implications, and there is a temptation to prefer one that suits one's personal preferences rather than one that intellectually best appears to reflect the world as it truly is. Huxley continues, "The philosopher who finds no meaning in the world is not concerned exclusively with a problem in pure metaphysics. He is also concerned to prove that there is no valid reason why he personally should not do as he wants to do. . . ."[37] A worldview that permits us to behave the way we want to, without feeling guilty about it, has powerful attractions: "The voluntary, as opposed to the intellectual, reasons for holding the doctrines of materialism, for example, may be predominantly erotic . . . or predominantly political. . . ."[38]

These reasons were exactly those of Huxley himself:

> For myself as, no doubt, for most of my contemporaries, the philosophy of meaninglessness was essentially an instrument of liberation. The liberation we desired was simultaneously liberation from a certain political and economic system and liberation from a certain system of morality. We objected to the morality because it interfered with our sexual freedom. . . .[39]

You can understand from this why materialism is a popular worldview and why an alternative like Christianity is so fiercely resisted. If we are just meaningless animals, then it's quite all right to behave like meaningless animals, with no deity we must be accountable to. The contemporary view is that all religions are false and arbitrarily chosen, so you might as well choose one that doesn't interfere with your personal moral behavior.

(As an interesting side note, the American Humanist Association has prettied up the implications of materialism, to cover over the obvious conclusion that life is meaningless in a random, non-directed, Godless world. According to the association's Web site, "Humanism is a progressive lifestance that, without supernaturalism, affirms our ability and responsibility to lead meaningful, ethical lives capable of adding to the greater good of humanity."[40])

Huxley observes,

> No philosophy is completely disinterested. The pure love of truth is always mingled to some extent with the need, consciously or unconsciously felt by even the noblest and the most intelligent philosophers, to justify a given form of personal or social behaviour, to rationalize the traditional prejudices of a given class or community.[41]

The Christian view is that religions are not all alike, not all false, not arbitrarily chosen or individually designed according to one's preferences. We are seekers of truth, absolute

Truth, and we believe and are convinced that we are on the right path in our faithful journeys with God. Thus, instead of a worldview that excuses our behavior, we are committed to one that directs it. Leading a directed life this way may be repulsive to some people, and they may choose an alternative worldview to escape such a "fate." But those worldviews, we believe, lack the integral wholeness, completeness, and objectivity that ours provides.

Do not be influenced, then, by claims that science or reason seems to require philosophical materialism. That is not the case.

Summary

A worldview is made up of the dispositions, beliefs, and assumptions that each person has worked out in order to make sense of the world and experience. While the Christian worldview shares much in common with the worldview of most modernists, it differs in one crucial area, by acknowledging God. As Stephen D. Schwarz says:

> Theism, the belief that God is, and atheism, the belief that God is not, are not simply two beliefs. They are two fundamental ways of seeing the whole of existence. The one, theism, sees existence as ultimately meaningful, as having a meaning beyond itself, the other sees existence as having no meaning beyond itself.[42]

Unfortunately, many of the professors at the university and many of the textbooks they use share a worldview that is hostile to the Christian worldview. Both modernists and postmodernists reject the transcendent realm, and, although their epistemologies are in conflict with each other, both reject Christian knowledge claims. The Christian must realize that these worldviews are often chosen for reasons other than their intellectual persuasiveness.

Questions for Thought and Discussion

1. For Christians in personal relationship with God, it sometimes seems odd to raise the question of his existence, as if someone should ask you why you think your mother or father exists. That issue aside, what is your view of discussing the existence of God with nonbelievers? Do you prefer the school of apologetics that brings forth evidence for the existence of God, such as Kenneth Boa and Robert Bowman's *20 Compelling Evidences That God Exists,* or do you prefer to argue for the reasonableness of the assumption of God, as has been done in this chapter? Defend your position.

2. This chapter provides several examples of scholars deeply interested in keeping God out of the realms of knowledge and education. Why do you think this is so? Can you identify several possible reasons?

3. Think about an important personal, spiritual, or relational decision you have made in the past. What assumptions (of belief, values, truth, expectations, and so forth) were behind the decision? Were you aware of these assumptions at the time? How easy or how difficult is it to identify assumptions behind your thinking?

4. The next time a nonbeliever accuses you as a Christian of being irrational (or of Christian faith as being irrational), what will be your reply? Try to be persuasive.

---

[1] Blaise Pascal, *Pascal's Pensées,* tr. Martin Turnell (New York: Harper & Row, 1962), p. 51.

[2] William J. Bennett, *The De-Valuing of America: The Fight for Our Culture and Our Children,* (New York: Summit, 1992), p. 27.

[3] For a helpful discussion of this idea, see Alvin Plantinga, "Advice to Christian Philosophers," *Truth Journal.* Retrieved from <http://www.leaderu.com/truth/1truth10.html>.

[4] Alvin Plantinga, "Theism, Atheism, and Rationality," *Truth Journal.* Retrieved from http://www.leaderu.com/truth/3truth02.html.

[5] Michael Rea, *World Without Design: The Ontological Consequences of Naturalism* (New York: Oxford University Press, 2002), p. 2.

[6] Ibid., p. 6.

[7] Quoted in Ronald H. Nash, *Faith and Reason: Searching for a Rational Faith* (Grand Rapids: Zondervan, 1988), p. 17.

[8] Ibid., p. 17.

[9] Quoted in William Dembski, *Intelligent Design: The Bridge Between Science and Theology* (Downers Grove: InterVarity, 1999), p. 125.

[10] Ibid., p. 125.

[11] *Genetics: Readings from Scientific American, With Introductions by Cedric I. Davern* (San Francisco: W.H. Freeman, 1981), p. 239.

[12] Quoted in Phillip E. Johnson, *Objections Sustained* (Downers Grove, IL: InterVarsity, 1998), pp. 71-72.

[13] Quoted in J. P. Moreland, "Academic Integration and the Christian Scholar." *The Real Issue.* Jan/Feb 2000, p. 9.

[14] Frederick Crews, ed., *Unauthorized Freud: Doubters Confront a Legend* (New York: Viking Penguin, 1998), p. 215.

[15] Ibid, p. 232.

[16] E. Fuller Torrey, M.D., *Freudian Fraud: The Malignant Effect of Freud's Theory on American Thought and Culture* (1992, rpt., New York: HarperPerennial, 1993), pp. 255-256.

[17] Dinesh D'Souza, *Illiberal Education: The Politics of Race and Sex on Campus* (New York: The Free Press, 1991), pp. 182-183.

[18] See the discussion in Dennis McCallum, ed., *The Death of Truth* (Minneapolis: Bethany House, 1996), pp. 199-203.

[19] Ibid., pp. 202-203.

[20] Paul C. Vitz, *Faith of the Fatherless: The Psychology of Atheism* (Dallas: Spence Publishing, 1999), p. 119.

[21] Ibid., p. 120.

[22] Quoted in Roy Abraham Varghese, ed., *The Intellectuals Speak Out About God* (Chicago: Regnery Gateway, 1984), p. 19.

[23] Ibid., p. 18.

[24] Ibid., p. 19.

[25] Ibid., p. 20.

[26] Judith Hooper, *Of Moths and Men: An Evolutionary Tale* (New York: W. W. Norton, 2002), p. xix.

[27] Ibid., p. xix.

[28] Ibid., p. 310.

[29] "Darwinism: A Time for Funerals," *Contrast* 2:2 (March-April, 1983), p. 4.

[30] Richard Milton, "THES and Darwin: The Open Society and Its Enemies," 26 June 2002, available at <http://www.alternativescience.com/thes_and_richard_dawkins.htm>.

[31] Ibid.

[32] Ibid.

[33] Quoted in Phillip E. Johnson, *Darwin on Trial* (Washington, D.C.: Regnery Gateway, 1991), p. 9.

[34] Milton, op. cit.

[35] Aldous Huxley, *Ends and Means* (New York: Harper, 1937), p. 312.
[36] Ibid., p. 312.
[37] Ibid., p. 315.
[38] Ibid., p. 315.
[39] Ibid., p. 316.
[40] See <http://www.americanhumanist.org>.
[41] Ibid., pp. 314-315.
[42] Quoted in Roy Abraham Varghese, ed., *The Intellectuals Speak Out About God*, p. 98.

Chapter 6
Science and Scientific Naturalism

*There is no doubt that the natural sciences enjoy an enormous
amount of prestige, even among their detractors, because of
their theoretical and practical successes. Scientists sometimes
abuse this prestige by displaying an unjustified feeling of superiority. Moreover, well-known scientists, in their popular
writings, often put forward speculative ideas as if they were
well-established, or extrapolate their results far beyond the
domain where they have been verified.*
— *Alan Sokal and Jean Bricmont*[1]

*The rationality evident in science has also been misinterpreted
to mean that science is the only rational exercise of the intellect in society, or at least the highest and most authoritative.
Some scientists, in their public appearances, can be noticed
playing up to this role, which seems to invest them as cardinals of reason propounding salvation to an irrational public. It
is probably a misperception to think of science as different in
kind from other exercises of the human intellect.*
— *William Broad and Nicolas Wade*[2]

6.1 In Praise of Science

Before we move into a discussion of scientific naturalism,
that philosophy that has unfortunately taken over science and
pressed the agenda of excluding God from the realm of
knowledge, let me say a few words about science itself and its
relationship to the Christian worldview. Fear sometimes
causes people's imaginations to run wild and create all kinds
of doomsday scenarios when a cherished idea or way of thinking appears to be threatened. So it is among some scientists,
when they hear scientism (the exaltation of science as the only

way of knowing) called into question or when they hear that science should be separated from materialist metaphysics or when comments are made that suggest that science might actually lead to God. Such statements are sometimes met with fearful reactions, with claims that these ideas are "anti-science," that letting God in the door will bring all science to a standstill, or that every scientific question will be answered by religious dogma.

In order to calm such fears, it wouldn't hurt to take a few moments to reassure all those in science that the Christian worldview, far from being an enemy, could be the best friend science has ever had.

Science and Christianity. It has been argued at length that modern science was not possible until the replacement of pagan understandings of the world with theistic, and more specifically, Christian ones. Charles Thaxton notes the hospitable climate for science in Christian Europe:

> It is by now well documented that modern science was born in Europe in a theistic culture. As much of this scholarship has shown, theistic belief in a Creator was not only a circumstance but a significant part of the cause of modern experimental science.[3]

Stanley Jaki goes a step further by identifying the birth of modern science with the recognition of the critical importance of the law of inertial motion by John Buridan in 1330. Jaki says,

> Belief in creation out of nothing and in time is the very opposite of paganism. Once that belief had become a widely-shared cultural consensus during the Christian Middle Ages, it became almost natural that there should arise the idea of inertial motion. . . . Insofar as that broad credal or theological consensus is the work of Christianity, science is not Western, but Christian.[4]

Jaki notes that "the essence of paganism, old and new, is that the universe is eternal, that its motions are without beginning and without end."[5] Only the recognition of a world with a beginning and an orderly continuity would make possible the theory and practice of scientific investigation. In fact, sociologist Rodney Stark argues that Christianity provided the positive encouragement for the rise of science:

> As noted, science consists of an organized effort to explain natural phenomena. Why did this effort take root in Europe and nowhere else? Because Christianity depicted God as a rational, responsive, dependable, and omnipotent being, and the universe as his personal creation. The natural world was thus understood to have a rational, lawful, stable structure, awaiting (indeed, inviting) human comprehension.[6]

Stark notes that "Christians developed science because they believed it could—and should—be done."[7] Science was (and is) a way of looking into the mind of God.

The Christian worldview supports the methods of science, including the use of investigation, experiment, reason, and inductive thinking. We believe that there is truth which can be known, or at least approached, when sought using the proper means and with an open mind. Objective knowledge is possible. Christianity is thus much closer to science than is postmodernism, which rejects traditional forms of reason and logic and which denies the objectivity of truth.

6.2 The Rise and Fall and Rise of Scientism

Scientism's Rise. Scientism has been defined as "the doctrine that science alone is capable of providing a true account of reality."[8] In other words, "the only facts are scientific facts,"[9] and all other statements, philosophical, aesthetic, moral, religious, and so on, are unintelligible or cognitively meaningless. Scientism can be traced to the rise of logical positivism in the 1920s and 1930s, and through influential philosophers of science like Alfred J. Ayer, Karl Popper, and W. V. O. Quine.[10] By the 1940s and 1950s science and scientism began to become confused, with scientism becoming mistaken for science itself, as the discoveries of science and technology seemed to promise an ever better future for humanity. Science began to take over some of the promises of traditional religion as it brought health and deliverance from disease. Antibiotics for physical well being, radio and television for enlighten-

ment, abundance of food and electric toothbrushes for a satisfying life—all these seemed to promise that science would
bring us "every good and perfect gift," save us from disease
and death, and answer all our material needs. Science was always offering something new and improved, while traditional
religion was increasingly viewed as old fashioned and even
"pre-scientific."

Moreover, in the form of evolutionary theory, science
could provide us with a modern, substitute religion that answers questions about our origin and purpose on earth. As
Princeton biology professor Edwin Conklin wrote in 1943,
"The concept of organic evolution is very highly prized by biologists, for many of whom it is an object of genuinely religious devotion, because they regard it as a supreme integrative principle."[11] Many people felt liberated and improved
(perhaps even "saved") by science. Those, like Aldous Huxley
(mentioned in the previous chapter), who wanted to be deliv-
ered from moral constraint welcomed all the more the metaphysical freedom promised by this view of science as modern
savior.

Many scientists themselves were happy to take on the role
of a new priesthood, offering pronouncements of trustworthy,
authoritative truth to the humble masses. A scientific answer
was reliable. Scientists could be counted on to give the truth,
objectively and accurately. Because areas of learning that were
non-scientific began to be viewed as something less reliable,
less meaningful, even less factual than scientific findings,
many areas of scholarship attempted to become more scientific, to benefit from the aura of respect surrounding science.
The social sciences began to emphasize quantification and the
use of statistics, for example.

The Fall of Scientism. But something happened along the
dusty road of history. Things began to go wrong with some of
the promises of science. A major earthquake in the compla-
cency over scientific progress occurred with the horrific thalidomide disaster, where the drug marketed as a sleeping pill
and cure for morning sickness in the late 1950s caused more
than 10,000 severe birth defects in Europe. Even though the
drug was never approved for use in the United States and was

banned in 1961, the shock of the tragedy was global.[12] Historian J. M. Roberts observes that in the last thirty years or so a groundswell of antagonism toward science has arisen in the West.[13] According to Roberts, beginning in the 1970s, "a new skepticism about science became very evident in western countries,"[14] and this skepticism or even hostility has continued to grow. Events occurred that led many people to believe that science had let them down. Roberts names the nuclear accidents at Three Mile Island and Chernobyl and even the Challenger space shuttle disaster as defining events that "awoke large numbers of people for the first time to the limitations and possible dangers of advanced technological civilization."[15]

Highly influential in this change in attitudes about science was Thomas Kuhn's *The Structure of Scientific Revolutions* (1962, second edition, 1970), in which Kuhn argued that science is not a linear progress of "the accumulation of individual discoveries and inventions,"[16] but a series of shifts in the way the world is viewed and in what is permitted to be considered science. What Kuhn called "normal science," the process of science between revolutions (or "paradigm shifts") he described as "a strenuous and devoted attempt to force nature into the conceptual boxes supplied by professional education."[17] Moreover, these conceptual boxes are only in part derived from observation and experience. Kuhn claimed, "An apparently arbitrary element, compounded of personal and historical accident, is always a formative ingredient of the beliefs espoused by a given scientific community at a given time."[18] For many, science came to be viewed as more intertwined with philosophy and even politics than the idealized story of purely objective experimenters pursuing truth for its own sake.

In 1975 philosopher of science Paul Feyerabend published *Against Method*, an analysis of the methods and epistemology of science and concluded, "The similarities between science and myth are indeed astonishing."[19] In his criticism of the attitudes and teachings of science, he used terms such as *fancies, totalitarian pretensions,* and *fairy tale.*[20] He concluded that just as the separation of church and state is viewed as an important principle in American policy, so should there be a separation of science and state, since science is often practiced as a kind of religion: "A science that insists on possessing the only correct method and the only acceptable results is ideology and must be separated from the state, and especially from the process of education. One may teach it, but only to those who have decided to make this particular superstition their own."[21] Like Kuhn, Feyerabend saw science as involved in subjective preferences in addition to objective analyses:

> We see: facts alone are not strong enough for making us accept, or reject, scientific theories, the range they leave to thought is too wide; logic and methodology eliminate too much, they are too narrow. In between these two extremes lies the ever-changing domain of human ideas and wishes.[22]

Feyerabend's ideas, like Kuhn's, have been highly influential in demythologizing science and the scientific process from a philosophical standpoint. However, events of a more objective nature during this period also contributed to the change in some people's attitudes about the practice of science.

In 1980 the U. S. Food and Drug Administration reported that "perhaps as many as 10 percent" of those doing clinical testing of drugs were doing "something less" than honest work.[23] In the spring of 1981 the U. S. Congress launched its first ever investigation into the problem of fraud in scientific research.[24] In 1982 an investigation of Industrial Biotest Laboratories (IBT), one of the largest drug testing laboratories in the United States, revealed that "of some 900 out of 1200 studies on chronic effects of various substances tested by IBT, the examiners on the Environmental Protection Agency (EPA) came to the conclusion that the majority of the reports on these studies were invalid" because of improper or fraudulent practices.[25] Popular books, such as *Betrayers of the Truth: Fraud and Deceit in the Halls Science* (published in 1982) and *False Prophets: Fraud and Error in Science and Medicine* (editions in 1986 and 1988) exposed the disparity between how scientists say science works and the way it often actually does work.

Perhaps just as damaging to the aura of science were the historical accounts in these books of closed minded scientific communities that had bigotedly rejected for years after their introduction such now-accepted ideas as continental drift, Ohm's law, Mendel's genetics, the germ theory of disease, and the use of antisepsis to prevent child-bed fever.[26] Not only did some scientists reject the real, but they sometimes embraced the imaginary. Non-existent "N-rays" were "observed by at least forty people and analyzed in some 300 papers by 100 scientists and medical doctors between 1903 and 1906,"[27] while non-existent "mitogenic rays" resulted in "some 500 publications in the 1920s and 1930s,"[28] and non-existent "polywater" produced "some hundreds of papers" between 1962 and 1971.[29]

(For an eye-opening book-length study of how scientists and medical doctors can be blinded to the facts by insisting on an erroneous theory they have been long committed to, even after convincing evidence of its falsity, see *Deadly Medicine: Why Tens of Thousands of Heart Patients Died in America's Worst Drug Disaster*.[30] The book is a stark revelation of the power of politics, economics, self-interest, and bias in the process of developing and testing new drugs.)

But Scientism is Not Science. None of these distressing events would be earth shattering to those who believed that scientists are ordinary human beings. As William Broad and Nicholas Wade observe, "Scientists are not different from other people. In donning the white coat at the laboratory door, they do not step aside from the passions, ambitions, and failings that animate those in other walks of life."[31] Their beliefs and desires, and their worldviews, animate them in ways similar to that of everyone else. They are subject to self-deception, "the human tendency for an observer to see what he wants to see" and to "unintentional bias in interpreting data, particularly when the scientist has some personal preference as to the outcome."[32] However, for a public that had come to believe that scientists were somehow perfect in their objectivity and function, these events came as a paradigm-shattering blow. Clearly, science had not been the best answer to every human problem or need, and its prideful promises could not be fulfilled. Broad and Wade identify the crux:

> Historians who have attempted to arrogate to science all credit for social or material progress, or for the triumph of reason over the forces of darkness and ignorance, also render science vulnerable to blame for all the deficiencies of modern societies. To a probably insalubrious degree, science has replaced religion as the fundamental source of truth and value in the modern world.[33]

In other words, if people have put their hope and trust in science for all good things, then when the technology or the medicine or the behavior recommended by "science" goes wrong, then science itself is to blame.

Such an anti-science attitude might go far in helping explain the rejection of reason and logic among many postmodernists, the embracing of herbal and even mystical remedies over those of traditional medicine, and the rise of power and politics over empirical proof in legislation, court cases, and so on.

Christians have reason to lament this bashing of science as a whole. While the hijacking of science by philosophical materialists with an anti-Christian agenda is wrong and needs redressing, science itself and the scientific method should be celebrated. Among the problems of science has been the claim of the total separation of fact and value, when in practice, values, however they may be submerged, are always present in the scientific enterprise. (Even the choice of what experiment to do reflects a value judgment.) The joining of Christian values to the scientific process would actually benefit science. When ethical issues such as those related to cloning and genetic engineering arise, a powerful value system would be more than helpful; it would be crucial in helping scientists to work for the benefit of humanity.

Benefits of Science. Those who speak against science often seem to be rather selective in their choice of examples. With one eye closed and the other shut, they rail at the evils that science has brought upon civilization. "Science has failed us," they say. "Science has given us nuclear weapons, toxic waste, and polluted air and water. Science promised to save us and didn't." But they make these criticisms while sitting in air conditioned offices, typing on personal computers, and sipping imported coffee, air-freighted on modern jets from Kenya or Jamaica. They are secure with their good dental and medical plans, and happily use their wireless phones to call the pizza parlor from their cars—cars which allow them to cover more distance in an hour than they could cover in three days just a little over a hundred years ago.

My father was a medical doctor, and in his memoirs he recounts what medicine was like as recently as the 1930s, before science brought us antibiotics, sophisticated medical diagnosis, and modern treatments.[34] Imagine contracting pneumonia or tuberculosis and having no remedy other than to "monitor" it. So I'm deeply grateful to science, for medicine, for technical improvements—blessings, I call them—like aspirin and cordless drill-drivers and digital copiers, and for the wealth of knowledge about the world. The scientific method, investigative instruments, the use of evidence in forensic science, all these are among the great benefits of science. Science is great. It makes my automobile tires last much longer than tires from twenty years ago, and it reveals to me the complexity of God's creation (from quarks to DNA).

Christians should be positive about science for several reasons that seem to escape the bashers. First, we have always known that science would not save us. We have another means of salvation. We never trusted science to answer all of life's questions, to be the sole source of truth, or to provide our life's philosophy. We have what we believe is a better episteme and ontological set than the one promoted by many practitioners of science.

Second, we believe that scientists are fallible humans like the rest of us, usually trying to do right but also subject to bias, pride, greed, and worldview preconceptions. We should be no more surprised to hear of a scientist cheating on an experiment or aggressively proclaiming the truth of a theory on the basis of poor evidence than we should be shocked to hear of a policeman, dedicated to upholding the law, instead taking bribes or dealing drugs. Even ministers and priests sometimes dramatically fail to live up to their callings. It is not, therefore, a matter of accusing scientists as a whole or science itself of lying or being dishonest. Experimenter error and unintentional bias—the powerful desire to see one's ideas find empirical support—do not necessarily involve dishonesty. The more that science can be disconnected from the factors that distort it, such as the materialist worldview, economic and political pressure to achieve certain results (such as the safety of a new drug), and social group pressures to conform to certain theories, the better off science and scientists will be.[35]

Third, where "science" has produced weapons of mass destruction, pollution, toxic waste, and so forth we see, not the failure of science, but the failure of a secular world—in the rush to exclude God—making very poor public policy, social, and political decisions that have misdirected the scientific enterprise or failed to manage it well. But that's another topic.

What we're critical of, then, is not science. What we as Christians object to is the materialist philosophy, the religion, that is attached to science by so many people, and the resulting "metaphysically correct" forced interpretations. The insistent confusion between science and materialism—indeed, the equation of the two ("science is materialism")—is false and must be rejected. To say that the answer to every question about the world must come from the natural world is not science but metaphysics, an article of faith. Truth should be pursued wherever it leads, even if it leads to God.

Sensitivity of Scientists. One reason many scientists are so quick to become angry and hostile when any opposition to "scientific findings" or theories is raised is that they have confused the ideal of science with its less ideal practice. According to Broad and Wade, "Researchers are imbued in their lengthy training with the notion that science is a realm of thought where logic and objectivity reign supreme. They are taught that science works just the way the [logical empiricist] philosophers say it should work. They learn the ideal as if it were reality."[36] Most scientists believe themselves and their discipline to be objective and unbiased, the clear route to truth. For example, anthropologist Glynn Custred says that science "is an open system where multiple hypotheses are encouraged, where evidence is continually scrutinized, and where different theories compete with one another in an open forum of free debate."[37] This is indeed the ideal view of science, how it should work, though it often is not how science actually does work.

Because many scientists hold this idealized view, any criticism or questioning of scientific processes or conclusions is declared to be "against science" or result in the accusation that the critic does not understand "how science works." Any questioning of the objectivity of scientists is taken as a personal attack, resulting in anger and hostility. "How dare you imply that I'm dishonest, a liar, and a conspirator," some will say. But experimenter effects (the tendency for researcher expectations to influence results), unconscious bias, and the honest desire to believe a theory do not imply dishonesty. When a scientist argues for a particular interpretation, he or she is probably genuinely convinced of that conclusion. It is not a question of lying or deceit (except perhaps in the case of unintentional self-deceit).

Scientism Lives On. While many in the general public have become skeptical of science (and whether postmodernist attitudes are the cause or the effect of this trend is open to question), many scientists still believe that science is the sole source of truth. This position is required by their adherence to scientific naturalism. However, it distorts science itself and attempts to force it to support predetermined views. In a more recent book than the one quoted above, philosopher of science Paul Feyerabend says that science has become ideological, oppressive, and dogmatic in the American educational system. He says,

> Scientific "facts" are taught at a very early age and in the very same manner in which religious "facts" were taught only a century ago. There is no attempt to waken the critical abilities of the pupil so that he may be able to see things in perspective. At the universities the situation is even worse, for indoctrination is here carried out in a much more systematic manner. Criticism is not entirely absent. Society, for example, and its institutions, are criticized most severely and often most unfairly and this already at the elementary school level. But science is excepted from the criticism. In society at large the judgement of the scientist is received with the same

reverence as the judgement of bishops and cardinals was accepted not too long ago.[38]

More than a decade earlier, physics professor Martin Eger noted this same unwillingness in science education to teach a skeptical approach to knowledge and the exploration of alternatives. Why, he asked, are students encouraged to be cautious of knowledge and conclusions in every arena other than science? If the goal of education is to learn how to think, how to evaluate ideas and arguments, why is science education so dogmatic? He asks:

> For if the core of rationality does include the two elements we have picked out—"criticism" and "alternatives"—then why should not the model [that is, science] exhibit them in greater measure than all other fields? . . . In morality, in politics, in social problems—criticism and alternatives are the hallmark of active reason. And in natural science, the pride of reason—there not?[39]

The problem, Eger thinks, lies in the dogmatic adherence to evolutionary theory and the insistence that it be accepted without question or qualification. Why he wonders, should this be so?

> If it is a good thing for children to consider all sorts of alternatives in moral decision-making, no matter how repugnant—stealing, cheating, betraying one's friends—all for the sake of developing critical reason and autonomy, then why, suddenly, when we come to evolution, is it far more important to learn *right answers* than to think critically? Why *just here* are certain alternatives taboo, even for the sake of discussion—despite the fact that being wrong about a scientific theory of remote origins can never have consequences as grievous as being wrong in one's moral outlook?[40]

The answer, of course, is that evolutionary theory is the foundation stone that currently provides the only reasonable support for materialism and the only available explanation for the living world when God is excluded from possibility. It is clear from this fact that no matter what, evolutionary theory must be protected, and for those committed to materialism, theism must be firmly rejected. Science, to those who follow scientism, has all the answers. Feyerabend concludes his comments quoted above this way:

> The move towards "demythologization," for example, is largely motivated by the wish to avoid any clash between Christianity and scientific ideas. If such a clash occurs, then science is certainly right and Christianity wrong. Pursue this investigation further and you will see that science has now become as oppressive as the ideologies it once had to fight.[41]

The problem facing the Christian in integrating scientific ideas with Christian faith, then, is not one of conflicting truths or the question of whether it is science or Christian faith that is "wrong." The problem is with a particular view of science (scientism), its claim to be the source of all truth, and the philosophy and interpretive claims made in the name of science.

6.3 The Definition of Scientific Naturalism

In this book I have tended to equate materialism and scientific (or philosophical) naturalism, and have implied that scientism is involved with both. The reason for this is that these ideas are overlapping and not clearly distinguished. Indeed, one is often seen to imply the others. As philosopher Michael Rea notes:

> Naturalism is identified sometimes with materialism, sometimes with empiricism, and sometimes with scientism; but all of these positions are equally difficult to characterize and, in any case, the identifications are controversial. It certainly carries a commitment to the thesis that there is nothing but nature, or nothing supernatural.[42]

Naturalism, then, is the philosophy or metaphysical position that everything knowable derives from an observation and interpretation of the natural world. Under this model of reality, only scientific knowledge, only empirically observable information is true. Other knowledge, such as religious principles, moral concepts like good and evil, aesthetic ideas like beauty, and ethical concepts like justice and mercy—none of this knowledge is true in any real sense, but is all merely subjective belief or "socially constructed" preferences. Under philosophical naturalism, all explanations for the world must be materialistic ones. There can be no soul, only the electrochemical functions of a brain. The powerful appearance of design in nature (in butterfly wings, crystals, metamorphosis, the eye) is only an appearance, because the idea of a Designer would be a non-material explanation. The equation seems reasonable then, that where there can be no knowledge of or from the supernatural world, naturalists are positing a materialist epistemology. Rea continues:

> Naturalism has always been associated with two related projects, both of which have roots in antiquity. The first project is that of trying to conduct all of one's philosophical theorizing in accord with the methods and results of the natural sciences. The second is that of trying to understand the world as much as possible in terms compatible with materialist assumptions.[43]

Methodological Naturalism. It is sometimes argued that the naturalistic approach to science can be divided in two. Philosophical naturalism is the metaphysical commitment to a non-supernatural world, where all truth lies in material nature. However, some say, scientists can put aside their metaphysical preferences and do science without them. This science looks the same as before, only now it is said to be guided by methodological naturalism. That is, believe what you like about God, whether you reject him or embrace him, but in science, do your work *as if* all answers derive from nature. Otherwise, it is said, whenever a difficulty is reached, someone will simply say, "Well, God must have done it that way." Those who promote methodological naturalism sometimes say that bringing religious ideas into the room is a "science stopper" because every unknown or every current mystery will be referred to an act of God and everyone will cease to try to solve scientific problems.

The fact that, as we saw, science rose in the Christian world and progressed for centuries before naturalism took over, ought to put this claim to rest. It is an objection that may sound good for about a second until you realize that it's a smokescreen for other issues.

6.4 Difficulties with Naturalism

At any rate, both philosophical and methodological naturalism are open to the same criticisms.

Arbitrary. Naturalism arbitrarily constrains the search for truth to a limited arena of investigation not obviously required by the need for knowledge about the natural world. William Hasker notes,

> Philosophical *naturalism* insists that the natural world is complete in itself, self-contained and self-sufficient. According to naturalism, everything which exists or occurs lies entirely within the domain of natural processes. Nothing comes into nature or influences it from outside. There is no "outside"; nature is all there is.[44]

But the claim that "nature is all there is" presents an unproven, assumed position.

Limiting. To restrict truth to natural explanations presents a truncated view of reality. Again quoting William Hasker,

> To the nonnaturalist, on the other hand, it may appear equally obvious that the naturalist is interpreting human life within a restricted and rather rigid conceptual scheme in spite of abundant evidence that the concepts are not adequate for the subject matter.[45]

Naturalism simply does not have the tools or ideas to explain satisfactorily the extensive non-material reality we know and experience. And to deny the reality of a realm (the supernatural) that is inexplicable with the tools of naturalism seems rather arrogant. Together, the arbitrariness of the source of truth (only in nature) and the limitations of the naturalistic model produce a Procrustean bed where all evidence must be chopped or stretched to fit. Phillip Johnson observes,

Of course, people who define science as the search for materialistic explanations will find it useful to assume that such explanations always exist. To suppose that a philosophical preference can validate a cherished theory is to define "science" as a way of supporting prejudice.[46]

In their book about fraud in science, William Broad and Nicholas Wade note that commitment to a method-controlling philosophy can result in error in spite of the ideal of objectivity:

> With some scientists, nevertheless, objectivity is only skin deep, not a sincerely felt attitude toward the world. Under its guise, a scientist can foist his own dogmatic beliefs on the world far more easily than could a plain demagogue.[47]

Exempt from its own rules. In his book-length study of philosophical naturalism, philosopher Michael Rea observes that naturalism's practitioners are involved in an inconsistency. Naturalists hold that all ideas are potentially falsifiable, and yet naturalism itself seems to be exempt from this belief:

> As I see it, the problem lies in the fact that (a) those who call themselves naturalists are united at least in part by methodological dispositions that preclude allegiance to views that cannot be called into question by further developments in science, but (b) no one seems to think that developments in science could force someone to reject naturalism.[48]

Rea concludes, "After all, if everything else is at the mercy of science, why not naturalism?"[49] Once again, we can see that naturalism is an arbitrary commitment, a philosophy standing before and outside of science, and not an essential aspect of science or the scientific method.

Intertwined with anti-religious bias. It should not be surprising that a philosophy that distinctly and explicitly excludes God and the supernatural is appealing to those who reject him, appealing both as a refuge and as a substitute religion of sorts. The hostility toward God has already been discussed, so just a brief mention will suffice here. Richard Lewontin clearly puts what he calls "Science" (with a capital S) in opposition to religion, claiming that

> the problem [in educating the public about science] is to get them to reject irrational and supernatural explanations of the world, the demons that exist only in their imaginations, and to accept a social and intellectual apparatus, Science, as the only begetter of truth."[50]

Here again we see scientism masquerading as science, with the confusion between the two abetted by philosophical naturalism's assumptions.

Psychologist Paul Vitz provides a provocative analysis in his book on the psychology of atheism:

> For men, God seems to function primarily as a principle of justice and order in the world—and only secondarily as a person with whom one has a relationship. In other words, God's law and providential control seem to be the central aspects of belief for men.
>
> We would expect, therefore, that men who become atheists will find a new principle with which to order the world. Thus, we expect male atheists to be quite explicitly atheistic and to have a new "divinity" that takes the intellectual place of God. . . . Many atheists today are well known as believers in science: they treat science as a worldview or personal philosophy, not just as an important methodology and type of knowledge.[51]

To choose a scientific method or set of working assumptions (such as naturalism) based on a rejection of God and to exalt science in God's place would seem to impact objectivity in a highly problematic way.

Philosophically irrational. Philosopher Alvin Plantinga argues that the naturalists' explanation of the origin of the mind makes naturalism itself irrational. Philosophical naturalists believe that our minds have evolved in a mechanistic way through chance and natural selection, for which the highest value is survival and reproduction, not something else like good ideas or truth or an accurate match between belief and reality. Therefore, Plantinga argues, there is reason to doubt the reliability of our minds and of the beliefs produced by our minds. He cites Richard Rorty as concurring that the idea of an evolved humanity being "oriented" toward truth is "un-Darwinian," and notes that Darwin himself had doubts about the trustworthiness of the human mind. Plantinga concludes: "Evolutionary naturalism, therefore, provides one who accepts it with a defeater for scientific beliefs, a reason for doubting that science does in fact get us to the truth, or close to the truth."[52]

6.5 Confusions About Science Caused by Naturalism

In order to understand the attitudes and reactions of some scientists either to the Christian worldview or simply to opposition to the worldview of scientific naturalism (and in particular, to its foundational creed, evolution), we need to know about how some scientists think. Here are some confusions.

1. The Equation Between Materialism/Naturalism and Rationality. The belief that reason is to be found only within the framework of materialist-naturalist epistemology gives its adherents several advantages. First, reason is, by definition, on their side. What a great feeling to have a metaphysical position that has reason for its support, especially when it *exclusively* has reason for its support. Of course, this was a much more powerful posture to adopt before the postmodernists arrived and said, in effect, "Reason? Pfft!" But for most people, who think that reason is useful and often reliable, it still has much weight. Educated people especially are interested in being reasonable and viewing the world through a lens of rationality. That's why this reason-implies-materialism ploy has been so effective in the past.

Second, if the materialists own reason, then all opponents are, by definition, irrational. Everything supernatural is irrational. Any talk about God is irrational. If one can irrationalize the opposition, then one need not take the opponent seriously. There are no logical or reasonable arguments to listen to, only irrational, blind, superstitious nonsense. Easy to dismiss. We've already seen in previous chapters that this equation is false, and that, if anything, the Christian worldview is more reasonable than the materialist one. And as we saw in Chapter

5, the argument over who is or is not rational is really an onto-logical one, based on one's deepest metaphysical assumptions, and not really a question of logic or the quality of thinking and argument. But you will discover that this possessiveness over rationality is fierce among the materialists, for to allow their opponents to have reasonable arguments would be to give them frightening power.

As a result, if you engage in a discussion with a material-ist/naturalist, you will probably discover that among the early tactics will be the attempt to irrationalize you. That is, you'll be asked some baiting questions designed to elicit a response that the materialist can seize upon as irrational or supersti-tious (not merely subjective), so that you and every argument or piece of evidence you may have to offer can be dismissed without a hearing. The better able you are to reason about your faith, the more powerful a witness you will become in this area.

If you look at some of the materialist, anti-religion maga-zines in your local bookstore, you'll see that many of them cling to the idea that reason is their ally, that reason alone is their guide, and that reason requires or at least clearly points toward adherence to their philosophical preferences. For ex-ample, the motto of *The Skeptical Inquirer* is "The magazine for science and reason." This "reason is on our side" is an insistent dogma among materialists, a dogma in need of more vigorous opposition by Christians.

2. The Equation Between Science and Materialism. The materialists desperately want science and reason to be seen as supporting what is in fact their metaphysical position, because first, reason and science are still respected as powerful, objec-tive tools for truth, and second, because the materialists see reason and science as setting them apart from what they view as irrational and unscientific religious types.

An interesting exchange took place a few years back in the pages of *The Humanist*, the magazine of the American Human-ist Association. Writing from a postmodern humanist perspec-tive, Professor Thomas Clark argued that in light of what postmodernism has done to destabilize the ideas of reason and science, those supports are not really of any weight any more.

But, he adds, "as humanists, we don't need to invoke reason or science to justify our preferences. . . . Instead, we are better served by the realization that these preferences are all the foundation we could ever have or need."[53] Humanists, he says, should stop resorting "to rather simplistic appeals to reason, science, and human nature to buttress their case against religion."[54] In true postmodernist form (and following philosopher Richard Rorty) Clark declares:

> Hence our conceptual schemes, our sciences, our rationalities, and our ethical beliefs all lack the absolute, objective grounding that the traditional philosophical project hoped to provide. Our choice among them becomes a matter of their relative utility for the purposes at hand — not a matter of discovering which of them establishes the one true picture of the world.[55]

Therefore, Clark says, "Rationalism . . . can be safely left behind once we see that preferences, values, and beliefs are as deep as we can (or need to) go."[56] And as for science, he adds, "But what we can't claim is that the humanist commitment to science gets things ultimately 'right,' and that therefore there is something cognitively defective or willfully recalcitrant about those who don't share this commitment."[57] Since both reason and science are "false gods" so to speak, they cannot be relied upon to support humanism. Clark concludes:

> Bereft of the reassurances given by God, a universal rationality, an ultimately objective science, or a fixed human nature, humanism will discover that its agenda still remains the same: to create the best solution to the human predicament that the desires, aspirations, and skills of its adherents allow.[58]

As you can see, what Clark is implying is that in a postmodern "anti-foundational" world, humanism is just as groundless, subjective, and non-rational as, um, Christianity. For the mainstream humanist, this is a horrible thought. If humanists cannot cling to reason and science for an objective

SCIENCE AND SCIENTIFIC NATURALISM ⌘ 117

grounding, then they must admit their philosophy is simply another metaphysical preference.

Of course, the article was soon answered in a subsequent issue of the magazine. Norman Haughness wrote that, while it is true that "we all, humanists and religious fundamentalists alike, are driven initially toward our beliefs by emotive engines . . . humanism's beliefs are . . . based in science. . . ."[59] Without this basis, Haughness says, humanism will have little credibility. In fact, "we'd find ourselves no better grounded than others whose imperatives are rooted in whim, ignorant fear, and dogma. This in turn, would vitiate the uniqueness of our claim to attention and the justification for our impulse to prevail."[60] He concludes that "the future of the world's humanist movement is threatened—not made more secure or better able to meet its formidable competition for humankind's allegiance—by relinquishing humanism's unique, distinguishing, and perfectly sound claim to a foundation in science."[61]

From this exchange, you can understand why the humanists and other materialists cling so desperately to the idea that science and reason support their philosophy, their metaphysics. If science and reason are neutral, or worse, if science and reason reveal God and show the reasonableness of theism, then the humanist boat is headed for the mud on the bottom. They know this.

The first point to remember here, then, is that the confusion between science and materialism is a conscious one, not an accidental one. Materialists strongly want to believe that science is on their side and cling desperately to that idea. The prestige of science, the benefits of technology (from a modernist perspective, at least) and the heritage of the Enlightenment that deeply honors reason and empiricism are all powerful entities that the materialists want to draw upon to support their beliefs. (And their beliefs, which often seem counterintuitive to many people, need some rather dramatic support to gain credence.)

The second point of importance is that in spite of this conscious confusion by the materialist/naturalist camp, reason and science actually better support the Christian worldview because Christianity is not reductionist the way materialism is. We don't attempt to answer spiritual questions with materialist explanations, for example. The fact that this argument is not often heard does not mean that it is not a good one.

3. The Conflation of Evolutionary Theory with All of Science. Some scientists believe that to criticize evolutionary theory is to criticize science itself, the scientific method, or "how science works." This conflation between philosophy and empirical science causes some scientists to claim that to criticize evolution is to criticize the way new medicines are developed or TV sets are engineered. This is a smokescreen, of course, but it arises so often that we should mention it. Physicist and philosopher Martin Eger notes:

> Anti-creationist writers routinely raise the fear of a scientific dark age if evolution is not taught within the framework of a totally dominant paradigm, if instead it is encumbered by distracting, useless comparisons with a theory long outworn. Often this warning is joined to a more general plea for keeping all our science at the forefront, lest we "inevitably recede into the backwater of civilization." "American science will wither. We will raise a generation of ignoramuses, ill-equipped to run the industry of tomorrow" (Asimov...).[62]

Our first reaction might be to think that those who equate evolutionary theory with science itself are interested in maintaining the link between materialism and science, because evolution is the foundational creation myth that supports an agnostic or atheistic view of reality. There is probably much truth in this. There seems to be an effort to connect evolution with every scientific topic, even when there is no compelling reason to do so. Evolution seems to get mentioned near the beginning of nearly every "science" program on TV, even if the topic is far from related to the theory. As a result, we are inclined to think that evolution has religious significance for many of those who profess it.

However, it should also be noted that the vigorous adherence to evolutionary theory is not very different from the adherence to other theories in the past. Many scientists come to accept a particular theory as a compelling view of reality and resist, often angrily, any effort to criticize or replace it. They argue that to reject the received truth would be to throw out many years of scientific progress and put an end to science as we know it. Thomas Kuhn reminds us of events in the history of science:

> And again, during periods of revolution when the fundamental tenets of a field are once more at issue, doubts are repeatedly expressed about the very possibility of continued progress if one or another of the opposed paradigms is adopted. Those who rejected Newtonianism proclaimed that its reliance upon innate forces would return science to the Dark Ages. Those who opposed Lavoisier's chemistry held that the rejection of chemical "principles" in favor of laboratory elements was the rejection of achieved chemical explanation by those who would take refuge in a mere name.[63]

The idea that "nothing makes sense" without the current theory is therefore not a new one. And we will see later on in Chapter 10, for the naturalist, who must insist on the material origin of life, evolution does possess a higher degree of probability than it does for the theist, simply because there is no good alternative explanation. Once the possibility of a Creator is eliminated, evolution looks like the only game in town.

4. Casting the Controversy Over Evolution as One of Science Versus Religion. The origin of this naturalist confusion goes back to the history of the university. Most of the universities in the world were started by Christians for the advancement of faith and knowledge. Both the Catholic church and many Protestant denominations started universities. As a result of the rise of empiricism and philosophical materialism, especially in the nineteenth century, many researchers at these universities prosecuted a strategy to throw off the control of the church and gain independence and power for themselves, all in the name of academic freedom. "One reason Charles Darwin was so touted by the British scientific establishment, while Alfred Russel Wallace, the codiscoverer of evolutionary theory, was practically blackballed," writes Gregg Easterbrook, "was that Darwin was an agnostic who threw the rector class into a tizzy, while Wallace was a believer who spoke about 'the unseen world of spirit.'"[64]

The leftover smoke from this nineteenth-century battle is with us still. Easterbrook adds:

> Patinaed with what seems like objective science, the notion of life as a vacuous accident is central to contemporary intellectual orthodoxy. But, while life may be pointless, that's an opinion, not an impartial induction. And it is surely an opinion leveraged by the desire of many thinkers to gain retribution against belief by treating it as dismissively as faith once treated science.[65]

A goal is to keep religious ideas from regaining any of the power or influence they used to have in the academic and especially scientific world. The fear of the loss of grant funding is sometimes raised. And the general fear of control from the outside is overwhelming.

Phillip Johnson argues that another reason motivates the scientific establishment to marginalize religion as mere belief. Science now enjoys (among modernists) the highest reputation not only as sole arbiter of truth but as virtual dictator of cultural norms. Our status as mere evolved animals has resulted in profound moral and social implications, all in the name of scientific fact. In order to maintain this monopoly, scientists must reject religious truth, which presents conflicting claims. To accept any religious ideas or thinkers as possessing "a genuine knowledge of God" would make them "dangerous rivals to the scientists as cultural authorities." Johnson continues, "The strategy that naturalistic philosophy has worked out to prevent this problem from arising is to label naturalism as science and theism as religion. The former is then classified as *knowledge* and the latter as mere *belief.*"[66]

Unless the controversy is cast in terms of science versus religion, how else could anyone countenance going to court to keep conflicting ideas or criticism out of the classroom? What other arena of knowledge uses the court system to rule out ideas that oppose the dominant ideology, as does the evolutionary establishment in seeking to ban in the public schools all discussion of weaknesses in evolutionary theory or alternatives to it? On the other hand, Johnson is right when he notes that we are not really talking about science versus religion but naturalism versus theism: "It would be much more accurate to say that it [the conflict] involves a clash between two religions and two definitions of science."[67]

6.6 Fact and Interpretation

If you've thought much about what makes false ideas believable, it may have occurred to you that the most credible falsehoods, whether urban legends or even postmodernist assertions, contain a small kernel of truth or at least a plausible core. A lie that is ten percent true has a much greater chance of being accepted because people can see that ten percent truth and recognize it as accurate. Similarly, one of the techniques that makes speculation in science so believable is that it is often connected to a factual base. Of course, that in some sense is the way inference works: Examine a number of facts and then construct a generalization about them. However, such inductive leaping sometimes becomes involved with naturalist metaphysics and reaches beyond the legitimate range of generalizing about the facts.

Confusion Between Established Fact and Theoretical Inference. One problem that occurs in scientific writing is the mixture of fact and inference without clearly identifying or differentiating one from the other. Note in this quotation from two physicists how the empirically observable and controversially theoretical are presented as if equally established:

> One may possess evidence in favor of a given theory that is so strong that to doubt the theory would be almost as unreasonable as to believe in solipsism. For example, we have good reasons to believe that blood circulates, that biological species have evolved, that matter is composed of atoms, and a host of other things.[68]

Well, yes, the circulation of blood was first observed and demonstrated in the seventeenth century by William Harvey. It is not a "theory." And atoms can be observed by using electron microscopes. Atoms are not theoretical anymore, either.

On the other hand, slime-to-the-sublime evolution is a theory, whose evidence is not so strong as to eliminate reasonable doubt. The mixture of these two types of scientific ideas as if they were the same is emblematic of the problem some scientists have. (Of course, if these writers mean by "species evolved" only that they have "changed over time" — one of the several definitions of *evolution*, then they could be absolved. For the problem with the meaning of the word *evolution*, see Chapter 9.)

But evolution is not the only theory presented as fact. When I was an undergraduate in the late 60s and early 70s, one of the burning political issues popular among professors was the idea of world overpopulation. A book required in at least two of my classes was *The Population Bomb*, published in 1968 by Paul Ehrlich. Ehrlich predicted a coming world disaster brought on by too many people and not enough birth control: "The battle to feed all of humanity is over," he said. "In the 1970s and 1980s hundreds of millions of people will starve to death in spite of any crash programs embarked upon now."[69] There was extensive discussion by professors about the need for birth control and, of course, abortion rights. You'll recall that the Supreme Court's decision in Roe Vs. Wade legalizing abortion did not occur until 1973. Thus, the population scare was a handy piece of propaganda in the battle to persuade us students about the need for legal abortions.

However, time passed and no mass starvation by the hundreds of millions occurred. Ehrlich was wrong and his book today is largely forgotten. Yet at the time, the "facts" were argued as if incontrovertible.

As we have just seen, one of the most problematic issues in science is the confusion — or the failure to distinguish — between empirically demonstrated scientific fact and highly extrapolated theoretical conclusions, those huge inductive leaps that reach inferences based on preferred outcomes. Phillip Johnson comments:

> . . . the Darwinist educators cannot afford to acknowledge to either their students or the public that there *is* a distinction between the data or testable theories of science, on the one

hand, and philosophical or religious claims that are made in the name of science, on the other. All Darwinist propaganda depends on blurring the distinction so that a credulous public is taught to accept philosophical naturalism/materialism as inherent in the definition of "science."[70]

Science as Fiction. Another problem area is the often too easy passage from the domain of fact into the domain of fiction when descriptions of supposed historical states and possible events are given. The silent movement from the known to the imagined is often not easy to discern. In the presentation of scientific ideas, narrative interpretations of a combination of facts and inferences often appear to represent historical facts or events more conclusively than they actually do. In other words, the description of what appears to be the case or what might have happened is presented as if it indeed is the case or did in fact happen.

Physical scientist William Romey, in his article, "Science as Fiction or Nonfiction?" says, "It is time to recognize the fictional dimension of all science and to acknowledge what is often thought 'pure' is a blend of fictional and nonfictional elements just as is true in history, biography, and in novels."[71] In the process of creating a story, there is a temptation to add details and create bridge information that helps to connect the pieces and fill in the gaps. Forming generalizations based on data requires a leap into the unknown, a leap beyond the evidence. As Romey notes, "Inference, by its very definition . . . involves a leap across a gap of unknown dimensions to a conclusion. Any inference, then, may not be far from a flight of fantasy."[72] He continues:

> When, in geology books and technical articles, we find details of what happened in a past long before the human species even existed and for periods in which only the most remote and fragmentary evidence exists, we know we are in a land very close to the land of fiction.[73]

A striking example of this kind of writing comes from anthropologist Raymond A. Dart, who, drawing upon his examination of fragmentary fossilized bones, wrote:

Man's predecessors differed from living apes in being con-
firmed killers; carnivorous creatures, that seized living quar-
ries by violence, battered them to death, tore apart their broken bodies, dismembered them limb from limb, slaking their
ravenous thirst with the hot blood of victims and greedily
devouring their writhing flesh.[74]

While Dart's comments are pure imagination, this mingling of fact and dressed up theoretical interpretation is quite
common, though usually in a less dramatic way, and presents
a genuine difficulty for the reader who wants to separate what
is actually known from what is concluded or believed. Inference and even creative speculation are fine, as long as they are
clearly differentiated from the actually known facts. (As we
have seen, sometimes what is a fact is problematic enough
without mixing it silently with interpretation.)

Computer graphics now allow this fictionalizing to appear
extremely realistic, as you may have noted if you've seen *Ju-
rassic Park* or science programs on television. The animated
movements, sounds, attitudes, and behaviors of various dinosaurs are all created by drawing inferences (and making
guesses) from the extant fossils. Was the animal aggressive or
passive? Was it upright or prone? How fast did it move? Similarly, reconstructions and models give a three-dimensional
seeming reality to long-extinct animals.

Misinterpretation of Scientific Findings or Theories. A
final problem with the confusion between fact (or in this case,
theory) and interpretation is the misinterpretation or misapplication of scientific theories for political or social purposes.
There is often an attempt to push every new theory in the direction of demonstrating that life is empty and meaningless.
One more "proof" of the futility of it all. Space does not permit
an extensive discussion here, but you may be familiar with
claims that Einstein's theory of relativity implies moral relativity, that Chaos theory "constitutes scientific proof of the hap-
hazard character of life,"[75] or that the Heisenberg principle of
uncertainty (in physics) means that we can't really know anything for sure. These are all wild misapplications of scientific
ideas to the cultural and social world. Once again, you can see
that the name of science is still so revered (except among

postmodernists) that lots of people would like to attach it to their pet social and political causes.

6.7 Implications for Integration: Archaeoraptor: A Case Study

In its November, 1999 issue, *National Geographic* ran an article about "new dinosaur fossils with stunningly birdlike bones and indications of feathers"[76] that the magazine claimed are missing links between birds and dinosaurs. Author Christopher Sloan claimed that "we can now say that birds are theropods just as confidently as we say that humans are mammals. Everything from lunchboxes to museum exhibits will change to reflect this revelation."[77] Star of the article was a fossil dubbed *Archaeoraptor*, which appeared photographed as both fossil and highly realistic three-dimensional reconstruction. The fossil had been thoroughly examined: "Scientists funded by *National Geographic* studied the animal, named *Archaeoraptor liaoningensis*, under ultraviolet light (above) and used CT scans to view parts of the animal obscured by rock," and concluded, "This mix of advanced and primitive features is exactly what scientists would expect to find in dinosaurs experimenting with flight."[78]

There you have it: The physical evidence of a fossil, a persuasive reconstruction, scientific analysis including CT scans (computed tomography, where a computer assembles multiple X-rays into images), together with the seemingly objective and uncontroversial conclusions.

However, there is a little more to this story. Storrs Olson, the curator of birds at the National Museum of Natural History at the Smithsonian Institution, was incensed. He wrote a blistering letter to the magazine, declaring that "*National Geographic* has reached an all-time low for engaging in sensationalistic, unsubstantiated, tabloid journalism."[79] Olson had seen the photographs of the fossils prior to publication and had "tried to interject the fact that strongly supported alternative viewpoints existed to what *National Geographic* intended to present, but it eventually became clear to me that *National Geographic* was not interested in anything other than the prevailing dogma that birds evolved from dinosaurs." It should be noted that Olson himself subscribes to evolutionary theory, but holds to a different evolutionary route for birds. Olson continued:

> Sloan's article takes the prejudice to an entirely new level and consists in large part of unverifiable or undocumented information that "makes" the news rather than reporting it. His bald statement that "we can now say that birds are theropods just as confidently as we say that humans are mammals" is not even suggested as reflecting the views of a particular scientist or group of scientists, so that it figures as little more than editorial propagandizing. This melodramatic assertion had already been disproven by recent studies of embryology and comparative morphology, which, of course, are never mentioned.

It seems ironic that a fellow evolutionist should be making the same kinds of complaints that often come from creationists, complaints about not mentioning the existence of opposing views or alternative interpretations.

Olson had more to say about the interpretations presented as facts:

> More importantly, however, none of the structures illustrated in Sloan's article that are claimed to be feathers have actually been proven to be feathers. Saying that they are is little more than wishful thinking that has been presented as fact. The statement on page 103 that "hollow, hairlike structures characterize protofeathers" is nonsense considering that protofeathers exist only as a theoretical construct, so that the internal structure of one is even more hypothetical.

Olson concluded his letter by calling the entire idea of the dinosaur-to-bird theory a "hoax" and a "faith":

> The idea of feathered dinosaurs and the theropod origin of birds is being actively promulgated by a cadre of zealous scientists acting in concert with certain editors at *Nature* and *National Geographic* who themselves have become outspoken and highly biased proselytizers of the faith. Truth and careful scientific weighing of evidence have been among the first

casualties in their program, which is now fast becoming one of the grander scientific hoaxes of our age—the paleontological equivalent of cold fusion.

Act Two of this drama began with a letter to *National Geographic* from Chinese paleontologist Xu Xing, who compared the magazine's specimen with another fossil and "concluded that *Archaeoraptor* is a composite," made by shoving together fossil pieces of a bird's body and a dinosaur's tail.[80] This revelation of the probability of fraud should not have been very surprising, since it has become known that large numbers of faked fossils, especially from China, have flooded the market. According to *New Scientist*, "Most of the beautiful Chinese fossil birds on sale have been embellished in one way or another. Some may be assembled from broken pieces of several fossils while others have had missing features added."[81] The article continues, "Some composites are even good enough to fool the professionals," and quotes Larry Martin of the University of Kansas: "I don't trust any of these specimens until I see the X-rays."[82]

But what about *Archaeoraptor*? Weren't there computerized X-rays examined by the experts? Well, yes. But now, in reply to the letter of Xu Xing, *National Geographic* said, "As we go to press, researchers in the U.S. report that CT scans of the fossil seem to confirm the observations cited in his letter."[83] Previously, when the fossil appeared to support the magazine's theoretical preferences, the computed tomographic analysis had supposedly shown the genuineness of the specimen, but when it was exposed as a fake, the same X-ray technique and further analysis "seemed to confirm" its fraudulent nature. Another look, using the same techniques, revealed a different interpretation. This is a good example of scientists finding what they want or expect to find. As the authors of *Forbidden Archeology* say (here discussing human fossils),

In the absence of direct knowledge of the past, any discussion of paleoanthropological evidence, which is always somewhat ambiguous, is certain to involve controversy, because of the differing preconceptions and methods of analysis of the participants in the debate. Empiricism thus becomes inextricably entangled with speculative modes of thought and deeply held emotional biases and prejudices. In most cases, the speculation and bias are carefully masked with a thin veneer of fact.[84]

Act Three involved media retractions of the story. An Associated Press article, "Scientists Confirm Mistake," announced the findings of a panel of scientists who had determined conclusively that the fossil was a fake, a composite.[85] *National Geographic* backpedaled by announcing, "Regardless of this week's conclusion, most scientists have been convinced for some time that birds descended from small, meat-eating dinosaurs."[86] Echoing this line, the AP article claimed, "Scientists have plenty of other evidence that birds descended from small, meat-eating dinosaurs, however, and the new report does not change that."[87] Audiences worldwide must be reassured that evolution is safe. And what of the evolutionists who oppose the dinosaur-to-bird theory? One news report included "a story about Dr. Alan Feduccia who is part of a small but vocal minority of scientists who believe that the dinosaur didn't give rise to the modern bird."[88] The phrase "small but vocal minority" is a common expression aimed at marginalizing a viewpoint the journalist rejects. This is a good case in point about how "consensus" sometimes works in science. The larger or more powerful group uses its power and influence to marginalize or silence the less powerful group. Soon the "small minority" of dissenters recognizes the handwriting on the wall and realizes that continued opposition may jeopardize research grants or publication in preferred journals, and grows silent.

What can we learn about integration from this little drama? There are several noteworthy items.

1. News reports and even scientific analysis are often not completely objective. Support for or opposition to various causes or ideas skews the reporting or the analysis. Many journalists' well-known support for abortion is an obvious case in point. In the case of Archaeoraptor, the fossil represented for the magazine support of a cherished belief, so it was welcomed with an enthusiasm that even other evolutionists objected to. There was no mention of alternative interpretations (as Storrs Olson noted), and the admission of a fake was much quieter than the proclamation of the original claims.

2. A double standard for evidence is sometimes apparent. Fossil or other evidence that appears to support a favored theory will often be admitted with less scrutiny than evidence that conflicts with a favored theory. Conflicting evidence is often submitted to intensely critical analysis, while favored evidence is accepted in an almost cursory way.

Since we have been looking at a fossil example of this fact, an example relating to fossils might be handy. Fossils that support current evolutionary interpretations are accepted even when found on the surface of the ground or turned in by farmers or amateurs, while fossils that conflict with current interpretations are often rejected because they were not found *in situ* (in the strata) but were turned in by amateurs or found on the surface.[89] In our current case, it's interesting to note that the *Archaeoraptor* fossil was "found" at a gem and mineral show in the United States, not in the strata in China, where it (that is, its pieces) originated. Such a fact did not deter *National Geographic* from heralding it as a missing link.[90] Whether you are studying archaeology or history or sociology, be aware of this double standard. Many people have a tendency simply to dismiss arguments or evidence that conflicts with their own position, when in fact those arguments and evidence may be substantial and worthy of consideration after all.

3. In time, many "facts" are overthrown or at least qualified. As we saw in earlier chapters, many students were faced with "facts" from Margaret Mead or Sigmund Freud, "facts" which were admitted to be false only after many years. It's good to be cautious about information that apparently conflicts with Biblical teaching, then, because in time that information may be shown to be false after all. My advice about simply filing away information until you have an opportunity to examine it may be extended here to filing away information that appears irreconcilable with your faith. Not every idea can be integrated successfully right away, because some ideas are merely propaganda, misinterpretation, or falsehood. It's all right to say, "I'm not sure about that," rather than to accept or reject a particular claim. *Archaeoraptor* was exploded in just a few months, but many other falsehoods have lasted (and many still last) for many years. Remember that you want to integrate your faith with learning in the sense of true learning, or truth, not with hostile interpretations or false ideas.

4. Falsehood never quite goes away. I used to tell my critical thinking students, in relation to the ability of urban legends to continue to circulate long after they were disproved that "undead information walks ever on." That is, even after something has been disproved, it can still be influential. Our fake fossil is a case in point. That issue of *National Geographic* will be sitting around, in millions of copies, with its false claims, for the foreseeable future.

5. Pictures are often more powerful than words. The reconstruction of *Archaeoraptor*, in its three-dimensional, colorful glory, is a powerful image. Why, you can see the creature, right there. Remember that reconstructions, computer simulations, dioramas and the like represent interpretations rather than known realities. View them with caution in the same way you handle all other kinds of information with caution.

Summary

While we don't view science as the savior of mankind, Christians welcome scientific progress, the scientific method, and the knowledge that the method of experiment has given to the world. The challenge we face as believers is that some insist upon mingling scientism and philosophical naturalism with science itself. Because many of the most vocal practitioners of science are interested in maintaining this confusion, the task of separating them will be difficult. As long as the naturalist/materialist camp can continue to assert that their philosophy — their religion — is science, then the truths of science relating to the creation and its Creator will be denied and suppressed.

Questions for Thought and Discussion

1. How would you define *science*? What is the definition of *science* in your major? If there is a difference between your definition and that of your major, explain why. What is the significance of any difference?

2. What impact does the definition of *science* in your major have on the determination of knowledge?

3. Have you encountered readings in your textbook or elsewhere that did not clearly distinguish between demonstrable facts and interpretations? How did you negotiate such materials?

4. What are some strategies you might adopt to make the best use of information and knowledge claims that you know come from hostile or limited worldviews?

---

[1] Alan Sokal and Jean Bricmont, *Fashionable Nonsense: Postmodern Intellectuals' Abuse of Science* (New York: Picador USA, 1998), p. 193.

[2] William Broad and Nicholas Wade, *Betrayers of Truth: Fraud and Deceit in the Halls of Science* (New York: Simon and Schuster, 1982), pp. 218-219.

[3] Charles B. Thaxton, quoted in Roy Abraham Varghese, ed., *The Intellectuals Speak Out About God* (Chigago: Regnery Gateway, 1984), p. 2. Thaxton provides a bibliography of nearly a dozen titles in support of his conclusion. See his endnotes 1 and 2 in the book, p. 12.

[4] Stanley L. Jaki, "Science: Western or What?" *Intercollegiate Review* 26:1 (Fall 1990), p. 8.

[5] Ibid., p. 8.

[6] Rodney Stark, "False Conflict," *The American Enterprise* 14:7 (Oct./Nov. 2003), p. 30.

[7] Ibid., p. 30.

[8] Avrum Stroll, "Twentieth-Century Analytic Philosophy" in Richard H. Popkin, ed., *The Columbia History of Western Philosophy* (New York: MJF Books, 1999), pp. 648-649.

[9] Ibid., p. 649.

[10] For a helpful discussion, see Stroll, pp. 621-651.

[11] Quoted in Norman Macbeth, *Darwin Retried: An Appeal to Reason* (Ipswitch, MA: Gambit, 1971), p. 127. Macbeth (who, for the record, is not a creationist) provides a very interesting account of evolution as a religion in Chapter 14, "Religion in Reverse."

[12] Interestingly enough, thalidomide has made a comeback as an effective treatment for some of the skin problems caused by leprosy. See, for example, "Thalomid (Thalidomide): Balancing the Benefits and the Risks," at <http://www.celgene.com/images/pdf/$FILE/Balancing.pdf>.

[13] J. M. Roberts, *Twentieth Century: The History of the World, 1901 to 2000* (New York: Viking, 1999), pp. 575-583.

[14] Roberts, p. 578.

[15] Ibid., pp. 578-579.

[16] Thomas Kuhn, *The Structure of Scientific Revolutions*, 2nd. ed. (Chicago: University of Chicago Press, 1970), p. 4.

[17] Ibid., p. 5.

[18] Ibid., p. 4.

[19] Paul Feyerabend, *Against Method* (London: NLB, 1975), p. 298.

[20] Ibid., pp. 300, 307-308.

[21] Ibid., pp. 307-308.

[22] Ibid., p. 303.

[23] Broad and Wade, p. 83.

[24] Ibid., p. 11.

[25] Alexander Kohn, *False Prophets* (New York: Barnes and Noble, 1988), p.180.

[26] Broad and Wade, pp. 134-137.

[27] Ibid., p. 113.

[28] Kohn, p. 23.

[29] Kohn, pp. 28.

[30] Thomas J. Moore, *Deadly Medicine: Why Tens of Thousands of Heart Patients Died in America's Worst Drug Disaster* (New York: Simon and Schuster, 1995).

[31] Broad and Wade, p. 19.

[32] Broad and Wade, p. 85.

[33] Ibid., p. 219.

[34] See Trester S. Harris, *Patients Are People, Too*, on my Web site at <http://www.virtualsalt.com/pp/>.

[35] As I write this, two articles have just appeared in my local paper. "Industry-Sponsored Research Biased?" notes that about "one-fourth of university-based medical researchers receive funding from drug firms," with the result that "industry-sponsored research tends to draw pro-industry conclusions," (Orange County *Register*, January 22, 2003, News 11), and "Officials See Rise in Lab Fraud," noting that testing laboratories "are increasingly being caught falsifying test results (Orange County *Register*, January 22, 2003, News 13).

[36] Broad and Wade, p. 127.

[37] Glynn Custred, "The Forbidden Discovery of Kennewick Man," *Academic Questions*, Summer 2000, p. 24.

[38] Paul Feyerabend, *Paul K. Feyerabend: Knowledge, Science, and Relativism, Philosophical Papers, Volume 3*, ed. John Preston (Cambridge: Cambridge University Press, 1999), p. 182.

[39] Martin Eger, "A Tale of Two Controversies: Dissonance in the Theory and Practice of Rationality," *Zygon* 23:3 (September 1988), p. 303.

40 Ibid., p. 300.

41 Feyerabend, *Knowledge, Science, and Relativism*, p. 182.

42 Michael C. Rea, *World Without Design: The Ontological Consequences of Naturalism* (New York: Oxford University Press, 2002), p. 21.

43 Ibid., pp. 22-23.

44 William Hasker, *Metaphysics: Constructing a World View* (Downers Grove, IL: InterVarsity, 1983), p. 108.

45 Ibid., p. 109.

46 Phillip Johnson, *Objections Sustained: Subversive Essays on Evolution, Law, and Culture* (Downers Grove, IL: InterVarsity, 1998), p. 73.

47 William Broad and Nicholas Wade, *Betrayers of the Truth: Fraud and Deceit in the Halls of Science* (New York: Simon and Schuster, 1982), p. 193.

48 Michael Rea, *World Without Design: The Ontological Consequences of Naturalism* (Oxford: Clarendon, 2002), p. 51.

49 Ibid., p. 52.

50 Quoted in Johnson, *Objections Sustained*, pp. 69-70.

51 Paul C. Vitz, *Faith of the Fatherless: The Psychology of Atheism* (Dallas: Spence Publishing, 1999), pp. 109-110.

52 Alvin Plantinga, "Darwin, Mind, and Meaning," Retrieved from UCSB Faculty-Staff Christian Fellowship, http://id-www.ucsb.edu/fscf/library/plantinga/dennett.html.

53 Thomas W. Clark, "Humanism and Postmodernism: A Reconciliation," *The Humanist* Jan-Feb 1993, pp. 18-23. Gayle Group reprint, p. 1

54 Ibid., reprint p. 1.

55 Ibid., reprint p. 2.

56 Ibid., reprint, p. 4.

57 Ibid., reprint, p. 5.

58 Ibid., reprint, p. 6.

59 Norman Haughness and Thomas W. Clark, "Postmodern Anti-foundationalism Examined, The Humanist, July-August 1993, pp. 19-22. Gayle Group reprint, p. 1.

60 Ibid., reprint, p. 2.

61 Ibid., reprint, p. 3.

62 Martin Eger, "A Tale of Two Controversies: Dissonance in the Theory and Practice of Rationality" Zygon 23:3 (September 1988), p. 313.

63 Kuhn, p. 163.

64 Gregg Easterbrook, "Science Sees the Light." *The New Republic* 219:15 (Oct. 12, 1998), pp. 24-30. Gayle Group reprint, p. 1.

65 Ibid., reprint page 2.

66 Johnson, *Objections Sustained*, p. 28.

67 Phillip E. Johnson, *The Right Questions: Truth, Meaning, and Public Debate* (Downers Grove, IL: InterVarsity Press, 2002), p. 60.

68 Alan Sokal and Jean Bricmont, *Fashionable Nonsense: Postmodern Intellectuals' Abuse of Science* (New York: Picador USA, 1998), p. 70.

69 Quoted in "Paul Ehrlich," *Overpopulation.com*. Retrieved from http://www.overpopulation.com/faq/people/paul_ehrlich.html>.

70 Johnson, *Right Questions*, p. 33.

[71] William D. Romey, "Science as Fiction or Nonfiction?: A Physical Scientist's View from a General Semantics Perspective," *Et Cetera*, 37:3 (Fall, 1980), p. 201.

[72] Ibid., p. 205.

[73] Ibid., p. 205.

[74] Quoted in Michael A. Cremo and Richard L. Thompson. *Forbidden Archeology: The Hidden History of the Human Race*. Rev. Ed., Los Angeles: Bhaktivedanta Book Publishing, 1998, p. 672.

[75] Easterbrook, reprint, p. 6.

[76] Christopher P. Sloan, "Feathers for T. Rex? New Birdlike Fossils Are Missing Links in Dinosaur Evolution," *National Geographic*, November 1999, p. 99.

[77] Ibid., p. 102.

[78] Ibid., pp. 100, 101.

[79] Storrs L. Olson, Letter to Dr. Peter Raven, November 1, 1999. Retrieved from <http://www.answersingenesis.org/docs/4159.asp?vPrint=1>. All subsequent quotations attributed to Olson are from this letter.

[80] Xu Xing, "Feathers for T. Rex?" in the Fourm (letters) section of *National Geographic*, March 2000, n.p.

[81] Jeff Hecht, "F is for Fake," *New Scientist*, Feb. 19, 2000, p. 12.

[82] Ibid., p. 12.

[83] *National Geographic*, March 2000, Forum, n.p.

[84] Cremo and Thompson, *Forbidden Archaeology*, p. 112.

[85] Randolph E. Schmid, "Scientists Confirm Mistake: 'New' Dinosaur a Combination of 2 Mismatched Fossils," Associated Press, April 7, 2000. Retrieved from <http://abcnews.go.com/sections/science/DailyNews/dino_mistke000407.html>.

[86] Quoted in Carl Wieland, "National Geographic Backs Down—Sort Of," *Answers in Genesis*. Retrieved from <http://www.answersingenesis.org/docs2/4273news4-11-2000.asp?vPrint=1>.

[87] Schmid, op. cit.

[88] "Piltdown Bird," *EXN.ca*. Retrieved from <http://exn.ca/Templates/webisode.asp?story_id=2001033054>.

[89] Cremo and Thompson make this point repeatedly, with numerous examples. See pp. 182-188.

[90] Sloan, p. 102.

Chapter 7
The Worldview of Postmodernism

People are always looking for ways to forget God, even if they have to give up reason in order to do it.
— Phillip Johnson[1]

The revolutionary spirit, which searches the world for things to hate, has found in Foucault a new literary formula. Look everywhere for power, he tells his readers, and you will find it. Where there is power there is oppression. And where there is oppression there is the right to destroy.
— Roger Scruton[2]

7.1 What is Postmodernism?

No doubt you have encountered someone who told you, "Well, that may be true for you, but it isn't true for me," as if truth is relative to the individual. Or you may have heard that we must not criticize the cultural practices of other nations, even if they involve burning alive the widows of men who have just died. If you have taken a literature class, you may have been told that a given work of literature or even a particular paragraph has not one but many possible meanings. All of these ideas are reflections of postmodernist attitudes.

Postmodernism has had a widespread influence on modern culture. Even most people who would not identify themselves as postmodernists have adopted or been affected by postmodernist doctrine. But just how can we define this worldview that is supposedly replacing modernism?

Some people like to think of postmodernism as relativism on steroids because it is so ruthlessly relativistic about everything. There are no more absolutes; nothing is true for everyone; there are merely "truths" relative to a particular culture, society, or individual. As Jim Leffel notes,

> Relativism says that truth isn't fixed by outside reality, but is decided by a group or individual for themselves. Truth isn't discovered, but manufactured. Truth is ever-changing not only in insignificant matters of taste or fashion, but in crucial matters of spirituality, morality, and reality itself.[3]

What's true or false, good or bad, depends on circumstances and context, or even personal taste. You can see already that postmodernism is positioned to be hostile toward both modernism, with its claim that scientific truth is universal, and Christianity, with its claim that spiritual truths are universal.

Relativism is not unique to postmodernism because the modernists/materialists had for a long while argued for relativism in cultural and moral values. Situation ethics is a good example of relativistic thinking coming out of the anti-metaphysical stance of modernism. Where there is no God, there is no standard for making fixed moral judgments or objective moral evaluations.

But postmodernism is much more elaborate and much more problematic in its implications. Postmodernists claim that we are imprisoned by the language we use, that our language controls our thoughts, and that therefore reason itself is unreliable, just a language game. Further, because language controls the way we think, our view of reality is individually or culturally constructed by those around us who use the same language. As a result, there is no such thing as a "correct" or "authoritative" viewpoint. There is no objective authority, and there are no standards other than culturally relative ones. One culture cannot understand another because their different languages create different realities.

For those of us who still believe in the usefulness of reason, the problems with postmodernist thought are obvious. Just in the realm of language and constructed reality, we might ask some interesting questions. If language constructs our reality, does someone who knows more than one language have two realities in his or her head? Why is it that so many written works can be successfully translated from one language to another? How can international business be so successful if one culture cannot understand another? And as Christians, we might add, How is evangelism possible if the postmodernist view of language and culture is correct? How has Christianity managed to spread throughout the world? How indeed did we in the United States even become Christians, having responded to the ideas of geographically and chronologically distant cultures?

A focus on opposition. Postmodernists are fond of using words that sound good and make the movement appear positive. They always seem to be writing and speaking about fairness, justice, equality, rights, tolerance, and respect. But in reality, these terms are very narrowly applied to specific groups (those they identify as the victimized and marginalized) and in specific ways. Indeed, one of the most distinctive features of postmodernism is not its apparently positive talk, but its relentless opposition to the common and traditional values of Western civilization. Postmodernism can be described as anti-tradition, anti-foundational, anti-bourgeois, anti-universal, anti-individual, anti-metaphysical, anti-authority, anti-patriarchal, anti-high art, anti-Eurocentric, anti-Western.

By extension of its opposition to authority, tradition, and universal values, postmodernists are also anti-Christian. Postmodernists reject views that include everyone, such as views of human nature or the claims of God on all people. Such claims, they say, are "totalizing" (and thus oppressive). In fact, "metanarratives" of every kind are to be rejected. According to Thomas Rudel and Judith Gerson, metanarratives are objectionable to postmodernists because, as they say, "Grand theories present comprehensive explanations of their subject matter which postmodernists repudiate as making false claims of universality, truth, and objectivity."[4] And of course, the grandest of all metanarratives is Christianity, which proposes a universal, transcendent truth, a fixed and inclusive human nature, the sovereignty of one God for all peoples, and so on. Postmodernists see people as inextricably entwined and defined by group identity (meaning gender and race, primarily), whereas Christianity claims, "There is neither

Jew nor Greek, there is neither slave nor free man, there is neither male nor female; for you are all one in Christ Jesus" (Galatians 3:28).

Just as a momentary aside, it is interesting to note that scientific naturalism has attempted to destroy the influence of
Christianity by defining it off the table (Christianity is religion
and not science, belief and not fact), while postmodernism has
attempted to produce the same effect by destroying the underlying concepts of truth and universality. Under a postmodernist worldview, Christianity is just another mythical, localized,
subcultural, tribal word game. With modernists, Christians
have common ground in the belief in reason and truth, so that
some sort of evidentiary or at least philosophical arguments
can take place, but with postmodernism, the very grounds of
commonality have been dissolved by the acid of relativism.
Modernists will say that the Christian worldview is wrong,
while postmodernists will say it is naïve or even morally objectionable.

Exaggeration on steroids. What makes postmodernism
plausible? As described so far, it would seem that postmodernism is almost silly and that no one of a reasonable tem-
perament would follow it. And yet, a large segment of the
university is postmodernist. And postmodernist ideas have
deeply influenced the culture (and ordinary people) as well as
even many Christians and Christian professors. Why?

Recall our discussion in Chapter 6 about what makes a lie
attractive or plausible. False ideas are sold on the basis of that
part of them that is recognized as true. In other words, many
postmodern concepts are built on a kernel of truth that has
been exaggerated beyond all reality, almost to the point of satire. And yet that kernel allows postmodernists to press their
ideas down the slippery slope to irrationality. When people
see the plausible kernel, they are more likely to accept the entire idea.

Let's look at a few examples to make this point clearer.
Here are some statements (call them propositions if you have
had a philosophy class) that are unobjectionable or even obvious truths, followed by their postmodernist exaggerations.

Truth #1: Your culture influences your beliefs.

Postmodern exaggeration: Your culture controls or determines your beliefs. Your whole view of reality is determined by your culture and your language. In fact, "All our thinking is a social construct."[5] We have been conditioned by our society to believe and think the way we do.

Comment: Obviously, the choices we think are available (both in consumer goods and ideas) influence the decisions we make. What is being discussed in the media or what we read has an effect on what we think. The attitudes and values of those around us cannot help but exert some influence on our thinking. So far, so good. However, we are able to recognize this influence and to respond to it. We have the ability to think about—and criticize—our culture, to research varying ideas and opinions, find other options, and even to develop our own version of culture. Further, it's hard to claim that we are products of "our culture," because today we are exposed to so many national and international cultural influences, it would be difficult to say, as philosophy professor Hugh Mercer Curtler notes, just what culture any of us actually belongs to. He says,

> Even in Plato's day an urban, sophisticated thinker who was aware of views held in other cultures, especially a thinker who traveled, might be said to be the product of several cultures.
>
> This is especially true today when a young woman might grow up in a working-class Iowa home, attend college at an elite East Coast college, spend years working in Europe, convert from one religious denomination to another, and belong to several clubs made up of men and women not at all like herself. What exactly is her culture?[6]

The same is true with our language. While it is true that language influences the way we express our thoughts, our thoughts precede the language we clothe them in. Most people have had the experience of trying to find the right word to express an idea or of saying, "That's not exactly what I meant, but I can't quite figure out how to say it better right now." So while language does have an effect on thinking, we are able to transcend this problem by exploring several words or phrases (or completely new sentences) to represent a single concept, learn a foreign language or use foreign words, or read books written by those in other cultures. Recognizing the influence of words (as arbitrary labels) is simply a part of good critical thinking, and we can all learn to resist such influence. The postmodernists are simply wrong in their assertion that language "radically controls thought."

Truth #2: Personal experience influences the way we interpret things.
Postmodern exaggeration: *We are "imprisoned by our point of view," and gender, culture, and language "inescapably determine the way we understand things."*[7]

Comment: It is true that some people who are not well educated have a tendency to generalize from single personal incidents, to see the world only in terms of their own limited experience. But one of the purposes of education is to bring us out of such a limited viewpoint, to learn not only about the experiences of others, but also their points of view, as well as about empirical studies that form more reliable generalizations and provide broader perspectives. And, as we will see more than once with postmodernist claims, this particular statement seems to refute itself. If external factors "inescapably determine the way we understand things," then this claim is not really true in any sturdy sense, but is instead merely the result of some deterministic effect of gender, culture, or language. In other words, the belief that this claim is true is determined by our limited point of view and is thus not an objective truth. There is an equal possibility that someone else could believe an opposite claim about knowledge because that claim was also determined by a personal viewpoint.

Truth #3: Some passages in some texts can be interpreted in more than one way. All interpretations are subject to later possible correction or revision.
Postmodern exaggeration: *Every passage in every text has an infinite number of interpretations. To say that one interpretation is "correct" is merely to "privilege" that interpretation. Since all inter-*

pretations are subject to correction, all interpretations are incorrect ("misinterpretations") and must always remain provisional.

Comment: In a given document, whether literature, law, history, or other text, some passages may not be quite clear, and some might be interpreted in more than one way, or even have more than one meaning (poetry is a good example of the intentional exploitation of multiple meanings). This is a far cry, however, from the fact that for the most part texts do yield a clear meaning in most places. "You shall not steal" is fairly clear in its meaning, even if we argue over whether a particular act constitutes stealing. The literary interpretive process of deconstruction, where every text is discovered to be a tissue of contradictions, evasions, and inconsistencies, provides the postmodernists with a tool for destabilizing language, texts, and culture. (See the section below for further clarification.)

Truth #4: What the author says he or she intended should not always be the last word in interpretation.
Postmodern exaggeration: The author's intent is completely irrelevant in interpretation.

Comment: While the "death of the author" and the rejection of authorial intent may have made high school English much more fun, allowing anyone's interpretation of a poem to be just as good as anyone else's, think what such a position does for interpreting the United States Constitution, the law, the Bible, a will, or any other document where the author's intent is clearly crucial to understanding the meaning of the document.

Truth #5: A word can refer to more than one thing; a thing can be referred to by more than one word.
Postmodern exaggeration: The play between word and thing is so limitless that the meaning of all language is indefinite.

Comment: If the meaning of all language is indefinite, then the meaning of this claim must be indefinite, too, since it is expressed in language. (Many postmodernist claims are self-refuting, as we will see later on in Chapter 9.) Anyone who likes puns or who has studied semantics knows how flexible language is and how words can cover many meanings. But the fact that the words are arbitrary symbols does not take away from the fact that we are capable of using them for quite precise communication.

Truth #6: *Authority is not the final word in analysis, and should be questioned.*
Postmodern exaggeration: *Authority should be completely rejected as totalizing and oppressive.*
Comment: As mentioned in Chapter 3, Section 3.4, authority is a major source of knowledge. Much of what we believe is based on or supported by authorities. Sometimes authorities are wrong or subject to their own biases, but that is not a reason for rejecting them altogether. And ironically, postmodernists do not really reject all authority. They merely reject some authorities and substitute others of their own preference. In other words, they "decenter" traditional authority (such as God, the Bible, Aristotle, Plato) and "privilege" the supporters of their own ideology (such as Marx, Derrida, Gramsci, Foucault).

Truth #7: *It's impossible to be completely objective.*
Postmodern exaggeration: *Since everyone is completely biased, it is permissible to promote your own biases and ideologies to whatever extent you wish.*
Comment: Pure objectivity is difficult, but it can still be a goal in our thinking. We can strive to recognize and resist bias, and this is the better choice than giving in to the most partisan ideological excesses in one's thinking and behavior. To use the claim of the impossibility of pure objectivity as an excuse to turn higher education into a system of political and cultural indoctrination is one of the more tragic trends wrought by postmodernist influence.

This list could be much longer, but it should suffice as is to give you an idea of how postmodernist ideas have been constructed by ballooning simple and rather ordinary truths into grotesque distortions of their former selves. When you encounter postmodernist claims, you should therefore neither swallow them whole nor reject them out of hand. Look for any bit of truth or wisdom in them (and it may be a rather small bit), save that, and protect yourself from the remainder of the excess.

Perhaps the next question to be asked is, Why? Where did all this come from and what are postmodernists thinking? A look at the historical factors behind the rise of postmodernism will help clarify the current situation.

7.2 The Historical Context

Back to the Nineteenth Century. The first fifty or sixty years of the twentieth century saw the decline of romantic ideals in the United States to some extent, accompanied by the rise of scientism, empiricism, and reason. There was a return to Enlightenment attitudes. Those old newsreels from the fifties you may have seen (the ones with the upbeat but corny music) trumpeted the "march of science" and showed men in white lab coats making all kinds of wonderful discoveries destined to save the world. Then, as we saw in Chapter 6, scientism (outside the natural sciences) began to lose its luster. A reaction against modernism began to set in and a new interest in the themes of the Romantic Era (rebellion, personal autonomy, distrust of authority) began to grow in popularity.

One way to put postmodernism in context, then, is to say that just as the Romantic Era in the 19th century represented a rebellion against the Enlightenment of the 17th and 18th centuries, so postmodernism is a new expression of romantic rebellion against the revival of Enlightenment Baconian empiricism of the early and mid 20th century. Call this cyclical history if you will, where movements replace each other in turn, and where postmodernism represents the swing back to romanticism. Another way to describe the situation is to say that postmodernism might be seen as the full flowering of the 19th century. Romanticism in the 19th century was interrupted by the industrial revolution. Now that we have passed industrialization and moved into the information economy, the work of the Romantic Era can continue.

Postmodern or Hypermodern? Another way to look at the rise of postmodernism is to say that what we are really seeing is not a rebellion or replacement of modernism but modernism taken to its logical extreme. In other words, postmodernism would better be labeled hypermodernism or radicalized modernism because its characteristics are actually extensions or completions of many modernist attitudes.[8] Those who agree with this label note that postmodernism involves "pushing the assumptions of modernism, with its skepticism and contempt for moral authority, to new extremes."[9]

There is some agreement between modernism and postmodernism that lends weight to the label of hypermodernism, including the continued anti-metaphysical focus. And, in fact, as far back as 1950, Arnold Lunn in his book *The Revolt Against Reason* traced some of the threads of what we now view as postmodern ideas to the sciences and social sciences themselves. He notes that the logical conclusion of philosophical materialism, announced by its advocates as far back as the late nineteenth century, is that "mental processes have no effect on physical processes," that "there is no such thing as free will and no such thing as free thought," and that "truth is unobtainable."[10] Lunn discusses the position of scientific naturalists who say that "there is no ground for believing our thoughts to be valid," and that "we are not interested in truth." He quotes Bertrand Russell in saying that man's "origin, his growth, his hopes and fears, his loves and beliefs, are but the outcome of accidental collocations of atoms" and notes that the psychological school of behaviorism, popular in the 1920s and 1930s, teaches that our beliefs are "imposed on us by irrational forces, our instincts, or sexual complexes, lust for power, etc."[11] Lunn quotes James Watson, one of the founders of behaviorism as saying, "Behaviorism claims that consciousness is neither a definite nor a usable concept."[12]

Lunn's comments and conclusion make us think that postmodernism may indeed have flowered out of modernist principles. He says,

> Behaviourism is welcomed not as the solution of an intellectual problem, but as the solvent of objective codes, the moral restraints of which are regarded as irksome. The essence of the revolt against reason is, as I have insisted throughout this book, a revolt against objectivity in general, in morals no less than thought.[13]

Lunn concludes that a truly consistent materialist, who believes only in a physical universe without transcendent values, must believe that all "moral restraints" are irrational. The true follower of scientism can be consistent only if he or she "repudiates all morality and surrenders the right to condemn any action however vile."[14] And in what appears to be a prescient insight into the double standard of the postmodernist mind, Lunn notes, "There is always some dogma to which the sceptic clings, some standard of absolute behaviour uninfected by his relativity."[15] This fact would seem to explain much about the current campus environment, where in the face of declared cultural and moral relativism, there exist stringent speech codes and seminars aimed at political thought reform.

So, Lunn, were he alive today, might say that what he saw in the 1950s and even earlier, possibly back to the rise of modernism or even back to the rise of Marxism during the industrial revolution, were the seeds of postmodernism.

At the same time, however, many of the advocates of modernism seemed to support the concepts of (scientific) authority, reason, and the progress of knowledge. In that sense, postmodernism's rebellion against these ideas make it different from merely an extension of modernism. In fact, the goal of many postmodernists is the destruction of the modern world itself. Taking to its logical conclusion of relativism the idea that our brains are nothing more than unreliable machines is only one factor in the rise of postmodernism. Politics also plays a large role. To see this the most clearly, we need to go back in time a bit.

The traditional, or orthodox Marxists were committed to a theory of history that emphasized the importance of economic and class struggles to produce revolutionary social change. These original followers of Marxist ideas believed that it was an inexorable historical progression (the result of a "historical determinism") for workers living in capitalist societies first to gain insight into their oppression, and then to revolt and overthrow their oppressors, thus ushering in a communist utopia. (Remember that Marx wrote in the 19th century, when there was a clash between romanticism and industrialization. It was easy to contrast the smoky reality of factory life to the romanticized and imaginary workers' paradise of communism.) The collapse of capitalism and the rise of the proletariat were both seen as inevitable events. However, Marx also had an explanation for the absence of worker revolutions in the face of their exploitation. Workers were not revolting because they could not understand their true situation. In today's terms, we might say that they had been brainwashed by the capitalist system:

> In the *German Ideology* (1845), Marx and Engels argue that under capitalism our social consciousness is distorted by the institution of private property, resulting in mere false consciousness, which tends to preserve rather than alter the present social situation; hence it conceals the contradictions inherent in modern industrial society.[16]

This idea of false consciousness was to prove useful again in the late twentieth century. After the loss of many millions of lives and the economic well being of hundreds of millions, after the worldwide collapse of communism, the failure of new revolutions, and the rush to imitate Western capitalist market structures among former communist nations, Marxism could be seen clearly to have failed as economics, as sociology, and as history. But as political ideology, with its division of all mankind into antagonistic classes, races, and genders, and especially the two categories of victims and oppressors, Marxism is still running—on its last set of retreads, perhaps, but still running—at the university. And the concept of false consciousness is now more handy than ever to explain the disconnect between theory and reality.

Attack the Culture. Rather than remain dispirited over the failure of a worldwide communist civilization to materialize, the Neo-Marxists, among whom was Antonio Gramsci, began to argue that changing the culture of capitalist society was a preliminary requisite to "the emergence of class consciousness" and the eventual revolution.[17] As David Horowitz notes, Gramsci argued for the takeover of the cultural and intellectual core of capitalist countries, and this activity explains why American universities have become such centers of political correctness and Marxist ideology:

The structural support for ideological conformity is intensified by the introduction of overt political agendas. These agendas were originally imported into the university by radicals acting as the self-conscious disciples of an Italian Marxist named Antonio Gramsci. As an innovative Stalinist in the 1930s, Gramsci pondered the historic inability of Communist parties to mobilize workers to seize the means of production and overthrow the capitalist ruling class. Gramsci's new idea was to focus radicals' attention on the means of intellectual production as a new lever of social change. He urged radicals to acquire "cultural hegemony," by which he meant to capture the institutions that produced society's governing ideas. This would be the key to controlling and transforming the society itself.[18]

Thus, Gramsci believed, according to Gene Edward Veith, Jr., that

cultural change must precede socialism. . . . Changing America's values is seen as the best means for ushering in the socialist utopia. This is why the Left today champions any cause that undermines traditional moral and cultural values and why leftists gravitate to culture-shaping institutions — education, the arts, and the media.[19]

In a sentence, "If you want to take over a country, Gramsci argued, do not assault the government; capture its culture."[20] Social transformation must be preceded by a transformation of values among the citizens: Gramsci argued that "the old order had to be rejected by its citizens intellectually and morally before any real transfer of power to the subordinate groups could be achieved."[21]

In "Restoring American Cultural Institutions," Jerry L. Martin explains Gramsci's plan, which you will likely recognize as being in process on your own campus:

Gramsci advocated a three-prong strategy. First, delegitimize existing norms and institutions. Second, infiltrate and co-opt existing institutions. Third, create alternative institutions.

> The first task is destructive — the delegitimization of tra-
> ditional values and institutions. This task requires a persis-
> tent critique of the culture and its norms. This is the task, in
> our society, of what Irving Kristol has called "the adversary
> culture" — a body of intellectuals criticizing everything from
> religion to capitalism to the patriarchal family. Gramsci's ar-
> gument that monogamy is a capitalist plot is an example of
> such a critique. . . .[22]

The attacks on Western civilization and the literary canon of
classic works, the criticism of "high art" as elitist, the rejection
of universal truths, the condemnation of "Eurocentric culture"
as racist and oppressive, and much more can all be seen to
make sense in light of Gramsci's plan to destroy the culture.
Martin continues by explaining the next step:

> The second prong is "cultural penetration," the infiltration
> and co-opting of existing institutions. It is necessary, he said,
> to "assimilate and conquer 'ideologically' the traditional in-
> tellectuals." Having delegitimized religion and traditional
> social norms, adversary culture intellectuals are in a position
> to define a new moral high ground based on ideological
> politics. The new moral high ground is what we would call
> political correctness.[23]

Thus, a subversive ideology is presented in the guise of
morality, so that in the names of fairness, justice, tolerance,
respect and so forth, we have the most unfair, unjust, intolerant, and disrespectful speech codes, divisive racial politics,
double standards, and the like. Further, since the ideology is
viewed in moral terms, any disagreement with it or opposition
to it is viewed as, in essence, immoral. There is no agreement
to disagree, no respect for different viewpoints. Those who
oppose what amounts to the party line are seen as racist, sexist, homophobic, intolerant, insensitive, "unevolved," or morally tainted. And they must be either punished or reformed or
both. As writer and former leftist Harry Stein has noted, there
is "something fundamental to the progressive mind-set: the
idea that politics is holy war, that one's adversaries are not

merely mistaken but evil, that they must be shown no understanding and allowed no quarter."[24]

Other Threads. The late-nineteenth-century philosopher Friedrich Nietzsche also rejected the "foundations of modern thought" because, he said, they were built on Greek and Christian ideas, which gave thinking a rational basis. Nietzsche objected to this because he believed that basing thought in rationality put limits on human advancement. According to Louis Dupre, "The primacy of the logos [reason], sustained since Socrates and deified in the doctrine of the Incarnation, implied for him a denial of the deeper impulse of life, a denial that exploded in the nihilism of late modern culture."[25] The romanticism of individual autonomy, the throwing off of all restraints and inherited truths, can be seen here as a thread leading directly to postmodernist ideas. It is also interesting that Nietzsche advocated the postmodernist dogma that "there are no facts, only interpretations."[26]

Other nineteenth-century philosophers that influenced postmodernist thought include Edmund Husserl, who emphasized the subjectivity of our experience of the world and whose ideas led to the claim that reality is, in fact, merely a social construct.[27] Martin Heidegger argued for the deconstruction of history and tradition in order to free us from the limitations of the past.[28] Heidegger exerted a substantial influence on such postmodern thinkers as Michel Foucault and Jacques Derrida.[29] And Hans-Georg Gadamer posited a theory of philosophical hermeneutics that claimed, "The meaning of the text is not reducible to the meaning intended by its author" but "always transcends what its author originally intended." In fact, "Textual meaning is nothing substantial in itself but exists rather in the form of an ongoing event that is the act of reading, an act that occurs ever anew."[30]

Herbert Marcuse. Another thread of influence in postmodernism comes from twentieth-century Marxist philosopher Herbert Marcuse. He followed the Neo-Marxist claim that those at the center of power "maintained their control by keeping the population 'manipulated and indoctrinated,' so that ordinary people 'parrot, as their own, the opinion of their masters,'" an echo of the idea of false consciousness.[31] Writing in the 1960s, Marcuse advocated the doctrine of "liberating tolerance," which meant that only some ideas should be tolerated. In contrast to "repressive tolerance," he said, liberating tolerance meant "intolerance against movements from the Right, and toleration of movements from the Left," including words as well as actions.[32] In order to combat the brainwashing that people had suffered by those in power, students would need to undergo a re-education, which amounted to nearly the opposite of current educational practices. There would have to be a systematic censorship of the wrong ideas (which he described as "regressive and repressive").[33] If you have ever wondered why the campus advocates of diversity never mention religious or political diversity—ensuring that Christians and conservatives are celebrated on campus, Marcuse supplies the answer with his concept of repressive tolerance.

Historical Summary. The short-term view of postmodernism is that it inherits the "obsessive denigration of the bourgeois" and arrogant detestation of all forms of authority popular among French intellectuals, who, in the twentieth century, have been its source of momentum.[34] The longer term view is that postmodernism derives from a long tradition of "left eclecticism unified by abhorrence of limits":

> The left eclectic has a distinctive orientation of character and sensibility, which draws him irresistibly on to appropriate new modes of thought that are new manifestations of the same disposition. It is no mystery that [nineteenth century] Rousseauism gave birth to Jacobinism, that romantic pantheism fostered naturalism, materialism and Marxism, that the various forms of psychoanalysis as well as radical feminism and sexual emancipation could be enlisted in the revolutionary cause, that gay studies and queer theory grew out of sexual emancipation, that not only Nietzsheanism and Heideggerianism but the whole romantic revolution culminated in postmodernism, etc.[35]

Hostility Toward Science. Now that we understand postmodernism as in part an extension of the romantic rebellion against the Baconian empirical world, the Enlightenment of the 17th and 18th centuries, we can also understand why postmodernists are so hostile toward science. Science is part of the modernist, empiricist worldview that the romantics rebelled against. Friedrich Nietzsche, who has been called "the real father of the postmodern movement,"[36] saw science as merely a tool for destroying religion and philosophy, but not ultimately valuable as a mode of truth:

> In *Human, All Too Human* (1878), he [Nietzsche] praises the spirit, if not the results, of science for enabling us to counter the illusions of religion, philosophy, and the arts. In his view, the sciences do not produce true results to replace the false beliefs of traditional religion, but they are useful for cooling down "the hot flow of belief in ultimate truths."[37]

Martin Heidegger proposed that "our scientific understanding of nature is no more than an interpretation of what is" and therefore had no claim to objective truth. In fact, he believed, no theory can ever reveal the way the world really is.[38]

More than its failure to produce "true results," however, science is viewed by the Neo-Marxists as a collaborator with capitalism, for it is "the ideology of science that produces the innovations and technologies that keep the capitalist engine running."[39] The postmodernists couple science, technology, consumer products, and the commodification of culture with the capitalist system they are bent on destroying.[40] Science invents those products that people buy, thus perpetuating the capitalist market system, and by extension, all the supposed evils of capitalism.

Thus postmodernists are "skeptical about the modern scientific enterprise and its claims about the truth, objectivity, and value of scientific work."[41] The postmodernist interest in destabilizing truth (in order to advance the postmodernist agenda) and the traditional Marxist opposition to capitalism thus combine to oppose the claims and products of science. And a society that has too many technological comforts is a society that will resist revolution because life is too good.

7.3 Postmodernist Anti-foundationalism

As T. S. Eliot observed more than half a century ago in his essay, "The Idea of a Christian Society," the leftist tendency (which he called Liberalism) is "a progressive discarding of elements" rather than a replacement of old with new. "For it is something which tends to release energy rather than to accumulate it, to relax, rather than to fortify."[42] The tendency is to criticize, oppose, or reject the ideas and values and traditions (viewed as constraints or old fashioned views) of the past, rather than to provide alternative value structures. The resulting nihilism, Eliot says, clears the way for the rise of pure power. In other words, once values are destroyed, totalitarianism will follow:

> By destroying traditional social habits of the people, by dissolving their natural collective consciousness into individual constituents, by licensing the opinions of the most foolish, by substituting instruction for education, by encouraging cleverness rather than wisdom, the upstart rather than the qualified, by fostering a notion of getting on to which the alternative is a hopeless apathy, Liberalism can prepare the way for that which is its own negation: the artificial, mechanised or brutalised control which is a desperate remedy for its chaos.[43]

Eliot wrote these words in 1939, just as Hitler was rising to power in Europe. Yet they serve as emblematic of the anti-foundationalism that underlies the postmodern movement today. Postmodernism is operating especially energetically in the first of Gramsci's three phases, the phase of destroying the current culture. We can see this more clearly by looking at the vocabulary of postmodernism.

Postmodernist discourse is encumbered by a substantial amount of jargon, which has given it the unflattering nickname of pomobabble. But by studying some of this diction, we can see what such discourse is up to. The anti-foundational nature of postmodernism, its unrelenting hostility to values, standards, tradition, universals, absolutes, and so on can be seen by the campaign to attack existing institutions and their ideals.

Hegemony. This word, which used to refer commonly to the dominant influence of one nation over another ("the hegemony of Britain over colonial America"), is now used almost as a synonym for oppression. We read about capitalist hegemony, Judeo-Christian hegemony, white male hegemony, or even the "hegemony of totalization" (you're being oppressed by those who believe in universals). Interestingly, no one seems to mention the hegemony of postmodernism in the humanities departments of the university. The idea is that alternative or dissenting voices are silenced by the sheer dominance of an idea, especially a traditional idea about values. While the traditional belief is that values can be liberating, the postmodernists believe that traditional values are victimizing.

Problematize. Take something long assumed to be good, such as "equal justice under law," and show that it is somehow not what it seems. Make it a problem. Reveal the hypocrisy of those who would maintain their own power behind the slogan. Show that the statement of an ideal has not been realized in every respect. Since few ideals have been fully achieved, such a problematization should not even require cleverness.

One of the complaints against postmodernist discourse is that problematization is viewed as an end in itself. Once the concept has been shown to be problematic, the writer may stop. No alternative or solution is necessary. After all, the underlying purpose at this stage is to destroy, not improve, the culture.

Decenter. Take something long treated as important, such as the idea of truth or the traditional literary canon, and push it aside in favor of another concept, such as power or third-world Marxist novels. In other words, marginalize what was once culturally or otherwise central. Postmodernists believe that the classics, like Shakespeare, or philosophers like Aristotle have been "privileged" because they help keep the oppressors in power. By decentering them, the oppressors can be overthrown.

Delegitimize. Attack not just the importance of a concept, but its very claim to validity. A popular technique among postmodernists is to claim that the idea is really a "code word" for some oppressive or evil concept or intent. Thus, for example, "cultural assimilation," one of the traditional goals of Americanization, is condemned by postmodernists as a code phrase for racist ideology.[44] The concept itself is rejected as illegitimate.

Deconstruct. Analyze a text and show that instead of actually meaning what it appears to mean, it actually means the opposite or has multiple meanings or contradicts itself or evades any identifiable meaning. The hoped-for result is to create a confusion about the work, weaken its effect, and thus render it powerless.

In his book, *Against Deconstruction*, Professor of German John Ellis describes the technique, saying that

> . . . deconstruction performs an operation that is variously described as undermining, subverting, exposing, undoing, transgressing, or demystifying; and it performs that operation on something variously thought of as traditional ideas, traditional limits, traditional logic, authoritative readings, privileged readings, illusions of objectivity, mastery or consensus, the referential meaning of a text, or simply what the text asserts or says.[45]

Deconstruction employs a host of these words of attack, criticism, and rejection. They include *destabilize, demystify, delegitimate*, and *demythologize*. Postmodern writers frequently use terms indicating hostility to their subjects, claiming that their arguments are *radically undermining, transgressing, disintegrating, bracketing out, short circuiting*, and so on. The ideas they attack are labeled with terms of insult such as *repressive, oppressive, patriarchal, privileged, hegemonic, ethnocentric, authoritarian* (used as a synonym for authority of any kind), *logocentric*. The words *hierarchical* and *conservative* are also used as insults because the concepts they embody imply that some ideas or works are better than others and that some elements of tradition or the past ought to be preserved and transmitted to future generations. Those who dare to object that there is still value in traditional ideas or methods of interpretation are scorned as *naïve, simplistic*, or even labeled with that popular mantra, *racist, sexist, and homophobic*.

In his book, *Tenured Radicals*, Roger Kimball says, "Given this intellectual climate, it is hardly surprising that criticism should degenerate into a species of cynicism for which nothing is properly understood until it is exposed as corrupt, duplicitous, or hypocritical."[46] The objective of postmodern scholarship, he notes, is "the destruction of the values, methods, and goals of traditional humanistic study."[47]

It is a staggering irony that the postmodernists are destroying the idea of high culture and exalting popular culture (often in the name of decolonization, egalitarianism, equality, or demarginalization) while at the same time decrying the evils of imperialist Western culture. It is precisely the evils of Western popular culture—violent and sexual Hollywood films, TV sitcoms filled with risqué language and suggestive jokes, soft-core pornographic novels, pop-fashion magazines with "sex tips for girls" and so on, that are flooding the rest of the world. It is not Aristotle and Shakespeare that the rest of the world needs less of, but magazines like *Cosmopolitan* and films like *Natural Born Killers*.

7.4 Postmodernism and Christianity

Some Christians think that postmodernism is not entirely without positive aspects and that in fact it can produce some benefits for the Christian faith. They point to the following:

- Tolerance for religious viewpoints. Unlike modernism's hostility toward religion, postmodernism welcomes religion.
- The dethroning of scientism. Postmodernists point out that science has been a false savior, and that there are alternative ways of knowing.
- Awareness of the theory-laden characteristic of knowledge claims. The understanding that knowledge claims are built upon a foundation of preconceptions has been particularly highlighted by postmodernists.

Unfortunately, these apparently compatible aspects are not really compatibilities after all, and for Christians to warm up to postmodernism is to make a fool's bargain. The tolerance for religious viewpoints comes only as those viewpoints are understood as (1) cultural or social expressions without genuine supernatural aspects and (2) all equally "valid" and all equally without truth content. Postmodernists were not the first to criticize scientism or philosophical naturalism. And the theory-laden quality of knowledge claims has long been known. How long? Here's Aristotle, writing in the fourth century B. C.:

> Since pure science or scientific knowledge is a basic conviction concerning universal and necessary truths, and since everything demonstrable and all pure science begins from fundamental principles (for science proceeds rationally), the fundamental principle or starting point for scientific knowledge cannot itself be the object either of science, of art, or of practical wisdom.[48]

While postmodernism has called these ideas to our attention once again or perhaps continued to emphasize them, it would be wrong to credit that worldview with originating them.

More significantly, postmodernism as we have seen is philosophically anti-Christian through its rejection of reason, authority, and foundational truth. And it is structurally anti-Christian also. That is, many of its goals require the rejection of Christian ideas in practical application. Let's look at just two aspects of this.

Multiculturalism. At the heart of Christianity (and at the heart of every reformer's ideals) is the idea that truth and the supreme virtues stand outside of every culture, allowing the wise and thoughtful to evaluate (on humanitarian or religious grounds) the benefits and liabilities of each culture. That is, Christianity condemns sin and injustice in every culture (including Western and American culture). The central claim of evangelism is, "Here is a better idea, one that will improve your lives, make you complete, rid you of harmful practices." Christianity teaches a universal human nature and a universal salvation, based on the common heritage from Adam and Eve, the common image of God in all people, and the specific teaching that all are welcome into the brotherhood of Christ. Once again let me quote: "There is neither Jew nor Greek, there is neither slave nor free man, there is neither male nor female; for you are all one in Christ Jesus" (Galatians 3:28). Quite the opposite of the postmodern mantra of "race, class, and gender," Christianity transcends racial, class, gender, and cultural differences, as it has since the beginning. At the end of the world, all believers will be one together:

> After these things I looked, and behold, a great multitude which no one could count, from every nation and all tribes and peoples and tongues, standing before the throne and before the Lamb, clothed in white robes . . . (Revelation 7:9, NASB).

Multiculturalism, on the other hand, is not what its name might seem to imply. It is not the same as cultural pluralism, or the American ideal of the melting pot, where people from many nations and ethnicities come together to find commonality in American values while maintaining individual aspects of their original cultures. It is not the same as the communitarian ideal like that expressed by Amitai Etzioni in *The Monochrome Society*, where "there are many more beliefs, dreams, and views that whites and nonwhites of all colors share than those that divide them."[49]

For the postmodernists, multiculturalism is about identity politics, where people are defined not as individuals but as members of a racial, ethnic, gender, or other group. Multiculturalism is a type of new tribalism, which furthers the postmodern agenda of destroying current society by inserting divisiveness, group rights, and victimization issues in place of the values of cooperation, assimilation, and common goals. It attempts to impose a set of politically correct beliefs upon each group and deny that any group member may have an independent idea.

At the heart of multiculturalism is cultural relativism, the idea that all cultures are of equal value and that therefore one culture cannot criticize another. Indeed, following the Marxist pipe dream of the pliability of human nature, multiculturalism denies that there is such a thing as a common human nature, since who we are is a product of our culture rather than a shared nature created by God. Cultural relativism implies that since all values are relative to a given culture, one culture cannot attempt to judge or to impose its values on another. "You can't criticize other cultures, because their solutions work for them." Of course, simply on humanitarian grounds, that's nonsense. *Of course* we can criticize the harmful practices of other cultures. Failure to do so lends implicit approval to some horribly inhumane practices, as Dinesh D'Souza notes:

> By insisting on the adaptiveness or functionality of all norms and practices, it [cultural relativism] compelled a suspension of critical judgment in assessing other cultures. . . . Such an approach sometimes required an averted gaze from practices such as witchcraft, mutilation, torture, female clitoral removal, destructive taboos, foot-binding, bride burning, blood feuds, the sacralization of disease, and horrendous sanitary practices. Instead of trying to rationalize indefensible customs, anthropologist Robert Edgerton protested, Western scholars should consider the possibility of maladaptive or dysfunctional practices.[50]

Certainly we in America can criticize the Illongot practice of relieving their grief "by hunting down strangers and cutting off their heads,"[51] just as those outside American culture have the right to criticize us for our historical treatment of American Indians, the practice of slavery, or the current glut of pornography, violent movies, and obsessive secularism.

Slavery, cannibalism, AIDS denial, tribal genocide, using a club to knock out a prospective bride, the list could go on with cultural features that are inhumane or that serve to hinder the progress and well being of a society. It seems that those who have discovered better cultural solutions to the problem of living should be able to share them with those who have not. In his book, *Sick Societies*, UCLA anthropologist Robert Edgerton supplies numerous examples where "traditional beliefs and practices are maladaptive because they endanger people's health, happiness, or survival."[52] He provides a powerful refutation to the idea that primitive or folk societies are well adapted while modern Western societies are not, and rejects cultural relativism in favor of "a form of evaluative analysis," where we are free to identify both adaptive and maladaptive characteristics of every culture.[53] The Rousseauian notion of the "noble savage" where primitive peoples are all happy and culturally well adapted, needs to be tossed into the trashcan of exploded myths.[54]

And this brings us to another difficulty with multiculturalism. It seems to imply that cultures are static and should be preserved as is, lest they be diluted, co-opted, damaged, or eradicated by Western culture. However, as Thomas Sowell points out, "Cultural features do not exist merely as badges of 'identity' to which we have some emotional attachment. They exist to meet the necessitites and forward the purposes of human life." The habit of all cultures interacting with each other, he says, is to adopt solutions which work better than current ones: "The historic sharing of cultural advances, until they became the common inheritance of the human race, implied much more than cultural diversity. It implied that some cultural features were not only different from others but better than others." His, and my, favorite example is the replacement of Roman numerals by Arabic numerals. When the West saw the advantages of using Arabic numerals, Roman numerals were effectively wiped off the face of the earth and were subsequently hardly ever used for any serious purpose.[55]

The point is that all cultures change. The more interaction a culture has with other cultures, the faster it changes, as it greedily adopts better solutions to the problems of living. One of the reasons so-called Western civilization developed such a superior culture is that it took the best ideas from so many other cultures. As Sowell notes, "Much of what became part of the culture of Western civilization originated outside that civilization, often in the Middle East or Asia." In fact, he says, "No culture has grown great in isolation. . . ."[56] Such a fact presents a warning to those who would isolate our American subcultures from each other in a "multicultural" new tribalism. Such an isolation will inhibit the free exchange of better solutions to the problems of living, and create more resentment and divisiveness as those subcultures that freely adopt new ideas succeed better than those who insist on remaining unchanged.

Perhaps a point of clarification is in order here. To criticize the dysfunctional elements in another culture or in one of our own subcultures is not to criticize or condemn the culture as a whole or those who live in it. Nor is such criticism to imply that the culture of the criticizer is superior in general to that of the criticized. Indeed, the criticizer may base the criticism not on a comparison with his or her own culture (an ethnocentric approach), but on the basis of transcendent or humanitarian or practical values.

As with many aspects of postmodernism, we once again run into logical problems. First, if we cannot judge other cultures, then we cannot judge that they are all equal. All judgment must take place according to some standard of measurement, and without a standard of measurement, there is no basis to proclaim equality. The idea of the equality of cultures or the claim that all cultures have acceptable features *as judged from within their own culture* thus becomes merely an ideological assumption bereft of rational support.

Second, how can the multiculturalists criticize Western and American culture if all cultures are equal and if we cannot make judgments about cultures? That seems to be inconsistent.

Third, even if "reforms" are instituted, it will be impossible to know whether society is progressing toward the neo-Marxist ideal of a classless society, since we cannot say that the culture of tomorrow is better than that of today. As Dinesh D'Souza says, "Strictly speaking, relativism does not permit social progress, because the new culture is by definition no better than the one it replaced."[57]

And finally, multiculturalism appears either illogical or hypocritical by first insisting on the value of other cultures and peoples, but then by denying them the same benefits of humanity and justice we enjoy. Once again, D'Souza:

> Moreover, as Leszek Kolakowski points out, it seems paternalistic to say that Islamic practices such as punishing thieves by cutting off their limbs represent legitimate judicial options—for those people. Such arguments, which imply that our kind of people deserve democracy and human rights but their kind of people do not, seem self-serving and may be destructive to the contemporary aspirations of millions of Third World peoples.[58]

The importance of the multicultural agenda as it relates to Christianity is that Christianity must be rejected as being in structural conflict with postmodernist goals. Christianity recognizes that while many cultural artifacts are unimportant and local to given cultures (hairstyle, body paint, dress, and so on), other practices are in need of reform (cannibalism for example). Members of other cultures where evil spirits are worshipped or placated need spiritual enlightenment in the form of the Gospel. Christian missionaries all over the world have always worked to bring humanitarian reform to cultures with cruel practices. Postmodernists reject all of these reformist ideas.

Radical Feminism. Radical feminists find postmodern theory very attractive for several reasons. The postmodern claims about the social construction of reality and the resulting illusion that people are exercising free will[59] helps feminists explain why so many women reject feminist ideology and claim, for example, that they are happy or that marriage is really a good rather than a bad institution. The radical feminists employ Marx's concept of "false consciousness," discussed above, to explain the self-deception that makes so many women believe they are happy and fulfilled even though they are really oppressed and victimized. Women suffer under the tyranny of men in a way similar to the way the workers suffer under their capitalist oppressors: "The struggle between women and their male oppressors is analogous to the struggle between the proletariat and the bourgeoisie in Marxism."[60]

The postmodern rejection of science takes on an anti-Christian tone in the hands of these feminists. A speaker at a feminist conference session on transforming the science classroom, according to Christina Hoff Sommers, "discussed how science was part of a discredited 'bourgeois' Christian legacy practically indistinguishable from imperialism, its cognitive core 'tainted by sexism and racism.'"[61] Science, like Christianity, is oppressive: A Women's Studies textbook asserts that "science is closely tied to the centers of power in this society and interwoven with capitalist and patriarchal institutions."[62]

According to the book, *Issues in Feminism,*

An even more perfect form of slavery was one in which the slaves were unaware of their condition, unaware that they were controlled, believing instead that they had freely chosen their life and situation. The control of women by patriarchy is effected in just such a way, by mastery of beliefs and attitudes through the management of all the agencies of belief formation.[63]

And, of course, religion in general and Christianity in particular is one of these oppressive "agencies of belief formation." The same book refers to the "virulent racism and misogyny of the religious and political right" and refers to the pro-family men's group Promise Keepers as "patriarchy-worshipping."[64]

The institution of marriage, that Christianity considers a sacred and lifelong bond, is considered by radical feminists as prison where "a woman's identity disappears."[65]

Feminism also finds the postmodern collapse of high culture and low culture attractive, for such leveling allows works of art and literature previously considered of lesser value to be brought to attention. Those involved in changing the writing of history, art, and literature to include emphasis on women are known as transformationists. Self-described "equity feminist" Christina Hoff Sommers describes the criticism of artistic standards by "gender feminists," saying that they oppose "the notion of masterpiece in art and the 'hegemony' of Greco-European-American standards." She continues, "In literature, as in the arts, gender feminists have made a sweeping attack on allegedly male conceptions of excellence."[66] But without the idea of excellence, she concludes, we lose the concept of truth:

If one believes that all knowledge is socially constructed to serve the powers that be, or more specifically, if one holds that the science and culture we teach are basically a "patriarchal construction" designed to support a "male hegemony," then one denies, as a matter of principle, any important difference between knowledge and ideology, between truth and dogma, between reality and propaganda, between objective teaching and inculcating a set of beliefs.[67]

The radical feminist attack on marriage, family, sexual morality, men in general, and many traditional institutions now viewed as patriarchal (and therefore deplorable), as well as Christianity itself shows the hostility of this postmodernist influenced movement toward the Christian worldview.

7.5 Implications for Integration

The postmodernist rejection of truth and reason has played right to the selfish desires of a narcissistic society. David McCallum says that "postmodernists argue that when people think they are being reasonable, they are actually just expressing their personal *experience* of enlightenment culture. Thus, *experience* is all we know or ever can know. Our *experience* becomes our reality."[68] Since it's easier to feel and experience than to think and reason about something, and since an emphasis on experience encourages self-indulgence, this doctrine has a powerful appeal. But experience is not truth, and our emotions are easily fooled.

More problematically, if Christianity itself begins to emphasize experience over truth, then it will be placed in the position of competing with alternative experiences that may be more exciting. This is the same problem that occurred in the 1960s, when some rather naïve Christians went around saying, "Jesus is better than heroin," and "Get high on Jesus." When some people told them, "Well, I've tried Jesus and I've tried heroin, and heroin is a bigger high," no argument was possible. We cannot guarantee a superiority of experience or feeling or pleasure. The New Testament makes no such promises. What we have with Christianity is not just one more choice of activities among many, "God as a hobby," but the challenge of truth. We don't ask others (or ourselves) to choose between God and bowling on the basis of which is more fun. We stand on truth and ask others to choose the truth. Postmodern churches that emphasize merely an experiential religion are pursuing the wrong path, in my view.

Even more than philosophical naturalism, postmodernism is categorically anti-Christian. The rejection of authority rejects God, The Authority; the rejection of stable textual meanings and specific interpretations rejects the usefulness and guidance of the Bible, the rejection of truth renders Christ's claims mere preferences ("Without truth, Christianity itself will vanish or be swallowed up in an ocean of subjective religious experience," says Dennis McCallum).[69] Postmodernism's divisiveness along class, race, gender, and cultural lines runs counter to the unifying teaching of Christian missiology. In place of a unified vision of humanity (neither Jew nor Greek, male nor female) we have a movement toward "the retribalization of the world."[70]

In presenting their ideas, postmodernists often attempt to couch them in high moral terms ("respect," "tolerance," "social justice") so that they appear attractive or at least unobjectionable. But underneath the euphemisms lies an agenda antithetical to Christianity and to human happiness. Be careful not to welcome a wolf in sheep's clothing.

Summary

Postmodernism represents the full flowering of a set of philosophical ideas aimed at throwing off authority and moral restraint. By denying the reality of reason, objective truth, and standards of judgment, postmodernists argue that power is the only determiner of whose ideas prevail. Postmodernism's rejection of individualism also portends the rise of totalitarian forms of government. The rejection—the demonization—of truth, faith, family and so on put postmodernism in direct conflict with Christianity.

Questions for Thought and Discussion

1. What postmodernist ideas or influences do you find in your classes, especially in the humanities and social sciences?

2. What postmodernist influences do you find in the cultural values and practices around you?

3. Postmodernists like to attack American culture. What aspects of American culture are valuable? What aspects are worthy of criticism?

4. When you encounter in a textbook or article a postmodern idea that seems to run counter to Christian truth (such as the postmodern view of marriage an instrument of patriarchal oppression), how might you counter this idea? Develop several general strategies.

---

[1] Phillip Johnson, *The Wedge of Truth* (Downers Grove, IL: InterVarsity, 2000), p. 38.

[2] Roger Scruton, "Why I Became a Conservative," *The New Criterion*. Retrieved online from <http://www.newcriterion.com/archive/21/feb03/burke.htm>.

[3] Jim Leffel, "Our New Challenge: Postmodernism," in Dennis McCallum, ed., *The Death of Truth* (Minneapolis: Bethany House, 1996), p. 31.

[4] Thomas K. Rudel and Judith M. Gerson, "Postmodernism, Institutional Change, and Academic Workers: A Sociology of Knowledge, *Social Science Quarterly* 80:2 (June 1999), pp. 213ff. Page 1 of InfoTrac reprint.

[5] Leffel, p. 35.

[6] Hugh Mercer Curtler, "The Myopia of the Cultural Relativist," *The Intercollegiate Review* 38:1 (Fall, 2002), p. 40.

[7] Roger Kimball, *Tenured Radicals*, Rev. ed., (Chicago: Ivan R. Dee, 1998), p. 91.

[8] Peter Augustine Lawler, "Conservative Postmodernism, Postmodern Conservatism," *Intercollegiate Review* 38:1 (Fall, 2002), p. 17.

[9] Gene Edward Veith, Jr., *Postmodern Times*, (Wheaton: Crossway Books, 1994), p. 41.

[10] Arnold Lunn, *The Revolt Against Reason* (London: Eyre and Spottiswoode, 1950), pp. 173, 175.

[11] Ibid., pp. 176, 177, 189.

[12] Ibid., quoted on p. 193.

[13] Ibid., p. 194.

[14] Ibid., pp. 180, 181

[15] Ibid., p. 181.

[16] Tom Rockmore, "Karl Marx," in Richard H. Popkin, ed., *The Columbia History of Western Philosophy* (New York: MJF Books, 1999), p. 554.

[17] David Ingram, "Continental Philosophy: Neo-Marxism," in Richard H. Popkin, ed., op. cit., p. 721.

[18] David Horowitz, "Missing Diversity on America's Campuses," *FrontPageMagazine.com*, Sept. 3, 2002. Available from <http://www.frontpagemag.com/articles/Printable.asp?ID=1003>.

[19] Veith, p. 161.

[20] Jerry L. Martin, "Restoring American Cultural Institutions," *Society* 36:2 (Jan-Feb 1999), pp. 35-40. Gale Group reprint, p. 2.

[21] John Fonte, "Why There Is a Culture War," *Policy Review* (Dec. 2000-Jan. 2001), p. 17.

[22] Ibid., Gale Group reprint, p. 2

[23] Ibid., Gale Group reprint, p. 2.

[24] Harry Stein, *How I Accidentally Joined the Vast Right-Wing Conspiracy (And Found Inner Peace),* (New York: Delacorte, 2000), p. 33.

[25] Louis Dupre, "Postmodernity or Late Modernity? Ambiguities in Richard Rorty's Thought," *The Review of Metaphysics* 47:2 (Dec. 1993), pp. 277-296. Gale Group reprint, p. 1.

[26] Rudolf A. Makkreel, "The Problem of Values in the Late Nineteenth Century," in Richard H. Popkin, ed., op. cit., p. 562.

[27] David Carr, "Husserl and Phenomenology," in Richard H. Popkin, ed., op. cit, pp. 677-681.

[28] Tom Nenon, "Martin Heidegger," in Richard H. Popkin, ed., op. cit., p. 684.

[29] Ibid., p. 690.

[30] G. B. Madison, "Hermeneutics: Gadamer and Ricoeur," in Richard H. Poplin, ed., op. cit., p. 708.

[31] Alan Charles Kors and Harvey A. Silverglate, *The Shadow University* (New York: HarperCollins, 1998), p. 68.

[32] Quoted in Kors and Silverglate, p. 70.

[33] Ibid., pp. 70-71.

[34] John M. Ellis, *Against Deconstruction* (Princeton, NJ: Princeton University Press, 1989), pp. 84-85.

[35] Jan Olof Bengtsson, "Left and Right Eclecticism: Roger Kimball's Cultural Criticism," *Humanitas* 14:1 (2001), p. 32.

[36] See Louis Dupre, op. cit., Gale Group reprint, p. 8.

[37] Rudolf A. Makkreel, op. cit., p. 561.

[38] Joseph J. Kockelmans, "Continental Philosophy of Science," in Richard H. Poplin, ed., op. cit, p. 695.

[39] Kenneth Allan and Jonathan H. Turner, "A Formalization of Postmodern Theory," *Sociological Perspectives* 43:3, p. 366.

[40] For a discussion of these connections, see Kenneth Allan and Jonathan H. Turner, op. cit., especially pp. 367 and 369.

[41] Rudel and Gerson, op. cit. Gale Group reprint, p. 2.

[42] T. S. Eliot, "The Idea of a Christian Society," in *Christianity and Culture* (1939; rpt., San Diego: Harcourt Brace, 1976), p. 12.

[43] Ibid., p. 12.

[44] Dinesh D.Souza, *The End of Racism* (New York: Free Press, 1995), p. 136.

[45] John M. Ellis, op. cit., p. 69.

[46] Roger Kimball, op. cit., p. 95.

[47] Ibid., p. 1.

[48] Aristotle, *Nicomachean Ethics*, 7.6.d, tr. Martin Ostwald. New York: Bobbs-Merrill, 1962.

[49] Amitai Etzioni, *The Monochrome Society* (Princeton: Princeton University Press, 2001), p. 7.

[50] Dinesh D'Souza, *The End of Racism* (New York: The Free Press, 1995), p. 154.

[51] Ibid., p. 155.

[52] Robert B. Edgerton, *Sick Societies* (New York: Free Press, 1992), p. 24.

[53] Ibid. See his conclusion on pp. 202-209.

[54] Ibid. See Chapter 6, where Edgerton makes the point that most cultures have features that cause discontent for many people in the culture.

[55] Quotations in this paragraph are from Thomas Sowell, "Cultural Diversity: A World View," available on Mr. Sowell's Web site at <http://www.tsowell.com/spcultur.html>. For awhile, Hollywood films used Roman numerals in their copyright notices in order to disguise how old the films were, but in recent years even that practice seems to have been largely abandoned.

[56] Ibid.

[57] D'Souza, p. 207.

[58] Ibid., pp. 383-384.

[59] Allan and Turner, p. 376.

[60] Tom Dixon, "Postmodern Method: History," in Dennis McCallum, ed., *The Death of Truth* (Minneapolis: Bethany House, 1996), p. 133.

[61] Christiana Hoff Sommers, *Who Stole Feminism?* (New York: Simon & Schuster, 1994), p. 83.

[62] Christine Stolba, "Lying in a Room of One's Own: How Women's Studies Textbooks Miseducate Students," *Independent Women's Forum*, 2002, p. 12. Retrieved from http://www.iwf.org/pdf/roomononesown.pdf.

[63] Quoted in Stolba, p. 18.

[64] Quoted in Stolba, p. 25.

[65] Phyllis Schlafly, *Feminist Fantasies* (Dallas: Spence Publishing, 2003), p. 78.

[66] Christina Hoff Sommers, pp. 63, 64.

[67] Sommers, p. 97.

[68] McCallum, *Death of Truth*, p. 239.

[69] McCallum, p. 249.

[70] Roger Kimball, *Tenured Radicals* (1990, rpt.: Chicago: Ivan R. Dee, 1998), p. 236.

Chapter 8
The Worldview of Christianity

Let them recognize that there are only two kinds of person whom we can describe as reasonable: those who serve God with all their heart because they have found him, and those who seek him with all their heart because they have not found him.

−Blaise Pascal[1]

For us as scholars this means that our agenda ought to be directed toward building for our community as solid a place in the pluralistic intellectual life of our civilization as is consistent with our principles. Helping to establish the intellectual viability of our worldview and pointing out the shortcomings of alternatives can be an important service to our community and an important dimension of our witness to the world.

− George Marsden[2]

8.1 Christianity and the Christian Worldview

In Chapter 5 we discussed the nature of worldviews, saying that a worldview is a personal theory of everything, a set of beliefs and values that help each of us make sense of the world or bring coherence to our experience. The Christian worldview is constructed from several elements.

- **The Bible**. Our knowledge of God, our purpose in life, guidance in daily living choices, the Gospel of Christ — all these elements of our worldview come from the Word we have been given. As we will see in a later chapter, understanding this book is crucial not only for constructing an accurate worldview but for performing the task of integration properly.

- **History**. Our faith has historical dimensions because God has interacted with his people in time and throughout history. How and why God has acted is important for our understanding of his ways.
- **Philosophy and Reason**. Again, we have already seen the role of philosophy in helping us develop a rational view of truth, reality, faith, and purpose. Philosophy and reason help us extend Scriptural truth to the general realms of knowledge, to specific problems, and to thinking about knowledge and reality.
- **Experience.** Our personal experience with God, with other people in Christian community, with those in the world at large, and all of our activities have an impact on how we build our worldview.
- **Learning**. What we hear, read, think about, all the knowledge we gain (learning about quarks, for example) helps us develop a more circumspect and coherent worldview (and honor our Creator God all the more).

That these last three elements of worldview construction will vary from person to person and will require a lifetime to work out fully reveals that there are, in fact, many "Christian worldviews," all with much in common but each with individual elements. One of the great features of the Christian faith is that it is simple enough for the simplest to understand and follow and yet it is ample for the greatest philosophers to find understanding and answers for their deepest questions. Thus, some Christians will not explore philosophy or learning to any great extent in the working out of their personal Christian worldview. On the other hand, highly educated Christians will explore the world of ideas, "taking every thought captive to the obedience of Christ" (2 Corinthians 10:5).

The Christian worldview does have many common elements, of course, as we have already seen in the discussions of previous chapters. Perhaps the best way to clarify the Christian worldview and to set it apart from the two other worldviews we have already looked at (naturalism and postmodernism) is to draw up a comparison of their positions on a number of crucial issues. By examining the similarities and differences among these views, we can gain a better understanding of all three. My first idea was to draw up a table with boxes for each issue and each position, but after some thought I realized that the table would run for several pages and create a cramped description. I have therefore decided upon a point-by-point descriptive comparison.

The particular topics of this comparison have been chosen especially with the goal of integration in mind, because it is on these topics that much of the conflict between worldviews occurs. Whether or not God is part of one's worldview has the most significant influence on one's conclusions about facts, but one's view of human nature (related to the God question) will be deeply influential about one's diagnosis of problems (such as social, psychological, historical, political, or economic) and their solutions.

8.2 God

Naturalism. God does not exist (atheism) or it is not known whether or not he exists (agnosticism) or else the question of God's existence is meaningless or unintelligible (positivism). The question of God and the supernatural is irrelevant to the living and learning of human beings. Since the only truth is scientific truth, there is no truth in any statements about God. Since God does not exist, religion itself, of any kind, is suspect, delusive, and possibly harmful.

Postmodernism. The idea of God, like all reality, is a linguistic construct, without any reference to an objective existence. God and religion have been created as tools of oppression by the powerful. As philosopher Michael Peterson says, "It is obvious to postmodernists that genuine knowledge of God is impossible because all supposed knowledge is embedded in language, all language is embedded in culture, and all cultures differ. The meta-narrative of God must be rejected along with all other meta-narratives."[3] Religion of any kind is all right as a social comfort, but any attempt to make truth claims or exclusivity claims ("This is the one true religion") will be rejected with hostility.

Christianity. God is an infinite, personal being who has created the universe and mankind and has revealed himself to us. He gives meaning to human life and action, and unifies the entire creation. He reveals himself to us through the natural world and through the Bible. He has come into personal contact with mankind through his son, Jesus Christ. Objective knowledge of God is possible. The existence of God gives purpose and direction to life and provides an objective foundation for knowledge and values. That we have been created by God and in his image allows us to place confidence in reason (though it is limited by the fall).

Comment. Belief in God is basic, rational, and natural, and it is supported by reason, evidence, and personal experience. In fact, it requires a substantial amount of "education" to draw most people away from belief in God. A long and deliberate rejection of faith, arising from the Enlightenment exaltation of reason and science, underlies the naturalist/modernist worldview; and a more recent but perhaps equally intense hostility underlies the postmodernist worldview. However, in an attempt to keep God from interfering with their projects, these worldviews have lost both comprehensiveness and correspondence. Neither view adequately explains the built-in longing for God that we experience.

It is important to understand that no worldview is neutral about God. As Ronald Nash explains, "Human beings are never neutral with regard to God. Either we worship God as Creator and Lord, or we turn away from God. Because the heart is directed ether toward God or against God, theoretical thinking is never as pure or autonomous as many would like to think." He adds that "some people who appear to reject Christianity on rational or theoretical grounds are, in fact, acting under the influence of nonrational factors, that is, more ultimate commitments of their hearts."[4] (These ultimate commitments help explain why arguing about religion is usually so futile. No argument is cogent enough for someone who is precommitted to nonbelief.)

8.3 Reality (Ontology)

Naturalism. The material world is all that exists. There is no supernatural realm, nor any supernatural being that relates to the natural world in any way. Therefore, ideas like justice, beauty, good and evil, spiritual fulfillment and so forth are merely subjective personal or social preferences. All of reality can be discovered through the scientific method of examining and testing the observable world. Because the material world encompasses all of reality, every explanation for every observed or felt phenomenon must, by definition, come from the natural world.

Postmodernism. It is impossible to access an objective reality, because everyone's view of reality is distorted by social, personal, and linguistic fictions that control perception and understanding. Every group or subculture has its own "reality," which it adheres to. All such "realities" are equally valid but not one is true in an absolute sense. What people think of as reality is actually a mental construct based on language, a word game. To believe that words represent something real is naïve.

Christianity. Reality includes both the material world and the spiritual world. Both exist in an objective way, outside human determination or subjective preference. There is a real world that can be known. Even when our knowledge of it is imperfect, true reality is still there. We live in an externally independent reality; we do not construct it with our imagination.

Comment. Much of reality is simply missed or explained away as a subjective preference by naturalism and postmodernism. Naturalism has a grip on material reality that postmodernism does not, yet neither worldview reasonably accounts for spiritual reality, emotional reality, ethical values, virtues, human nature, and the like. To continue to ascribe these real things merely to feelings, physical processes, linguistic constructs ("honor is only a word") and the like seems less adequate than to credit their ontological status.

8.4 Knowledge and Truth (Epistemology)

Naturalism. The observation of physical nature is the source of all truth. Knowledge means scientific knowledge. No answer to any question can be ultimately true unless it references only the natural world. Hence, if an examination of evidence might otherwise lead one to see a supernatural Designer, that answer must be rejected because it is not confined to the physical world. Any scientific discovery or interpretation that includes the supernatural is *by definition* "pseudoscience."

Postmodernism. Truth is a subjective, personal, and culture-bound belief that varies from time to time, person to person, culture to culture. There are no absolute truths, no transcendent truths, no truths that can necessarily be applied from one group, person, or culture to another. Another way of looking at this is to say that there are many "truths," perhaps an infinite number, but none are universal or applicable to everyone.

Christianity. There are absolute, transcendent truths, made possible by the existence, creation, and sovereignty of God. Knowledge comes from scientific observation, from Biblical revelation, and from reasoning about the world and experience. Truth and knowledge find their fixed foundation in the Creator, who has made nature, physical laws, moral laws, and spiritual laws.

Comment. Both naturalism and postmodernism suffer from epistemological difficulty because both make claims that are in logical conflict with their own assumptions. For example, naturalism's claim that all truth must derive from observation or experiment is a claim that cannot be derived from observation or experiment: it is a metaphysical assumption. And postmodernism's claim that all truth is relative and subjective implies that such a claim is itself relative and subjective and thus not generally true or objective. See the discussion of self-refutation in the next chapter for further details. Christianity is the only worldview of the three that is logically consistent in its epistemic foundations.

8.5 Reason

Naturalism. Reason can operate only on the information provided by an examination of the physical world or by logical deduction, as in mathematics. Reason and observation (or experiment) alone can tell us everything that can be known about the world and ourselves.

Postmodernism. Not only is the idea of objective reason merely a Western cultural myth, but the belief in reason is also a harmful myth, helping to preserve the power of the white European male way of thinking, at the expense of alternative and equally valid ways of thinking. Reason and logic interfere with the freedom to think in broader ways, such as believing self-contradictory truths. Reason is only one type of word game among many possible types. As a result, reason is not a guide to any kind of ultimate truth or knowledge.

Christianity. Even though reason has suffered some loss of power as a result of the fall, and even though it therefore cannot lead us to every truth by itself, reason is still a powerful, useful, and usually reliable tool for understanding our world. In fact, reason is necessary to help us make decisions, gain insight into God's creation, and learn new knowledge. Reason must be supplemented by revelation to gain the fullest knowledge about reality, but it is the friend and ally of faith.[5]

The role of reason in the Christian worldview has sometimes been an object of debate, but generally Christian thinkers have recognized the value and character of rationality in the faith. Just as an example, Nathaniel Culverwell wrote *A Discourse of the Light of Nature* in 1652, a book in which he argued for the value and role of reason in the Christian life, and where he frequently remarked upon the close relationship between reason and faith:

> . . . Reason and faith may kiss each other. There is a twin light springing from both, and they both spring from the same fountain of light, and they both sweetly conspire in the same end, the glory of that being upon which they shine. So that to blaspheme reason, 'tis to reproach heaven itself, and to dishonour the God of reason, to question the beauty of his image, and by a strange ingratitude to slight this great and royal gift of our creator.[6]

Comment. Naturalism runs into problems with the concept of reason because of the often expressed doubt that a brain produced by randomness can be a reliable instrument for understanding the world. Even Darwin himself worried about this problem: "But then with me the horrid doubt always arises whether the convictions of man's mind, which has been developed from the mind of the lower animals, are of any value or at all trustworthy. Would any one trust the convictions of a monkey's mind, if there are any convictions in such a mind?"[7] The current view of naturalism, that thinking is a function of brain states, is similarly problematic. As William Hasker explains, to believe that thinking is physically determined means "that rational thinking is an impossibility" because no one's "thinking is guided by rational insight; rather, it is guided entirely by the physical laws which govern the brain's functioning, which proceed with no regard to whether the thought processes they generate correspond to principles of sound reasoning." He concludes that "if all human thought is physically determined, then no one ever thinks rationally."[8] And as mentioned earlier, Richard Rorty claims that our species evolved with an orientation, like all other species, for reproduction, not for finding truth. To believe that we are oriented toward truth is "un-Darwinian."[9]

And the postmodernist view of reason, that "there is no such thing as 'rationality' other than that contextually defined by the practices of a group," causes us to wonder just how to understand the reasoned arguments of postmodernist ideology.[10] Postmodernists often write reasoned arguments to each other and to those outside their own group. Are we to take them seriously?

8.6 Human Nature

Naturalism. Human beings are the product of an undirected material process with no goal in mind, and their habits and nature are the product of the activity of random molecules. Many naturalists are determinists, believing that our actions are determined by our biological processes and that we therefore do not really have free will to make decisions. Those parts of human nature the naturalists do not like (such as the innate spiritual strivings of the heart) are dismissed as holdovers from our rise "from the sludge to the judge." What is commonly called human nature is a combination of genetic determination and social conditioning.

Postmodernism. Human beings are conditioned by their social environment, which determines what they think and how they act. Postmodernists thus adopt classical Marxist theory that human nature is pliable and can be changed. (Hence the desire of Marxists to bring about a communist utopia where there is no greed, selfishness, crime, class warfare, etc.) People in different cultures will have different natures. Even subgroups within a given culture will be so different that they may be unable to understand each other. Hence the emphasis on tribalism and group identity.

Christianity. All humans worldwide share the same humanity and are equally valuable because they have all been created by God. Humans in fact share the image of God. Human nature includes spiritual as well as biological (genetic) components. It does not change. We are all created to desire spiritual fulfillment and we are all tempted by sin, for example.

Comment. The Christian view that all humans share a common nature, resulting from their creation in the image of God, reveals that all people are equally valuable children of God. The fact that human nature does not change means that eternal and traditional solutions to human problems remain as applicable today as they always have. Many solutions to the problems of human life (hygiene, human rights, freedom) are therefore applicable across cultures.

Philosophy professor William Hasker says that "surely one of the acid tests for a world view is whether it is able to provide a consistent, coherent, and acceptable account of the nature of humanity."[11] It is here especially that both naturalism and postmodernism seem to fail glaringly. As for naturalism, Hasker notes,

> Naturalism typically expresses itself in metaphysics through such viewpoints as behaviorism, mind-body identity theory and scientific determinism. . . . The naturalist is likely to feel that, whatever the difficulties and obscurities of particular points, the naturalistic understanding of man is obviously correct and the resistance to it is the result of sentimentality and superstition. To the nonnaturalist, on the other hand, it may appear equally obvious that the naturalist is interpret-

ing human life within a restricted and rather rigid conceptual scheme in spite of abundant evidence that the concepts are not adequate for the subject matter.[12]

We all have many experiences, beliefs, feelings, and ideals that seem inadequately explained by the doctrine that they simply arose as byproducts of our undirected, meaningless rise from lower life forms.

The postmodernist view that human nature is a social product and that paradise on earth can be achieved by the right kind of social engineering, seems too obviously counter to our experience of even our own humanity. Whether we examine other peoples, our friends, or the pages of history, human nature appears to be much better described by the Christian worldview than by what is clearly an ideology "overthrown by the experience of every hour."[13]

8.7 Ethics and Values (Axiology)

Naturalism. There are no fixed, eternal, or even completely objective values. Two essentially naturalistic ethical movements arising from within naturalism are pragmatism ("If it works, it's true") and situation ethics ("Maybe cannibalism is okay if you're starving in a lifeboat"). Morality is personal, and ethical behavior derives from social consensus. Neither is fixed in any unchangeable laws.

Postmodernism. Values, like other ideas, are culturally determined and culture bound. The belief in cultural relativism — that all cultures are equal in value and that no culture is better than another — is a foundational principle of postmodernist ethical theory. Hence, tolerance is a key virtue. Any criticism of another culture's values is condemned as oppressive, intolerant, and ethnocentric. Values and ethical rules differ among groups within a culture as well as across cultures. Michael Peterson explains the implications of the postmodernist attitude: "According to this model of education, the postmodern educated person, the one who really knows what is going on, must renounce fidelity, loyalty, faith, courage, and dedication to a cause, since these once-admirable qualities are merely fictions that enable a dominant social group to maintain power."[14] In fact, literature or other writing that expresses values or a moral position is merely "propaganda."[15]

Christianity. Ethical rules derive from eternal values. Values and morals derive from an eternal God who created humankind and the values necessary for a fulfilled life. Revelation in the Bible, historical experience, and philosophical reasoning have identified the permanent values that apply to every human being. These values are objective "in the sense that their truth is independent of human preference and desire."[16] That is, we cannot alter them just because we feel like it or our attitudes or circumstances change. Because human nature does not change, ultimate human values do not change. Cultural relativism is rejected. We have the right, even the duty, to criticize elements in other cultures (and in our own) that are inhumane or harmful. For example, the practice of burning alive a man's widow (suttee) is wrong, regardless of which culture practices it.

Comment. The only way to have a reliable ethical system is to base it on an objective and fixed foundation. Of the three worldviews, only Christianity provides a stable base for values. The other systems can offer only cultural, social, or personal value systems, subject to flux and whim or political power. On the other hand, "A Christian and theistic position holds that moral principles are objectively meaningful and absolute because they reflect constant moral realities inherent to creation."[17] Even from the standpoint of consistency, as Hugh Mercer Curtler notes, cultural relativism is "an absurd view," because "no one would hesitate, in practice, to condemn another (regardless of that person's cultural background) for activities they regard as morally offensive." He adds, "If it is wrong to violate the dignity of the human person in our own culture, as it surely is, then it is wrong in any culture whatsoever."[18] Postmodernists especially see themselves as standing on moral high ground as they condemn the things they dislike. And yet, on what basis can they make moral judgments when their own position condemns such judgments?

8.8 Humanity's Challenge

Naturalism. The largest problems facing mankind are ignorance, superstition, and technological inadequacy. Resisting the rule and control of science holds mankind back. Metaphysical schemes and beliefs are harmful to human progress. Humanity's greatest challenge is allowing science to gain further control over nature and mankind.

Postmodernism. The largest problems facing mankind are capitalism, oppression, and white European male hegemony. The marginalization of non-Western cultures and voices and the oppression of victim classes are the real challenges. Capitalist structures are so distorting that many people suffer from false consciousness and may think they are happy because they do not recognize their true oppression and victimization. Thus, the ills of life result from social, economic, or political systems rather than personal behavior or morality.

Christianity. In a word, the deepest problem with mankind is sin. In the history of mankind, pride, greed, selfishness, jealousy, hatred and so on—all the darker sides of our fallen nature—are the problems. The Seven Deadly Sins make a good list: pride, envy, anger, greed, lust, gluttony, and sloth. Sin is made even more problematic by many people's insistence on rejecting God. The separation from God initiated by the fall has resulted in the problems of humanity today.

Comment. The first rule of problem solving is to identify the actual problem. If you try to solve the wrong problem, the real problem will not go away. More technology will not eliminate pride. Destroying capitalism will not eliminate greed. Changing political structures will not eliminate lust. And continuing to reject God will not bring about happiness.

8.9 The Solution to Humanity's Challenge

Naturalism. Reason and science will save mankind, helping to bring about a better world free from disease, superstition, hunger, and pain. We must invent our own solutions. As Stephen Jay Gould says, we "must establish our own paths in this most diverse and interesting of conceivable universes— one indifferent to our suffering, and therefore offering us maximum freedom to thrive, or to fail, in our own chosen way."[19]

Postmodernism. The marginalization and eventual destruction of Western culture will help bring about a revolution in which a classless utopia can emerge. Emphasis on the struggle in terms of race, class, and gender will empower those marginalized groups to rise up and replace the dominance of the current system. Celebrating group differences will eliminate oppression. Since human nature is not fixed, but subject to molding by economic and political systems, the destruction of capitalism, modernism, and Christianity will cause "all historically known forms of human misbehavior (crime, greed, selfishness, lack of compassion, envy, etc.) . . . to 'wither away.'"[20]

Christianity. In a word, the solution to the problems of humanity is reconciliation. Personal and in some cases corporate repentance needs to be made, together with a turning to God. Receiving forgiveness of sin and salvation through Christ is essential. A new life with new attitudes, beliefs, and behaviors must begin. Humility is needed to take these steps. (It might be argued that it is precisely the resistance to humility that makes naturalism and postmodernism so appealing. Pride in the authority of science or in the position of cultural critic offer attractive incentives to those who cannot stand the idea of submission to God.)

Comment. Naturalism and postmodernism have similar hopes of bringing about paradise on earth. Naturalism seeks to solve human problems through technology. And, of course, technology can help and has helped us live much healthier and more comfortable lives. Postmodernism, advancing a neo-Marxist view of human nature and society, seeks to bring about a just social order through a change in human nature (resulting from a cultural and economic revolution). Neither system, however, adequately addresses the real needs of people, such as the need for meaning and purpose in life, a solution to the personal problems of living, spiritual hunger, and the need for moral guidance.

8.10 Implications for Integration: The Hermeneutics of Integration

Because the Bible is the foundation stone for the Christian worldview, those who would attack our worldview often begin with the Bible. "The Bible is not a science textbook," they say. That's true. The Yellow Pages is not a science textbook, either, but both the Bible and the Yellow Pages are filled with facts about the world. Nevertheless, a proper understanding of the Bible is crucial to an effective and accurate integration. The Bible includes many genres (poetry, history, laws, proverbs, prophecy, and so on) and it conveys the truth using several methods of expression (literal, metaphorical, and so on), in multiple contexts (textual, historical, theological).

Hermeneutics (the study of interpretation) is a large field that deserves some serious study. We face the challenge of interpretation in Scripture just as we face the challenge to interpret nature or human actions or any other events. Life is about interpretation. It is not self explanatory. *Integration, in fact, often means the integration of interpretations.* For our purposes, we will merely sketch out a few ideas that are directly useful to the integration issue.

Biblical Framework. The Bible presents the basic framework of reality upon which we can build a Christian worldview. From this fact, we understand:

- There is no conflict between Scriptural truth and any other truth. Apparent conflicts involve conflicts of interpretation (either of Scripture or of external facts). All truth is God's truth, and God does not contradict himself.
- The Bible's main emphasis rests in presenting historical and theological truth.
- The Biblical framework of reality includes a Creator God, the divinely created and self-fallen human nature, Scriptural principles for living, meaning and purpose in life, and so on. The most important concerns are who God is and who we are (and how we can return to God).

Message Versus Method. In interpreting the meaning of Biblical passages, we must remember that the writers use several methods to convey their ideas. It is important not to confuse how an idea is expressed with what idea is being conveyed. Methods of expression include the following.

- *Phenomenological.* Just as we do today in ordinary conversation, the Bible often uses a phenomenological approach to describing events. That is, the description matches the common sense, apparent, observed phenomena of life. For example, we, along with Scripture, refer to sunrise and sunset, even though we know that the sun does not revolve around the earth. The sun appears to be setting, so that's what we say. Scripture was written to be accessible to its first audience, and this approach makes sense. It does not imply, however, that Scripture is teaching as true the phenomenological description—that the sun really does move around the earth. Similarly, when Jesus says that the mustard seed is "smaller than all the seeds that are upon the soil" (Mark 4:31), he is making a recognizable, common sense observation. If he had added, "except for some other seeds, like orchid seeds," he would have received blank looks.

- *Analogical.* The Bible uses ideas that its audience would understand because those ideas were common at the time. This usage does not mean that the Bible is teaching as true those ideas. For example, Jeremiah says that God tests the kidneys (Jer. 11:20), knowing that his audience would understand that to mean the emotions. Even today, we say things such as, "My heart is happy," as a kind of analogy to represent our feelings.

- *Metaphorical.* The Bible makes use of many metaphorical expressions, especially in describing God and theological ideas, because those ideas are so abstract and difficult for us limited mortals to grasp. And we understand that such expressions are not literal. For example, when we read the many Scriptures that refer to the hand of God, we no more believe that Scripture is teaching an anthropomorphic God who has actual hands that we believe it teaches that he has wings when we read in Psalm 17:8, "Hide me in the shadow of Your wings."

- *Rhetorical.* The Bible also uses various rhetorical devices to convey meaning. When Jesus tells us in Luke 14:26 that we cannot be his disciple unless we hate our father and mother, he is using hyperbole to make his point. He is not contradicting the commandment to honor our father and mother.

We can see, then, that truth can be conveyed through a number of "literary" methods that do not involve making an absolutist or "scientific" claim. Bastiaan Van Elderen sums up:

> Under the concept organic inspiration we imply that the Bible was written under the inspiration of the Holy Spirit by men who used the language, culture, cosmology, thought forms, categories, understanding of nature and reality — all these of their environment and times. After all, this revelation had to be intelligible to the contemporaries of the authors.[21]

Integration and Norms. The true work of the integration of faith and learning lies is connecting Biblical norms with scholarly disciplines. Biblical rather than secular ideas of justice, right conduct, the role of government, human spiritual needs, and so on are at the heart of the challenge. The Christian worldview is, in part, a moral and psychological worldview that conflicts with many schools of thought. We will look at these issues in more detail in coming chapters.

Summary

The Christian worldview, as a Christ-centered "theory of everything," begins with a proper understanding of the Bible and extends through philosophical exploration into a conceptual scheme that encompasses all knowledge and all life. This worldview is distinctively different from those of naturalism and postmodernism.

Questions for Thought and Discussion

1. Describe what you think are the essential elements of a Christian worldview.

2. When you encounter a passage in the Bible that you do not understand, what is your method for gaining understanding?

3. Christians sometimes disagree over the role of reason in the life of faith. What is your own view and why? Is reason a reliable friend or something else?

4. How does your own worldview compare to the general Christian worldview described in this chapter?

---

1 Blaise Pascal, *Pensees*, tr. Martin Turnell (New York: Harper and Row, 1962), p. 40 (Lafuma 11).

2 George Marsden, "The State of Evangelical Christian Scholarship," *Reformed Journal* 37:9 (Sept. 1987), pp. 12-16, reprinted in *Discipleship and the Disciplines: Enhancing Faith-Learning Integration* (Coalition for Christian Colleges and Universities, 1996), Unit 1, p. 20.

3 Michael L. Peterson, *With All Your Mind: A Christian Philosophy of Education* (Notre Dame, IN: University of Notre Dame Press, 2001, p. 90.

4 Ronald Nash, *Faith and Reason: Searching for a Rational Faith* (Grand Rapids: Zondervan, 1988), pp. 28-29.

5 For a charming point about the relation between reason and faith, see Samuel Johnson, "The Vision of Theodore, Hermit of Teneriffe," available online at http://www.virtualsalt.com/lit/theodore.htm.

6 Nathaniel Culverwell, *An Elegant and Learned Discourse of the Light of Nature* (London: 1652. Reprint Toronto: University of Toronto Press, 1971), p. 13. I have modernized some spelling and typographical features of the original.

7 Francis Darwin, ed., *The Life and Letters of Charles Darwin* (New York: D. Appleton and Company, 1888), p. 285.

8 William Hasker, *Metaphysics: Constructing a World View* (Downers Grove, IL: InterVarsity Press, 1983), p. 48.

[9] Quoted in Alvin Plantinga, "Darwin, Mind, and Meaning." Retrieved from University of California at Santa Barbara Faculty Staff Christian Fellowship, http://id-www.ucsb.edu/fscf/library/plantinga/dennett.html.

[10] Richard Rorty, quoted in Carol Iannone, "PC with a Human Face," *Commentary* 96:6 (June, 1993), p. 48.

[11] William Hasker, op. cit., p. 72.

[12] William Hasker, op. cit., p. 109.

[13] This is a phrase from Samuel Johnson, from another context, which I have forgotten.

[14] Michael Peterson, op. cit., p. 90.

[15] David M. Whalen, "'A Little More than Kin and Less than Kind': The Affinity of Literature and Politics," *Intercollegiate Review* 37:1 (Fall 2001), p. 25.

[16] Ronald Nash, op. cit., p. 41.

[17] Michael Peterson, op. cit., p. 103.

[18] Hugh Mercer Curtler, "The Myopia of the Cultural Relativist," *Intercollegiate Review* 38:1 (Fall 2002), pp. 38, 39.

[19] Quoted in Phillip Johnson, "The Religion of the Blind Watchmaker," *Christian Leadership Ministries*. Retrieved Feb. 21, 2003 from <http://www.clm.org/real/ri9203/watchmkr.html>.

[20] Paul Hollander, "Marxism and Western Intellectuals in the Post-Communist Era," *Society* 37:2 (Jan-Feb 2000), p. 26.

[21] Quoted in Sidney Greidanus, "The Use of the Bible in Christian Scholarship," *Christian Scholar's Review* 11:2 (March 1982), pp. 138-147, reprinted in *Discipleship and the Disciplines: Enhancing Faith-Learning Integration* (Coalition for Christian Colleges and Universities, 1996), Unit 4, p. 18.

Chapter 9
Evaluating Worldviews

*The most decisive form of criticism in classical apologetics is
to show that a non-Christian belief or objection is logically
self-defeating or self-referentially incoherent. This criticism
is applied especially to relativism, both in Eastern religion and
philosophy and in the New Age movement and postmodernism. All these movements are regarded as self-refuting and
therefore incoherent on their face.*
     — Kenneth Boa and Robert Bowman[1]

*What unifies naturalists is just a shared set of methodological
dispositions. Furthermore, these dispositions preclude naturalists from justifiably believing that their research program is
one that ought to be shared by others, or that it is the only one
that issues in justified belief. For to think such things is to
suppose in part that the epistemic status of scientific reasoning
is open for philosophical debate. But the project of using philosophy to justify science is a project that naturalists reject.
Thus, given their methodological dispositions, they lack the
resources for converting descriptions of their research program
into theses about how inquiry ought to be conducted.*
     — Michael Rea[2]

9.1 Integration as Critical Thinking

  The integration of faith and learning involves the interac-
tive comparison and analysis of the cognitive content of the
Christian worldview (Christian knowledge) with the knowledge claims, assumptions, and methods of the various disciplines, schools, and studies. In other words, it is not just a
learning task, like memorizing or studying, but an evaluative
and coherence-building task, a task of critical thinking. You'll

recall that in Chapter 5 discussing worldview issues, we said that the basic ontological question we all face is, "What makes the world make sense?" What assumptions and what conclusions help us make sense—that is, come to a reasoned understanding—of the world as we experience it?

Critical thinking helps us develop propositions, conclusions, systems of thought and worldviews that allow us to make sense of our lives and of the cosmos. And critical thinking helps us make choices about the worldview possibilities themselves. We want to adopt a worldview that is free from poor thinking, free from logical fallacies, and free from logical inconsistency.

This chapter provides some specific tools of critical thinking related to the issues of integration, tools for evaluation of particular knowledge claims and of worldviews themselves. We want to be sure that the ideas we are asked to integrate make sense and are fair representations of what is known or believed. Bias and ideology all too often distort information.

As we begin to think about integrating the knowledge arising from our Christian worldview with the knowledge claims made from within other worldviews, we should first apply some thinking to the quality and adequacy of all three worldviews (Christianity, naturalism/materialism, and postmodernism). In the previous chapter we saw some pronounced differences among the worldviews. In this chapter we will look more closely at how well the worldviews stand up to a structural analysis. Philosophers have developed several tests that allow us to evaluate worldviews or metaphysical schemes and to determine how well each can serve as a "personal theory of everything."

In his book, *Metaphysics: Constructing a World View*, William Hasker says, "Metaphysical theories can be judged on the basis of their factual adequacy, logical consistency, and explanatory power."[3] To these, philosophy professor Ronald Nash adds the test of "practice," the livability of the person's philosophy.[4] Let's examine our worldviews using these tests.

9.2 Factual Adequacy

The first test of a worldview is that it has to meet the correspondence test of truth. That is, the truth claims of the worldview, its description of the world and of ourselves, must agree with our personal observations and experiences of the world. This does not mean that our worldview cannot sometimes correct a misperception or mistaken belief (as when we realize that we are seeing a mirage instead of real water in the roadway ahead). But generally the worldview itself "must be consistent with what you know by other means to be true," as William Hasker says.[5] Those other means of knowing may include not just observation and experience, but reason and even revealed truth (as in the Bible).

Naturalism and Factual Adequacy. Through its reliance on experiment, observation, reason, and a common sense set of ontological assumptions (such as the reality of the external world, and the existence of cause and effect) naturalism possesses a high degree of factual adequacy — as far as it goes. However, as philosopher Ronald Nash observes, included in factual adequacy must be adequate treatments of both the "outer world" (the worldview "should help us to understand what we perceive") and the "inner world" (the worldview must "fit what we know about ourselves.")[6] By its denial of the supernatural, and the consequent rejection of ontological status for the most important meanings of life and experience, naturalism is factually adequate for only a small portion of reality. Further, by attempting to explain those non-physical realms by purely material means, naturalism yields a twisted caricature of important phenomena such as morality, ethics, spiritual truth, aesthetics, and wisdom.

Postmodernism and Factual Adequacy. While the principal factual adequacy weakness of naturalism is truncation or its shrunken view of reality, the principal factual adequacy weakness of postmodernism is its lack of correspondence to reality as perceived and lived by ordinary people. The relativism underlying postmodernism renders its claims to knowledge powerless and incredible, since all such claims are admittedly subjective and localized. Postmodernists cannot properly describe their knowledge claims as truth claims, since truth in any sturdy sense is rejected as a language game. Relative and transitory and culture-bound ideas do not satisfy the need for factual adequacy.

Moreover, postmodern thought requires elaborate logic-chopping mechanisms in order to explain claims about reality that appear counterintuitive and experientially absurd. The example of false consciousness is just one of these. "You are not really happy. You only think you are. You are really oppressed. You just don't know it, so we are going to free you from your oppression for your own good." Such arguments are often seen not only as irrational but as cynical excuses for denying individual autonomy and imposing social control.

Christianity and Factual Adequacy. Of the three worldviews we are considering, Christianity alone encompasses the natural world, the moral universe, reason, human nature, hunger for God—it alone is adequate to explain the physical, moral, emotional, and spiritual dimensions of reality. The Christian worldview is superior to naturalism by holding truth to be the ultimate value, wherever the knowledge of it may come from or lead to, rather than arbitrarily limiting both the source and the end of knowledge to a single (naturalistic) realm, and the Christian worldview is superior to postmodernism by adhering to a rational and objective system. Unlike some religions, which devolve into an irrational mysticism or which make claims in clear contradiction to everyday experience ("Physical illness is an illusion"), Christianity describes the world as it is, and the resulting Christian worldview therefore meets the test of factual adequacy very well.

9.3 Logical Consistency

Whatever one's explanation of the world (worldview), it should make sense in a logical, consistent way. The law of non-contradiction tells us that we cannot rationally believe in a universe that contains round squares or objects that are all black and all white at the same time. To do so is to commit the fallacy of contradictory premises: "If an object is both stationary and traveling at an infinite rate of speed, how long will it take to meet itself?" Such a question may be amusing, but it is a logical absurdity. Both premises (a stationary object and the same object traveling at an infinite rate of speed) cannot both be true at the same time.

Self Referential Absurdity. A similar problem occurs when a statement is made that, when applied to itself, results in a logical impossibility or an obvious falsehood. For example, to say, "There are no true statements," results what Ronald Nash calls "logical nonsense."[7] Applying this claim's denial of truth to itself makes it false, thus leaving open the possibility that there are true statements. Or, if the statement is true that there are no true statements, then it proves itself false by being a true statement in contradiction with its claim. (Feel your head spinning yet?)

Statements or theories that, when applied to themselves, involve this kind of contradiction commit the logical fallacy of self-referential absurdity, also known as self-refutation. Such statements are either internally contradictory or entail another claim that is false or contradictory.

The classic example is the philosophy of logical positivism. The positivists (popular during the 1930s) argued that the only true statements were those whose terms agreed by definition ("All bachelors are single men") or those that were provable by experiment. Because the founders of positivism were scientists, they concluded that "only the factual propositions of science satisfy this condition."[8] The positivists were happy to say that statements about philosophy, metaphysics, religion, ethics, values and so on had no meaning at all because none of those statements could be proved empirically. You could not answer the question, "Does God exist?" with *either* a Yes or a No because the question itself was meaningless.[9]

Then someone pointed out that the central claims of positivism were neither true by definition nor provable by experiment. That meant that the claim that "any meaningful sentence will pass the test of empirical verification"[10] was itself meaningless because it could not pass that very test. There was no experiment possible to design that would prove that statement true. As Arnold Lunn pointed out, "Just as the logical conclusion from Marxist or Freudian philosophy is that no philosophy (including Marxism and Freudianism) can possibly be true, so the basic premise of logical positivism refutes logical positivism.[11] What the positivists refused to acknowledge, that all worldviews rest on unprovable metaphysical assumptions, had destroyed their philosophy. Positivism quickly died out among philosophers. Unfortunately, leftover positivist biases still linger among many people, who continue to claim that experiment is the test of all truth, even though there has never been an experiment that establishes that claim. And many of these same people refuse to see the metaphysical quality of their belief, its essentially religious nature.

Naturalism and Logical Consistency. Philosophical naturalism, originally buttressed by positivistic theory, still suffers from the flaws of positivism. Naturalism asserts that all truth is scientific truth, discovered by either experiment or reason (inductive processes based on observation and analysis). However, this assertion itself is an unprovable metaphysical assumption not subject to any sort of experimental analysis. The same argument holds for all the other assumptions of naturalism, as discussed in Chapter 5. There is no empirical proof or demonstration that truth exists, that the external world is real, or that you are really reading this rather than dreaming that you are reading this. Naturalists desire to deny or gloss over the assumptions that form the foundations of their ontology and epistemology, largely because they wish to avoid facing up to the religious or metaphysical basis of their worldview, and such a denial must be seen as a form of logical inconsistency. To be consistent, naturalists must admit that their system is not based on empirically demonstrable truths.

In his book, *World Without Design*, philosopher Michael Rea notes that naturalists are inconsistent in the application of their theory of truth. He notes that, on the one hand, naturalists reject any beliefs that cannot be questioned and possibly proved false by new scientific discoveries. On the other hand, none of the naturalists appears willing to believe that any discovery of science could lead them to reject naturalism. But Rea asks, "After all, if everything else is at the mercy of science, why not naturalism?"[12] Rea continues by noting that the one thing naturalists seem to agree on is the rejection of the supernatural. However, he says, this is an arbitrary and unscientific position: It is clear that naturalists respect the natural sciences as absolutely authoritative with respect to what there is and what the world is like. Naturalism demands that we follow science wherever it leads with respect to such issues. . . . But then naturalism, whatever it is, must be compatible with anything science might tell us about nature or supernature. Thus, no version of naturalism can include any substantive thesis about the nature of nature or supernature.[13]

To argue that naturalism requires such a thesis, namely that there is no supernature, is arbitrary and logically inconsistent with the presuppositions of naturalism itself.

Further, Michael Peterson calls our attention to the deterministic implications of naturalism, the idea that our mental processes are caused by our physical processes, since according to naturalism our mental processes *are* our physical processes. He notes that "if naturalism really is true, then the belief that it is true cannot be rationally held. This is because the naturalist is implicitly stating that his belief is caused rather than free."[14] In other words, naturalism implies that we are compelled or determined to believe the things we do and that we cannot help ourselves or our thoughts. If our beliefs are simply the product of physical processes rather than the free conclusions of careful reason, then those beliefs are not true in any objective sense.

Postmodernism and Logical Consistency. The attempt to build postmodernism on a foundation of relativism presents such logical difficulties that it is no wonder that postmodernists reject traditional reason and logic. Their system is simply incompatible with what most of us would consider clear thinking. (And this may explain why so many postmodernist texts are written so incomprehensibly.)

At its theoretical level, postmodernism is freighted with inconsistencies:

- Truth is held to be local, socially constructed, a tool of those in power, a language game, and yet these ideas are presented as truths in some wider ranging if not absolute sense.

- The claim that "there are no facts, only interpretations" (adopted from Nietzsche)[15] is a fact claim that therefore involves a self-referential absurdity.
- Traditional reason is rejected as a product of the old and discredited patriarchy, yet the calls for rejecting reason are presented by means of reasoned argument.
- Postmodernism rejects totalizing views and metanarratives that claim to generalize about the world or truth or humanity, yet postmodernism itself is itself a large and comprehensive metanarrative.
- If we cannot judge other cultures because we are blinded by our own, then we can neither say that our culture is defective or that all cultures are equal. Or, we can say it, but we cannot know it because to know it would involve judgment.
- Postmodernists reject authority, which they regard as arbitrary and oppressive, but most of them revere certain writers like Louis Althusser, Jacques Derrida, Michel Foucault, Antonio Gramsci, and Herbert Marcuse, all of whose works are quoted almost like scripture by their adherents.[16]

Williams College student Wendy Shalit summed up her experience with postmodernist education in an article she wrote at the end of her sophomore year. Describing the required learning at her college as the "New Canon," she reveals the practical inconsistencies of postmodernist theory:

> The prerequisites for entry into the New Canon are more daunting, involving, among other things, a talent for overlooking contradictions: one must not be a racist, sexist, or ethnocentric unless one happens to be black or a woman; one must be positively sympathetic to diversity of gender, race, and sexual orientation but not to diversity of ideas; one must never admit a devotion to truth except to the truth embodied in the harassment code; one must deride the "notion" of historical fact but never question the facts of those who tell their own "survivor stories"; one must cleanse oneself of fidelity to the fixed meaning of texts, except to the texts of the postmodernists.[17]

As was mentioned in Chapter 7, deconstruction is the postmodern method of taking apart literary and other texts to show that their apparent meaning is merely an arbitrarily privileged meaning and that no text has an exact meaning or a fixed interpretation: "All interpretations are misinterpretations." And yet, during a dispute with a critic, Jacques Derrida, a leading advocate and practitioner of deconstruction, accused his critic of misunderstanding him and not grasping what Derrida meant.[18] If the author's intended meaning is irrelevant to the exposed meaning, as the deconstructionists argue, then it is absurd and illogical to argue that one's intended meaning has been missed. If deconstruction is a valid and worthwhile method of textual interpretation, then it must apply equally to texts of the traditional canon and to texts by the deconstructionists themselves. (Surprisingly, the deconstructionists never seem to take apart the texts of their Marxist friends or of their fellow deconstructionists.)

Yes, postmodernism is a confusion of inconsistencies. Postmodernists argue that our culture determines our values and that all values are culturally relative. We are trapped by these oppressive norms. But how do we know they are oppressive? Gene Edward Veith, Jr. observes: "Postmodernists, more than most people, complain about how various power structures are unfair, and they are always demanding sensitivity, tolerance, and justice. Do they not realize that they are appealing to transcendent, authoritative moral absolutes?"[19] If we are trapped by our culture, how can postmodernists, trapped by the oppressive values of the culture, see well enough to criticize it? And if there are no absolute values, by what standard do they measure unfairness or injustice? And if they reject authority, by what authority do they insist that something be done to remedy the situation? If the "authority" behind their push for change is merely political power, how persuasive is that to those not in their camp?

Postmodernists argue that the difference between truth and propaganda is merely a matter of semantics. As we have seen, postmodernists like to use sneer quotes to enclose words like *truth*: How quaint of you to be interested in "truth." "In fact," as Gene Edward Veith, Jr. notes, "according to postmodernist ideology, *everything* is fiction; all truth is an illusion created by social conventions."[20] Here is another instance of self-referential absurdity. If everything is fiction, then the claims, interpretations, and philosophy of postmodernism are also fiction, and fiction is merely an entertainment we need not take seriously if we don't want to. As Michael L. Peterson has remarked, "Postmodernism cannot avoid being self-refuting if it follows its own tenets."[21]

The Reasonableness of Christianity. Ronald Nash says that "even though most people who reject Christianity treat it as a refuge for enemies of reason, the truth is that there may be no worldview in the history of the human race that has a higher regard for the laws of logic."[22] Christianity recognizes that the physical, rational, and metaphysical realms must work together to present a logically consistent worldview. While at the heart of Christianity is a personal relationship with Christ, and while some aspects of the faith are inaccessible to reason (too complicated for reason, we might say), our faith is quite reasonable. It involves logically consistent, non-contradictory, and non-self-refuting ontological and epistemological presuppositions that provide a stable foundation for examining and building Christian truth. It is informed by an objective and unchanging source of transcendent truth (that's the Bible near your elbow), always ready to challenge and correct any human departures into unbiblical thought.

Dennis McCallum offers the analogy of viewing a painting. You can look at a painting and believe that it is beautiful, even though you may not be able to prove that it is beautiful. Yet your belief is not irrational. Your belief is based on direct personal experience and is therefore fully compatible with reason.[23] In fact, your experiential knowledge supplements what you can know about the painting by reason. Seventeenth century philosopher and mathematician Blaise Pascal wrote, "Faith does indeed tell us what the senses do not tell, but does not contradict their findings. It transcends, but does not contradict them." Reason, he says, recognizes that there are truths not discoverable by reason.[24]

Christianity makes sense. It hangs together logically. It makes the world make sense. It makes *us* make sense (and that's quite an accomplishment). That's why Paul is described as reasoning with his audience so often (see, for example, Acts 17-19). What we believe cognitively about our worldview affects how sturdily we adhere to it. We need a structure for knowledge not only that coheres but that includes every realm of reality: physical, mental, spiritual, and so on. And as Dennis McCallum says, only a worldview that includes God "is consistent with its own presuppositions."[25] Non-theistic worldviews run into logical complications by restricting or distorting their descriptions of reality.

9.4 Explanatory Power

When detectives examine a crime scene, their goal is to develop a narrative of events—a story—that explains as many of the details of evidence as possible in as plausible a way as possible. In other words, they develop a hypothesis that covers the facts. Similarly, a worldview might be seen as a hypothesis that aims to take into account as many of the observed phenomena of the world, life, and experience as possible in a coherent, unified way. The more phenomena that can be reasonably and plausibly explained by a given hypothesis, the greater is that hypothesis' explanatory power. Philosopher William Hasker describes the explanatory power of a worldview as ideally providing unity, causality, comprehensiveness, and simplicity.[26]

As we said at the beginning of Chapter 5, a worldview is a personal theory of everything, an explanation that includes everything we believe and experience. A worldview that explains only part of what we know to be true will have less explanatory power than one that explains more. Just as the best hypothesis for the detective is the one that explains best the most evidence, so the best worldview is the one that explains best the most of reality. Ronald Nash says,

> When faced with a choice among competing touchstone propositions of different world-views, we should choose the one that, when applied to the whole of reality, gives us the most coherent picture of the world. After all, Gordon Clark explains, "If one system can provide plausible solutions to

many problems while another leaves too many questions unanswered, if one system tends less to skepticism and gives more meaning to life, if one world-view is consistent while others are self-contradictory, who can deny us, since we must choose, the right to choose the more promising first principle?"[27]

Naturalism and Explanatory Power. Naturalism generally has great explanatory power over the biological and physical world, which explains its popularity (its exclusivity) for those who insist on keeping supernatural explanations out of consideration. In spite of its many problems (some would say fatal problems), the theory of evolution provides a comprehensive and unifying explanation for the biological world while some aspects of theoretical physics, geology, and chemistry explain our observations of the physical world. Those who promote naturalism attempt to weld it to the demonstrable facts of science, such as chemical processes, metallurgy, technology, and the scientific method. The package of interpretation and explanation provided by naturalism has some comprehensiveness to it. However, even in its own realm of the natural world, this worldview does not adequately—that is, within its own non-metaphysical constraints—explain the front end of things—where everything came from in the first place. Gregg Easterbrook explains:

> Suppose you accept the Big Bang theory of the origin of the universe. . . . You believe that . . . all the potential of 40 billion galaxies . . . was packed into a point smaller than a proton. . . . Next, you believe that . . . the universe expanded from a pinpoint to cosmological size in far less than one second—space hurtling outward . . . at trillions of times the speed of light. . . . Further, you believe that . . . the only reason our universe is here today is that the Bang was slightly asymmetrical, its yield favoring matter over antimatter by about one part per 100 million.[28]

Easterbrook comments that while this scenario is the currently accepted one, "for sheer extravagant implausibility, nothing in theology or metaphysics can hold a candle to the Big Bang.

Surely, if this description of the cosmic genesis came from the Bible or the Koran rather than the Massachusetts Institute of Technology, it would be treated as a preposterous myth."[29] The theory leaves unanswered or only gamely answered those uncomfortable questions, such as, "Where did that first particle come from?" "What caused the Big Bang?" "How did the cosmos assemble itself with stable physical laws?" "How did the cosmos just happen to arrive in a state so favorable to self continuance and life?"

At the small end of naturalism, the level of particle physics, we find another challenge. George Gilder writes,

> Scientists no longer see the foundation of all matter as inert, blind, impenetrable, blank particles. Rather, physicists now agree that matter derives from waves, fields, and probabilities. To comprehend nature, we have to stop thinking of the world as basically material and begin imagining it as a manifestation of consciousness, suffused with sparks of informative energy.[30]

Behind or underneath the many dozens of subatomic particles does not seem to be what we would call stuff, but something more like an idea, an intelligence, a Mind. And naturalism seems unable to explain the origin of information (such as that encoded in DNA).[31]

More problematically, however, is the failure of naturalism to include non-material reality in its worldview. Naturalism's attempt to explain all reality in terms of materialist and natural processes creates a truncation of explanation and a distortion of the non-empirical world. Michael L. Peterson says, "Metaphysics, theology, ethics, and aesthetics are disciplines that naturalists have either denigrated or dismissed because they do not contain information that can be measured or transmitted empirically. This has contributed to a kind of intellectual imperialism in which all fields of inquiry are forced to conform to the standards of one particular field."[32] And the standards of that particular field include its metaphysics.

Overall, then, the explanatory power of naturalism is limited to the realm of the natural world itself, and even there we can find room to question its adequacy.

Postmodernism and Explanatory Power. Postmodernism's origin in politics, philosophy, and literary criticism, together with its rejection of science, puts it in a singularly awkward position as a comprehensive worldview. Postmodernism attempts to explain everything, but does so in terms of political power, or the claim that people are trapped by their race, gender, or socioeconomic class. Its rejection of objectivity and truth and science and metaphysics makes postmodernism into a kind of secular mysticism that draws upon an alternate reality to explain how the world works. Based on neo-Marxist ideology, it offers what those standing at arm's length must conclude is an eccentric and irrational explanation of things. Every problem in the world is simply not reducible to issues of race, class, or gender. Not only its logical problems (discussed above) cause it to lack explanatory power and credibility, but so do its claims that those who do not see the world in the politically correct ideological terms are blinded by "false consciousness."

Perhaps it is no wonder that postmodernists are so intent on undermining such concepts as truth, objectivity, fact, logic, and reason, because measured by any of these yardsticks, postmodernism falls short in explanatory power.

Christianity and Explanatory Power. Of the worldviews discussed here, the inclusiveness and comprehensiveness of the Christian worldview give it the most complete and robust explanatory power. The Christian worldview includes explanations for both the natural world and the supernatural world, together with clarifying foundations for the realms of ethics, values, and human nature. It supplies an explanation for the beginning—before that first particle proposed by the Big Bang, God is. It supplies an answer to what is at the bottom of particle physics, who is that Mind underlying matter. It explains where information came from. It explains the source, foundation, and objectivity of transcendent value: the existence of truth, the stability of human nature, (created in the image of God, though now fallen), and the basis for believing that rational thinking is possible.

One of the strengths of the Christian worldview is that it allows the truth to reveal itself wherever it may lead, whether through the natural world or into the supernatural, whether that truth is humbling for mankind or uplifting. Naturalism is constrained by an anti-supernatural prejudice and postmodernism is constrained by an ideological agenda. Only the Christian worldview is willing to say, "Let truth reign. Let truth lead where it will." And that truth leads to the source of truth, God. As a result of this willingness to follow truth, the Christian worldview provides the most comprehensive and reasonable worldview. It welcomes the facts of science (whatever issues it has with some of the interpretations of science), and it welcomes the knowledge of truths inaccessible to science.

9.5 Livability

As professor Ronald Nash observes, "It is one thing for a worldview to pass certain theoretical tests (reason and experience); it is another for the worldview also to pass an important practical test, namely, can the person who professes that worldview live consistently in harmony with the system he professes?"[33] Remember that a worldview makes sense out of the world and experience, not only theoretically but practically. An adequate worldview must be not only intellectually and philosophically compelling, but it must also work as a source of decision making and the discovery of meaning in everyday life. A properly constructed worldview must contain beliefs that can be lived. We must "walk the talk" and accept the consequences of our beliefs. In other words, a worldview is not just an explanation, but it is also a guide.

Human beings seem to have an innate, non-culture bound sense that they can improve themselves, strive for goodness, and find meaning and purpose in their existence. A worldview that conflicts with this innate sense is open to question on those grounds alone. That is, a worldview that cannot help us to live better lives may mean that it does not adequately represent a true account of some part of our existence, whether the world around us or the world inside us or the world above us. We may have a very idealized worldview that is difficult to live up to, that asks us constantly to strive to be better, that is so perfect that we constantly fail to attain its highest goals, and that's okay. Such a worldview may still be proper, especially if it includes a reason for our failure to live up to it (such as human imperfection, the fall, and sin). But a worldview that is impossible to act upon rationally or consistently ought to be questioned. A worldview that offers no guidance in decision making, that cannot be lived, that answers the questions about inner life in a way that lacks sense, must be viewed with skepticism.

Most people, regardless of their worldview, maintain a set of active criteria they use for decision making. Many of these criteria have moral implications. In other words, most people have a set of principles that guide them when they are faced with the temptation — or opportunity — to steal, lie, cheat, help the needy, be generous, etc. A livable world view must be one that (1) logically includes the criteria actually employed by the individual and (2) produces at least general conformity between the criteria and the individual's behavior. For example, a worldview that denies the reality of choice is inconsistent with a set of criteria that help make choices. And an individual who believes that moral judgments are merely personal and arbitrary but who argues that certain social or political conditions are objectively wrong is not living in conformity with the stated worldview. In cases where people fail to live up to their worldview principles, they should be willing to admit that they have failed to meet their ideal and desire to change. The Christian who cheats on his or her income taxes or who steals music or computer software should be willing to recognize the inconsistency and stop the wrong behavior. On the other hand, someone who denies the objectivity of moral judgments but who refuses to stop making such objective judgments reveals that his or her worldview is ultimately not livable.

Naturalism and Livability. There are not enough antidepressants and suicide hotlines in the world to deal with the practical implications of naturalism if everyone accepting that worldview attempted to live strictly according to it. While some followers of naturalism claim to be able to find harmony between naturalism and a meaningful life, such a harmony is strictly illogical. As Arnold Lunn has noted, a first problem with naturalism is that we cannot know anything: "The consistent materialist (or naturalist, using the word in its philosophical sense) must admit that truth is unobtainable" because we have no reason to believe that our electrochemical brain processes produce valid results in thinking.[34] So we are left with what might seem very much like a postmodern relativism. Yet most naturalists insist on the idea of truth, especially in regard to naturalistic theorizing.

But more significantly, if, as Bertrand Russell has said, man's "origin, his growth, his hopes and fears, his loves and beliefs, are but the outcome of accidental collocations of atoms,"[35] then it follows to say, "The only consistent materialist is the man who behaves as if moral restraints were irrational."[36] Many followers of naturalism enjoy the sexual liberation implied by its tenets (as we saw with Aldous Huxley in Chapter 5), but most believe that others should not steal from them or lie to them or cheat them. Many are moral activists in one cause or another, such as human rights or animal rights. But why? When, as Russell says, "the soul's habitation" must be built "on the firm foundation of unyielding despair," why should the pursuit of justice or rights matter?[37] And in a meaningless, accidental cosmos, what standard do we use to argue for justice in the first place?

Here is a physics professor commenting on the implications of a naturalistic worldview:

> The whole incredible big bang story with its climactic human ending is merely the result of physical and chemical processes that are completely random, accidental, and meaningless. We may think we're pretty good and important, but there is absolutely nothing in the blind, meaningless events to suggest the slightest purpose, value, or significance in our existence.[38]

If this is so, why does this person appear to live as if his life had some meaning or purpose? He's written a couple of books, teaches college physics, wants to understand the cosmos. It's one thing to fall short of one's ideals or philosophical principles, but quite another to live in contradiction to them. To claim that life has no meaning but to live as if life does have meaning or to claim that there is no free will or choice in life but to live as if choice is important reveals a weakness in the livability of that worldview.

The truth is that most followers of naturalism partially adhere to some semblance of the leftover Christian worldview that still informs much of Western society. These people still believe in a practical way in justice and injustice, right and wrong, fairness and unfairness, and many of the concepts that give life meaning, purpose, and direction. Some of these feelings are the God-created, inborn part of our human nature and some belong to the Judeo-Christian tradition. This sense of values is irrational for the naturalistic worldview, but it is necessary for life itself. In a word, no one can realistically live out the worldview of naturalism.

Postmodernism and Livability. The rejection of reason and of the definiteness of language, together with the embracing of relativism, make postmodernism the least livable of the worldviews. The rejection of reason, if genuinely applied, would make argument, understanding, judgment, and decision making impossible. Neither explaining nor trying to understand the philosophy of postmodernism would be possible. And the rejection of a stable understanding or meaning of texts would make society itself impossible, for it would put an end to communication.

As a thought experiment, imagine that a postmodernist's house burns down. He calls the insurance company and says, "My house burned down. My fire insurance policy says I'm covered." The insurance company also has a postmodernist worldview, so it says, "Well, we interpret 'covered' to mean that your house has or had a roof, not that we will pay you money if your house burns down." Since all interpretations are misinterpretations, and many are equally "valid" in a relativistic sort of way, does the fire victim simply say, "Okay," and hang up?

Even more complicating is the relativism of the postmodernist outlook. The anti-foundationalism, the rejection of standards or acceptable judgments of value (other than certain ideological preferences, such as tolerance) makes the negotiation of everyday life difficult, if not impossible. According to Michael L. Peterson, "Relativism treats all of life's major options as if they were of equal value, as if there really is no firm truth about anything: there are no standards, no absolutes, no reasonable guidance about how to live a decent human life."[39] In such a case, how can life be lived rationally and meaningfully, making personal progress in some direction (moral, spiritual, intellectual)?

If I am a postmodernist, who claims that all ethics are relative, that should mean that if you steal from me, I won't object, since your ethics may permit that and who am I to judge? But chances are, if you steal from a postmodernist, you are just as likely to have the police after you as if you steal from a naturalist or a Christian. But by calling the police, the postmodernist reveals an inability to accept the consequences of his or her belief. To argue that the rules against stealing are acceptable even though socially constructed would not provide much of a rebuttal for anyone who then claims to reject such social constructs or for someone who then says, "Well, I'm from a different culture." The point is that relativism ultimately denies a solid basis for living.

Lastly, postmodernists may say that truth is relative to individuals, but when an issue of fact involves them, they quickly come to see truth as objective. Suppose, for example, that an airliner crashes, killing a postmodernist's loved one. When the investigators are asked what caused the crash, would the postmodernist accept an explanation that "we believe the cause of the accident was different for different people,"[40] explaining that "what's true for you may not be true for me"?

Christianity and Livability. Much as many people seem to want to deny standards, authority, values, and rules, the fact is that moral and other structures provide the framework that allows both freedom and rational decision making. The belief in transcendent foundations for values gives us reason to adhere to those standards and values. On the other hand, if our beliefs are "imposed upon us by irrational forces, our instincts, or sexual complexes, lust for power, etc."[41] then there is no reason to accept any beliefs, including those of naturalism, and if our beliefs are merely the products of culture, language, or arbitrary power, then there is no reason to accept any of them, including postmodernism (which is the source of this belief about beliefs).

Christianity has given us a worldview that is not easy to live up to, because of our fallen nature and the many temptations that surround us constantly. Yet it provides standards and goals that make life meaningful, rewarding, purposeful, joyous, and satisfying. Sometimes this worldview seems counterintuitive, as when it tells us that one of the keys to happiness is unselfishness rather than selfishness. Our nature tells us that if we are not happy by being selfish, what we need is a whole lot more selfishness. But the Christian worldview tells us the opposite: happiness comes by giving and by thinking of others.

Overall, Christianity is a highly livable worldview because it provides the coherent, practical structure and values for the pursuit of rational living. Christian teaching matches the experience of everyday life and gives meaning to our every feeling and activity.

9.6 Knowledge Claims and Ideology

As a freshman just entering the university, I thought that I was going to observe the calm and reasoned operations of pure intellect, where a better argument would instantly be recognized by all and the weaker argument happily discarded. While that was sometimes the case, I discovered what I thought was an odd situation. Often, when a student raised an objection to an idea, or even asked a question that seemed to imply that the idea could be questioned, he or she was met, not with further clarification or additional arguments, but with anger and even scorn. To challenge some knowledge claims, it seemed, was off limits. But why such anger?

Pascal's Headache. In his book *Pensees*, Blaise Pascal provides us with the insight. He writes:

> Epictetus asks much more forcibly: "Why are we not angry if someone says that we have a headache and are angry if someone says that we are arguing badly or making a bad choice?" The reason is that we are quite certain that we have

no headache . . . but we are not so certain that we are making the right choice.[42]

Anger at disagreement, it seems, may be a sign of emotional rather than intellectual commitment to an idea. With an intellectual commitment, if someone challenges a belief, the challenge is accepted as a possible clarification or correction of error: "I'm sorry, but there were thirteen original colonies in the U.S., not twelve." But with an ideology, the commitment is much deeper. Ideologues are often deeply emotionally committed to their ideas, and to question them is to threaten their commitments and possibly even their personal identity. We find this anger response both among the naturalists and among the postmodernists.

I mentioned in an earlier chapter the emotional outburst, replete with mockery and sneering, that my anthropology professor made when he attacked the idea of continental drift in the late 1960s. Philosophical naturalists are especially prone to anger when anyone questions the conclusions surrounding origins. Michael Cremo and Richard Thompson note that

> put-offs and put-downs . . . are, for a good many scientists, still the favored methods for dealing with evidence that has uncomfortable implications for established views on human evolution. They avoid acknowledging anomalous evidence, never discuss it on its merits, and if pressed, simply ridicule it and those who support it.[43]

The response to Jonathan Wells' book *Icons of Evolution*, pointing out numerous errors in biology textbooks (such as the peppered moth experiments), was "wild and furious denunciation; the outpouring of warmth has been a firestorm of vilification; and if the superlatives become any more spiteful I may have to enter the witness protection program."[44]

Scorn, of course, is not a rebuttal, much less a refutation of any idea.

An Ideology Test. One way of helping you discover whether a claim has a solid basis or is perhaps based too much in ideological commitment is to ask one or two of the following questions. Try not to have an accusatory tone of voice, but ask with genuine interest and see what the response is. If you receive a calm, fact-based answer or some good explanation, then the idea is likely held on rational grounds. On the other hand, if your question is treated with anger, resentment, and scorn, you may have unearthed an ideological or philosophical commitment.

- *How do you know that?* (To be more polite, ask, "How do we know that?" thus showing a willingness to accept the idea.)
- *What is the evidence for that claim?* (See how specific your answer is. If the answer is that "It's in all the literature," ask for one or two specific sources. If the answer is "Everyone agrees," be careful.)
- *What is the evidence against that claim?* (Most fact claims are actually inferences, and few inferences explain all the evidence. There is usually some evidence that conflicts with any given knowledge claim.)
- *Is there any alternative to that idea?* (What other theories or schools of thought are there?)
- *Does anyone oppose that idea?* (The answer to this will tell you how the professor perceives the opposition. For example, "Only fools and madmen oppose this concept." Or religious nuts, of course.)

Political Correctness. One of the prominent features of the academy, among both naturalists and postmodernists, but especially among postmodernists, is political correctness, the idea that all members of the community must subscribe to a certain set of accepted ideas and judgments. Understanding the origin and history of political correctness will give us some insight into the ideological character of some areas of the university.

According to historian Frank Ellis, political correctness began in the 1920s "as an ideological criterion of Marxism-Leninism."[45] From the outset, "To be politically correct meant to be consistent with, not deviating from, the party line o[n] any given issue."[46] Political correctness was viewed as a necessary solution to the problem of a small group facing opposition by a larger world:

> Lenin believed that if a small revolutionary party was to maintain its sense of purpose and seize power, then it had to avoid becoming just a forum for discussion, with all the infighting and factionalism that involved. Party discipline and the sense of purpose could only be maintained, according to Lenin, if there was a rigidly enforced party line on all questions: from the materialist explanation of knowledge and reality . . . to a free press or the role of women in the future communist utopia. . . .[47]

Here we see the difference between the play of ideas and ideology. In an ideology, there is a predetermined, correct answer to each problem. Since "what is called objective knowledge is a part of the bourgeois conspiracy to retain power and control so that the working classes can be exploited,"[48] it is both logical and permissible to develop a revised truth (a truth based on political agendas) and even a revised science.[49] The supposedly bourgeois concepts of reason and proof are rejected, freeing the ideologues to advance their ideas without the need to argue their merits. "Liberated from the burden of proof," Ellis says, "Lenin and his successors were allowed to claim superior insight."[50]

There are two important consequences for the modern university. First, according to Ellis, "Absolute theoretical certainty . . . justified all means necessary to bring about the new society" including censorship and the suppression of open discussion.[51] Campus speech codes and the prohibitions against certain views in the name of tolerance or avoiding offense are examples of this, as are some courses where only a single point of view is permitted. Second, a society that was constructed "incorrectly" was justifiably to be torn down and rebuilt.[52] Anger, moral outrage, and the stance of attacking current values and institutions are the expected consequences of viewing the status quo as politically incorrect. As Ellis notes, "Contemporary political correctness pursues the same policy [as the Leninists] by dominating public discourse and creating a climate of fear such that 'incorrect' opinion is declared illegitimate, extreme or racist and so on."[53]

One way to implement the new ideological thinking and to change people's minds about various issues is to take control of the language, which is seen as "a series of ideological rituals" in order "to use language as a weapon." Current terms are redefined with new meaning and new terms are used to replace others.[54] For example, the term *sex* is dropped and replaced by *gender*, which is defined as a sex role, thus making it subject to change, argument, construction by society, or even individual preference. Or the neutral term *critic of homosexual behavior* is never used because the pejorative term *homophobic* (fear of homosexuality) allows critics of homosexual behavior to be attacked each time they are described.

Ideological pressures apply to both students and faculty. Speaking as a faculty member, Ellis says that

> anyone who has taught at an American university can testify that enormous psychological pressure is brought to bear on academics and students to submit to the general line on all issues dealing with multiculturalism, race, and feminism. The atmosphere is not one which is conducive to asking awkward questions. It is one of coercion."[55]

The problem facing one interested in integrating faith and learning when confronted with ideological stands is that those committed to ideology demand absolute assent and compliance. What is presented is not an idea for analysis, not one point of view or interpretation, but *the correct view*. However, even apart from the integrative question, remember that you are attending the university to learn how to think, not to memorize ideology. Always feel free to question even "the correct view."

9.7 A Handful of Fallacies

In his classic work, *Historians' Fallacies*, David Hackett Fischer identifies literally dozens and dozens of logical fallacies committed by historians in their arguments, analyses, and interpretations.[56] (His book, by the way, will reward anyone in any discipline with many valuable insights.) In courses on critical thinking, the number of fallacies taught is usually only thirty or forty. Here, we have space for just a few of the most common, together with a limited number of examples. The presence of fallacies in thinking and arguments is often an index to the degree of ideological bias, so you should be aware of some of these.

Argumentum ad Hominem. This fallacy involves attacking a person or the person's reputation instead of responding to the person's ideas or argument. Arguments and evidence and interpretations are to be countered by other arguments and evidence and interpretations. When someone resorts to an *ad hominem* attack, it appears that he or she does not have any good opposing arguments. You'll find this fallacy when a writer or speaker refers to opponents as "crackpots," "an unqualified nobody," "failure to grasp the obvious," and so on. Professor John Ellis remarks that *ad hominem* is popular among postmodernists who engage in deconstructionist literary theory. He observes that

> the dramatic denunciation of the person of common sense and received opinion is an important part of its [deconstruction's] intellectual orientation. . . . The test of whether they [opponents] have sufficient intellectual sophistication to discuss deconstruction will be that they are able to appreciate so sophisticated a position. Those who question that evaluation ipso facto fail the test and deserve to be regarded with scorn.[57]

In another example of attacking the messenger instead of the ideas, physicists Alan Sokal and Jean Bricmont, authors of *Fashionable Nonsense: Postmodern Intellecutals' Abuse of Science* were criticized at a conference for being "socially conservative Marxists" and for "sharing the values of Rush Limbaugh," quite a slam when made by academics against their colleagues.[58] They had dared to criticize the inappropriate way some postmodernists use scientific concepts to support their ideas.

Emotive Language. The fallacy of emotive language occurs when words with emotional overtones are used in place of argument. Words with heavily laden emotional qualities or with positive or negative connotations are used to attack or support a person or an idea. Ideas the writer or speaker approves of are labeled with positive emoters: *generous, progres-*

sive, compassionate, advanced, tolerant, authentic, inclusive, fair, just. Those ideas that the writer or speaker dislikes are labeled with negative emoters: *reactionary, patriarchial, bourgeois, repressive, racist, sexist, elitist, homophobic (not heterophobic), simpleminded, simplistic, naïve, oppressive, ethnocentric, hierarchical.* At the university, even the word *conservative* is usually spoken as a term of contempt, just like *fundamentalist.* The problem with the use of emotive language is that it confuses the right use of many terms. To call someone a conservative (or a communist) just for the effect of the word is unjust. But if the person referred to really is a conservative (or a communist) then that label is accurate. The difficulty lies in the ease with which opponents get labeled as racists, sexists, reactionaries, and so forth, simply for effect.

I've cited the book *Forbidden Archeology* several times in this book. What I didn't bother to tell you, because I considered it irrelevant, was that the book was written by a couple of Hare Krishna monks. This fact was not lost on Jonathan Marks, who reviewed the book in the *American Journal of Physical Anthropology.* Marks writes:

> The best that can be said is that more reading went into this Hindu-oid creationist drivel than seems to go into the Christian-oid creationist drivel. At any rate, this is a must for anyone interested in keeping up with goofy popular anthropology; at well over 900 pages, it is a veritable cornucopia of dreck.[59]

The review offers no evidence or arguments to rebut any of the claims made in the book. (The book may have errors, but the reviewer prefers name calling to rebuttal.)

It's useful to note in passing that in the academy, *creationist* is a term of insult, so that anyone or any idea opposing evolutionary theory is immediately labeled a creationist. Those studying intelligent design theory are labeled "intelligent design creationists" (though the two ideas are distinct, since some adherents to intelligent design subscribe to some aspects of evolutionary theory as well). We have seen in earlier chapters that both Richard Milton and Judith Hooper were labeled with the hateful term *creationists* for their criticisms of some aspects of evolutionary theory. Both firmly and clearly denied the charge. In a similar vein, David Berlinski wrote a criticism of the misapplication of a study relating to the evolution of the eye, when some writers claimed the study involved a computer simulation even though it did not. For his pains, he was lumped in with the creationists. He says, "As I have many times remarked, I have no creationist agenda whatsoever and, beyond respecting the injunction to have a good time all the time, no religious principles, either."[60] Rather than admit that someone with no commitment to divine origins could find fault with evolution, the critics rush to label each critic as a *creationist* for its emotive effect and then dismiss the criticism.

Equivocation. The fallacy of equivocation occurs when a single word is used in an argument with two different meanings. Often the term will change meanings during the course of the argument. Consider this little dialog:

> "I don't believe in UFO's."
> "Oh, everyone believes in UFO's."
> "Really? How?"
> "Well, a UFO is an object flying the sky that you can't identify. You've seen a light or something moving around at night sometime and you didn't know what it was, right?"
> "Yeah."
> "So then you believe in UFO's."
> "Oh, okay. When you put it that way."
> "So you agree, then, that aliens are visiting us regularly."
> "Huh?"

The single, most stupendous equivocation in the history of knowledge surrounds the use of the word *evolution*. When you are first introduced to the term, you may be told that evolution means "change over time." Well, my hair used to be brown and now is gray, so I guess that's change over time, so I guess I believe in evolution. Or you will be told that evolution means "a change in gene frequency."

Thinking back again to my undergraduate days, I recall getting into a letter writing discussion in the campus paper over evolution. This was before Kettlewell's work on the peppered moth had been exposed as unreliable, so I took it at face value, pointing out that all a change from mostly light moths to mostly dark moths represented was a change in gene frequency. My correspondent wrote back, calling into question my intelligence, and insisting, with exclamation points that "a change in gene frequency *is* evolution!" Well, by that definition, I guess we are all evolutionists, since we can see how varied dogs are in all their breeds. We recognize the flexibility of the genome to produce varied colors in roses and so forth or bacterial resistance to antibiotics. But then, if that variation within limits, a kind of horizontal change back and forth, is what is meant by *evolution*, then what word do we use to describe vertical change, the theory of the rise of life from molecules to mankind? Why, the same word. You can see the problem. Do we believe in evolution or don't we? Well, that depends on what you mean by evolution. Using a single word to mean two quite different things—confusing horizontal variation with vertical, increasing complexity of development—seems to be a trick designed to confuse us. (And using the term *microevolution* to describe variation within limits seems disingenuous.)

One of the factors that made me suspicious of evolutionary theory as an undergraduate was just this kind of procedure. All the evidence offered for evolution was of this variation sort: DDT resistance in house flies (which lost their resistance after the DDT was removed), Darwin's finches with their varied beaks, the peppered moths, and so on. Each little example of variation was followed by the claim that this was evidence or even proof for large-scale evolution. I kept wondering, "Is this all the evidence they've got?"

Other words are frequently equivocated in argument, where one definition seems to be in play until you accept it, and then the meaning changes as a means of getting you to agree with some questionable conclusion. In some cases, the meaning of a word continues to expand until it encompasses huge numbers of things or people that are not traditionally considered accurately labeled by the term. Watch out for expanding definitions of words like *disabled, abused, racism, sex-*

ism, and so on that are often ballooned in order to expand victim groups or oppressor groups or both.

Begging the Question. This fallacy occurs when a point to be proved is used as part of the evidence later on in the argument. Another term for this is circular reasoning. A simple example would be, "Science is the search for naturalistic explanations for all of reality. Therefore, there are no supernatural explanations for any of reality." You can see that this is a question-begging (that is, circular) definition, where the argument's conclusion is necessarily true because of the way the definition is constructed.

An example of a question-begging argument is the way homology is described in some biology textbooks. Jonathan Wells notes, "Many biology textbooks define homology as similarity due to common ancestry, yet claim it is evidence for common ancestry." He cites examples from five recent textbooks.[61]

In another article, Wells gives an example of a journal that defines science as meaning evolution, so that any opposition to evolution is non-scientific:

> When [Michael] Behe submitted an essay to another biology journal, the editor wrote back: "As you no doubt know, our journal has supported and demonstrated a strong evolutionary position from the very beginning, and believes that evolutionary explanations of all structures and phenomena of life are possible and inevitable. Hence a position such as yours, which opposes this view on other than scientific grounds, cannot be appropriate for our pages." Since Behe's essay dealt with evidence for his position (the hallmark of scientific reasoning), the phrase "other than scientific grounds" simply reflects the fact that for this journal, "science" is equated with "evolution."[62]

9.8 Implications for Integration

The next two chapters present some practical strategies for doing the work of faith and learning integration. You now are aware of the kinds of preparation and understanding you need to bring to this work. Here is a brief summary of the tools you will need to sharpen as you develop your personal integration.

- *Worldview orientation and epistemological awareness.* Much of the discussion in preceding chapters has laid the groundwork for helping you understand the nature of knowledge claims, the orientation of various claimants, and the way disciplines work.

- *Biblical knowledge and hermeneutics.* In order to integrate academic learning with your faith, you need a clear and appropriate understanding of what that faith is. You must have a good knowledge of the Bible and the proper means for interpreting it accurately. These characteristics, like your personal Christian worldview, will develop over a long period. You will not have a perfect understanding at the outset.

- *Wide ranging general knowledge and a circumspect view of your discipline.* Supplement your textbook reading and lecture notes with information from books, articles, Web sites and so on and with information from outside your major to give you a better sense of context, where the information is coming from, what critics say about it, what other possible positions there are, how it fits into a larger picture.

- *Critical thinking.* Learn how to analyze, how to spot fallacies of reasoning, how to detect bias and exaggeration. Study some semantics to understand how language is used and abused. How are terms defined? Just what does the writer or speaker mean by *multiculturalism, diversity, feminism, racism, patriarchalism*, and so on? And once defined, are the terms used consistently in keeping with their definition?

- *Philosophical context.* Read a book on the history of philosophy, especially 19th and 20th century movements to see how certain ideas have influenced current worldviews, what concepts are in play, what ideas have been debated, fought over, or suppressed.

Summary

A critical analysis of the three worldviews under discussion, on the basis of factual adequacy, logical consistency, explanatory power, and livability, together with the subjective nature of ideological commitment, reveals some challenges for integration. Good thinking habits and careful analysis of all knowledge claims are necessary in order to approach integration without being confused by questions of information quality.

Questions for Thought and Discussion

1. Can worldviews overlap? Can there be Christian postmodernism or naturalistic Christianity (with a purely historical Jesus)? What might be the nature of overlap? (Some possibilities: syncretism, a blending of elements; compatibilism, a finding of commonality; accommodation, a subordination of elements from one worldview to another; dilution, the weakening of the claims of one worldview's elements; two realms, identifying separate domains of operation or relevance for each worldview.)

2. Frank Ellis, quoted above, says that at the university, students (as well as faculty) are pressured to toe the politically correct line on a number of issues. He says, "The atmosphere is not one which is conducive to asking awkward questions." How should a Christian respond in class or in a course paper, where a grade may be at stake, to the presentation of coercive ideology and the expectation of agreement?

3. What does it mean to be an open-minded Christian?

4. Explain to an anti-intellectual Christian friend why it is important to learn about ideas and knowledge claims you be-

lieve to be wrong, yet which dominate the academy and society.

---

[1] Kenneth D. Boa and Robert M. Bowman, Jr., *Faith Has Its Reasons: An Integrative Approach to Defending Christianity* (Colorado Springs: NavPress, 2001), p. 136.

[2] Michael C. Rea, *World Without Design: The Ontological Consequences of Naturalism* (Oxford: Clarendon Press, 2002), pp. 72-73.

[3] William Hasker, *Metaphysics: Constructing a World View* (Downers Grove, IL: InterVarsity Press, 1983), p. 26.

[4] Ronald Nash, *Worldviews in Conflict* (Grand Rapids: Zondervan, 1992), p. 62.

[5] Hasker, p. 26.

[6] Nash, pp. 58-59.

[7] Nash, p. 84.

[8] Avrum Stroll, "Twentieth-Century Analytic Philosophy," in Richard Popkin, ed., *The Columbia History of Western Philosophy* (New York: MJF Books, 1999), p. 623.

[9] Nash, p. 85.

[10] Stroll, p. 623.

[11] Arnold Lunn, *The Revolt Against Reason* (London: Eyre& Spottiswoode, 1950), p. 222.

[12] Michael Rea, *World Without Design* (Oxford: Oxford University Press, 2002), pp. 51, 52.

[13] Rea, p. 55.

[14] Michael L. Peterson, *With All Your Mind: A Christian Philosophy of Education* (Notre Dame: University of Notre Dame Press, 2001), p. 37.

[15] See Roger Kimball, *Tenured Radicals*, rev. ed. (Chicago: Ivan R. Dee, 1998), p. 181. Also see his discussion of "The New Sophistry" on pp. 185-190.

[16] For a discussion of the pose of rebellion belied by the desire for authority among postmodernists, see Frank Ellis, "Political Correctness and the Ideological Struggle: From Lenin and Mao to Marcuse and Foucault," *Journal of Social, Political, and Economic Studies* 27:4 (Winter 2002), p. 428.

[17] Wendy Shalit, "A Ladies' Room of One's Own, *Commentary* 100:2 (August, 1995), p. 33.

[18] See the discussion in John Ellis, *Against Deconstruction* (Princeton: Princeton University Press, 1989), pp. 13-14.

[19] Gene Edward Veith, Jr., *Postmodern Times* (Wheaton, IL: Crossway Books, 1994), p. 62.

[20] Veith, p. 95.

[21] Michael L. Peterson, *With All Your Mind: A Christian Philosophy of Education* (Notre Dame, IN: University of Notre Dame Press, 2001), p. 89.

[22] Nash, p. 74.

[23] Dennis McCallum, *Christianity: The Faith that Makes Sense* (Wheaton: Tyndale House, 1992), p. 10.

[24] Blaise Pascal, *Pensees*, tr. Martin Turnell (New York: Harper and Row, 1962), p. 141.

[25] McCallum, p. 38.

[26] William Hasker, *Metaphysics: Constructing a World View* (Downers Grove, IL: InterVarsity Press, 1983), p. 28.

[27] Ronald Nash, *Faith and Reason: Searching for a Rational Faith* (Grand Rapids: Zondervan, 1988), p. 51.

[28] Gregg Easterbrook, "Science Sees the Light," *The New Republic*, 219:15 (Oct. 12, 1998), pp. 24ff; Gale Group reprint, p. 1.

[29] Easterbrook, Gale Group reprint, p. 1.

[30] George Gilder, "The Materialist Superstition," *Intercollegiate Review*, 31:2 (Spring, 1996), p. 8.

[31] Stephen C. Meyer, "The Origin of Life and the Death of Materialism," *Intercollegiate Review*, 31:2 (Spring, 1996), p. 39.

[32] Peterson, p. 38.

[33] Nash, *Worldviews in Conflict*, p. 62.

[34] Arnold Lunn, *The Revolt Against Reason* (London: Eyre & Spottiswoode, 1950), p. 176.

[35] Quoted in Lunn, p. 177.

[36] Lunn, p. 180.

[37] Quoted in Lunn, p. 177.

[38] Roger S. Jones, *Physics for the Rest of Us* (1992). Reprint New York: Barnes and Noble, 1999, p.131.

[39] Peterson, p. 115.

[40] The idea and phrasing are from Kenneth D. Boa and Robert M. Bowman, Jr., *Faith Has Its Reasons: An Integrative Approach to Defending Christianity* (Colorado Springs: Navpress, 2001), p. 185.

[41] Lunn, p. 189.

[42] Blaise Pascal, *Pensees*, tr. Martin Turnell (New York: Harper and Row, 1962), pp. 86-87 [Lafuma 188].

[43] Michael Cremo and Richard Thompson, *Forbidden Archeology: The Hidden History of the Human Race* (Los Angeles: Bhaktivedanta Book Publishing, 1998), p. 114.

[44] Jonathan Wells, "Critics Rave Over *Icons of Evolution*: A Response to Published Reviews," *Center for Science and Culture*, June 12, 2002. Retrieved from http://www.discovery.org.

[45] Frank Ellis, "Political Correctness and the Ideological Struggle: From Lenin and Mao to Marcuse and Foucault," *Journal of Social, Political, and Economic Studies* 27:4 (Winter 2002), p. 409.

[46] Ibid., p. 418.

[47] Ibid., p. 411.

[48] Ibid., p. 413.

[49] Ibid., p. 414.

[50] Ibid., p. 415.

[51] Ibid., pp. 415-416.

[52] Ibid., p. 415.

[53] Ibid., p. 423.

[54] Ibid., pp. 422-423.

[55] Ibid., p. 434.

[56] David Hackett Fischer, *Historians' Fallacies: Toward a Logic of Historical Thought* (New York: Harper & Row, 1970).

[57] John Ellis, *Against Deconstruction* (Princeton: Princeton University Press, 1989), p. ix.

[58] Alan Sokal and Jean Brickmont, *Fashionable Nonsense: Postmodern Intellectuals' Abuse of Science* (New York: Picador, 1998), p. 210.

[59] Quoted in Michael Cremo, *Forbidden Archeology's Impact*, 2nd ed. (Los Angeles: Bhaktivedanta Book Publishing, 2001), p. 93.

[60] See the letters in "A Scientific Scandal? David Berlinski and Critics," on the *Commentary* Web site, at http://www.commentary.org/berlinski.htm.

[61] Jonathan Wells, "Critics Rave Over *Icons of Evolution*: A Response to Published Reviews," *Center for Science and Culture*, June 12, 2002. Retrieved from http://www.discovery.org.

[62] Jonathan Wells, "Catch-23," *Center for Science and Culture*, July 1, 2002. Retrieved from http://www.discovery.org.

Chapter 10
Joining Faith and Learning

To integrate means to blend or form into a whole. In this sense, integration occurs when one's theological beliefs, primarily rooted in Scripture, are blended and unified with propositions judged as rational from other sources into a coherent, intellectually adequate Christian worldview.
— J. P. Moreland and William Lane Craig[1]

Belief in the divine incarnation of Jesus Christ implies the conviction that the natural and supernatural connect, rejecting the notion that an impassible chasm exists between the transcendent and the mundane. Christian scholars will not discount natural phenomena and processes. Indeed, they will be more sensitive to the ways in which God is present in the ordinary, in the empirical objects of their study — nature, art, literature, human societies, history. Believing that empirical realities touch metaphysical ones, Christian scholars will consciously operate in a spiritually open universe, and in their work they will challenge the common conclusion that materialism is the best explanation of reality. They will give attention to the wider context of their work, including its spirituality, and be intentional about expressing their academic agenda and priorities as shaped by their spiritual sensibilities.
— Jeff Childers[2]

10.1 The Meaning of Integration

From the discussions of earlier chapters, you can understand the challenge of integrating ideas and knowledge claims from competing worldviews that either contain a mixture of fact and often biased interpretation (as with naturalism) or reject the possibility of common ground by rejecting reason, objectivity, and evidence (as with postmodernism). And yet disciplines that have been built on or influenced by competing worldviews still contain much truth, useful knowledge, and important ideas that can be mined from them. The need for analysis and filtering is a significant challenge.

Another challenge facing us as integrators is the tendency of scholarship to divide and compartmentalize itself into narrow specialties, each with its own methodology, and sometimes even its own epistemology. For example, what used to be called philosophy included what we now call philosophy, science, theology, and ethics. These disciplines have branched off over the years. More recently, where postmodernism has taken over or become a powerful worldview in many fields (including literature, education, law, and social science), those fields have effectively changed worldviews and now include ideas quite incompatible with the ideas of the sciences.

And a third challenge is that human knowledge of all kinds is always in flux, requiring that we accept it tentatively or provisionally. Long-held beliefs that seemed to have good experimental evidence are suddenly overthrown by yet better evidence. So we develop the habit of being careful or skeptical about knowledge, learning current ideas without necessarily committing to them. There is a danger in this, of course, and recent generations of students have been criticized for having no commitments, for cynically writing out what the professor seems to want without believing a word of what they say. But sauce for the goose is sauce for the gander, they say, and this pose of being noncommittal is exactly what many professors themselves adopt. "The world is so complicated that it is naïve to believe anything," some professors say. I trust you will not fall into this trap, but that you will work diligently to separate the knowledge that is worthy of commitment from that which may need more time to assess. Without commitment, without working all knowledge together (including Christian revelation), there can be no integration and hence no holistic intellectual life and hence no wisdom. To be wise, to be able to make good judgments about life choices, requires commitment to truths.

Integration seeks to unify faith with every other aspect of learning, not just one of them. The challenge is enormous. It's a two-way process, with faith informing learning and learning informing faith. In the discussions below, we look at some practical approaches to the construction of this unified view of all knowledge.

10.2 General Approaches to Integration

When looking at integration from the standpoint of connecting the Christian worldview to various academic disciplines as a whole, there are several possible approaches, each resting on its own idea about what integration means. It is useful to take a look at the alternatives for bringing faith and learning into relationship, to make use of or incorporate faith into learning and learning into faith. This section covers the general or philosophical level of integration, the kind of master strategy or strategies that can be used.

The Two Realms Approach. As mentioned in Chapter 2, the two realms view is scarcely an approach to integration because it argues that disciplinary knowledge and Christian faith (or theology) exist in separate realms that are essentially mutually exclusive. Disciplines are studied according to their own rules and epistemology and Christian faith is a separate and, practically speaking, irrelevant issue. Allan Sandage, when asked, "Must there necessarily be a conflict between science and religion?" answers, "In my opinion, no, if it is understood that each treats a different aspect of reality."[3] In this approach, the connection between these separate aspects of reality seems tenuous at best, thus precluding the kind of unified and coherent worldview Christians ought to be working on. While this approach has the benefit of eliminating worrisome conflicts between disciplinary claims and theological claims, the lack of integration and the upholding by default of disciplinary claims has the effect of marginalizing Christian knowledge in relation to the larger world of ideas. The result is also an incoherent worldview that holds inescapably conflicting ideas.

The False Distinction Approach. Followers of the false distinction approach claim that integration is not necessary because "all knowledge is one." Knowledge, by its nature and from whatever source, and God by his sovereignty, automatically produce integration whenever the Christian learns. Learning the complexities of, say, metamorphosis also teaches us about the creativity of God. Once again, this approach has the benefit of denying that conflicts exist. However, this very denial is unrealistic. As we have seen in earlier chapters, the claims about what constitutes knowledge are in conflict because the worldviews are in conflict. It seems apparent that anyone who has engaged the world of ideas, where interpretations and conclusions about the same facts differ profoundly, and where argument is possible over what exactly a given fact is—this experience reveals that there is no automatic integration. Whether we are learning about a theory like behaviorism or discussing the ethics of stem cell research, the Christian worldview has much of relevance to bring to the issue.

The Compatibilist Approach. This approach emphasizes that Christian faith and the academic discipline share common points of agreement or certain basic assumptions (such as the reliability of reason, the methods of evidence, the existence of truth). It also believes that at least some and perhaps many of the knowledge claims of the discipline are compatible with those of the Christian worldview. Integration therefore involves identifying, connecting, and elaborating these points of commonality. Compatibilists also believe that in some cases disciplinary knowledge represents only a partial view of the wholeness of truth and that Christianity can supplement or complete this partial view. This approach has the advantage of allowing a Christian perspective to be put on secular claims; and by identifying shared assumptions and ways of knowing, it can prevent students from fear of or hostility to learning. Thus, compatibilist efforts can help defuse antintellectualism. The drawback to compatibilism is the danger that it will downplay the real conflicts between Christianity and the discipline's claims or its methodological worldview. Conflicting ontologies and epistemologies cannot really be reconciled to any meaningful degree. Fundamental differences result in fundamental issues that need to be addressed directly. Compatibilism may be a good starting point or an adjunct to other forms of integration, but is likely not sufficient on its own.

Examples of compatibilist efforts include these:

- Seeking common ground between faith and the scholarly discipline (basic assumptions about reason, truth, evidence)
- Identifying compatibility between Christian and secular ideas (e.g., Christianity and stoicism, Aristotle and Christianity on ethics or friendship)
- Using Christian and Biblical examples and illustrations to show the application of disciplinary concepts
- Comparing Biblical teaching to good practice (e.g., the use of honest scales as enjoined by Proverbs 16:11)
- Showing that Christianity is relevant to learning, that the Bible has much to say about knowledge (human nature, beauty, history, etc.)
- Decompartmentalizing faith and knowledge to merge faith and learning by applying Biblical knowledge to subject matter
- Experiencing in practice the idea that all truth is God's truth
- Recognizing that apparent conflicts between faith or Biblical knowledge and what is taught may derive from interpretation and thus not automatically accepting information that appears to conflict with Biblical knowledge

The Transformationist Approach. Transformationists assume, similar to the compatibilists, that the content of the discipline has some commonality with the Christian worldview, but transformationists also believe that the discipline itself has been arbitrarily truncated or narrowed by its omission of Christian insights. What is lacking in the discipline can be supplemented and completed by the Christian worldview. Just as important, the Christian worldview serves as a source of error correction for the areas where the discipline has misinterpreted fact, presented ideology as truth, or made truth claims that are not supported by the evidence or revealed knowledge. Transformationists want to reform the discipline by testing its claims and separating real knowledge from false knowledge. This approach has the benefit of recognizing that most disciplines develop their knowledge claims based on naturalistic or postmodern worldviews, which can skew the interpretations and theories developed as a result. Transformationists recognize the powerful role that ideology plays in many disciplines and they seek to identify and correct the tendentiousness of such scholarship. The drawback to this approach is that it involves much more effort, hard thinking, and assumption seeking than does compatibilism. It is also likely to result in hostility from the secular academy, which will reject any attempted corrections to the disciplinary systems already established. (All change, even from those who share the discipline's worldview and assumptions, is usually received with hostility. It is the nature of change.)

Examples of transformationist efforts include these:

- Upholding Biblical authority in the world of knowledge
- Applying Biblical principles and texts to specific disciplinary situations
- Asking integrative questions that require a connection between faith or Biblical knowledge and disciplinary knowledge
- Advocating the existence of truth, reason, meaning, and interpretive standards against postmodern rejection
- Differentiating between knowledge claims and genuine knowledge
- Using Christian worldview knowledge to test and correct claims made by the discipline (e.g., relating to human nature)

The Reconstructionist Approach. Reconstructionists assume that the discipline is "so deeply permeated with anti-Christian assumptions"[4] that it must be rejected outright and remade from the ground up from a Biblical foundation. Significant figures in the area may have clearly anti-Christian agendas behind their theories and claims, making other forms of integration unworkable.

Examples of reconstructionist efforts include these:

- Employing the Christian worldview as the organizing principle that informs and interprets the subject area and all knowledge.
- Replacing assumption sets underlying the discipline (e.g., replacing philosophical materialism with theistic assumptions)
- Proposing new theoretical and experimental approaches to generate knowledge in the subject area
- Identifying alternative interpretive schema for the analysis of data and evidence
- Upholding the primacy of truth over intellectual fashion, ideology, political correctness, or "idols of the tribe."

Which Approach? Of these alternative approaches to integration, then, which is the best one? At this point, it is crucial to remember that the goal is not simply to connect faith and learning or to overlay learning with a "faith perspective." The concept of integration refers to a process that will produce a unified, coherent system, an interrelationship, a holistic understanding, a seamless landscape of truth where the physical, spiritual, and rational all combine into one realm. In other words, integration is about the building of one's worldview, not simply learning about something in a Christian way. Therefore, the Christian worldview does more than make faith "relevant" to learning.

The answer to "Which approach?" will become clear if you think for a minute that (1) disciplines vary widely in their content, philosophy, and methods, (2) most disciplines have more than one school of thought, and (3) even within schools of thought controversy, change, adaptation, and development are common. For these reasons, then, a combination of the last three approaches (compatibilist, transformationist, and reconstructionist) will likely be the most useful, depending on the circumstances. The goal is to integrate faith and learning, to develop and apply the Christian worldview, to welcome worthy knowledge, to avoid being taken in by false knowledge claims—not to apply mechanically some mental formula. Integration is a complex and lifelong practice, and will require a number of methods and approaches.

10.3 Specific Approaches to Integration

Ultimately, integration comes down to specific cases and specific techniques. This section discusses several ways to integrate a given viewpoint or even a specific knowledge claim. The approach chosen depends on the circumstances. Here are some common situations that may occur when a knowledge claim is brought into relationship with the Christian worldview.[5]

There is no apparent overlap or conflict. Depending on the discipline or subdiscipline, much or even most of the content may be entirely harmonious with the Christian worldview. Even in science, which is often put at odds with faith by some naturalists, probably at least 80 or 90 percent is compatible with Christian knowledge. The melting temperature of lead is not subject to worldview conflict. The same holds for nearly all of empirical science and technology. (It's the *meaning* of some findings that creates many of the conflicts.) Similarly, many theological claims are not in conflict with any knowledge claim made by any discipline. Statements about the nature of angels do not conflict with the findings of any discipline (though, of course, such statements are rejected by both naturalists and postmodernists as unintelligible).

Those who argue for the two realms approach often cite items that fall into this category to show that religion and scholarship are separate realms. Christians do mathematical equations the same as atheists do, they say. Or the Christian worldview is irrelevant to the number of electrons in an atom of gold. Quite so. There are many such areas where content is generally neutral. However, remember that many areas of seemingly objective learning are accompanied by less than objective interpretation. Even in mathematics, which many people like to cite as being impervious to integrative issues, we have fields like chaos theory, which some are attempting to interpret as being hostile to theism.

The claims are complementary but separate. In some cases, a Biblical or theological understanding and a disciplinary understanding of the same event may represent, as More-land and Craig say, "two different, complementary, noninter-acting approaches to the same reality."[6] The effect of prayer to bring physical healing and the medical observation of the healing would be an example. Another example would be the spiritual process of rebirth and joy following a salvation ex-perience and the psychological description of it. In these cases, we have two complementary views of the same phenomenon. Note that the naturalists will assert that the psychological (or electrochemical brain activity) is the *only true* explanation of the reality (once again indicating the reductionist nature of the naturalist worldview), while the Christian can accept both and see a more complete view of reality.

Some of the worldview assumptions agree. As different as the worldviews are, there is some overlap in the assump-tions or presuppositions, especially between naturalism and the Christian worldview, as we saw in Chapter 6. More than that, in some cases the assumptions underlying the Christian worldview may support the findings of a discipline better than the discipline's own assumptions. As Moreland and Craig say, "Some have argued that many of the presupposi-tions of a realist understanding of science . . . (e.g., the exis-tence of truth, the rational, orderly nature of reality, the ade-quacy of our sensory and cognitive faculties as tools suited for knowing the external world) make sense and are easy to jus-tify given Christian theism, but are odd and without ultimate justification in a naturalistic worldview." Similarly, they ar-gue, philosophical concepts such as "critiques of epistemologi-cal skepticism and defenses of the existence of a real, theory-independent world and a correspondence theory of truth . . . offer justification for some of the presuppositions of theol-ogy."[7] Many ideas in philosophy can be seen as highly suppor-tive of aspects of the Christian worldview. And, in fact, much of the power behind integrative issues, worldview awareness, and apologetics now comes from philosophy.

Disciplinary knowledge and Christian knowledge may support each other. A scientific theory like the Big Bang pro-vides support for the theological claim that the universe had a single-point beginning in time. The second law of thermodynamics provides support for the idea that the universe has a finite life and is not eternal. In the other direction, the medical observation that religious people generally live healthier and happier lives is supported by Scriptural principle. The importance of nurture in childrearing is similarly supported.

Some people caution us not to depend too heavily on current disciplinary knowledge for faith support because, as we have noted, such knowledge is subject to change. For example, if the Big Bang theory is eventually rejected and replaced, we would not want to have committed to it so foundationally that our apologetic was damaged as a result. It is best, therefore, when we find harmonious features in science to say simply, "Current scientific theory supports the Christian view."

There is an apparent conflict between the disciplinary claim and the Christian worldview. Sometimes the claims in a disciplinary area are in conflict with those arising from the Christian worldview. A common example is that of the mind-body problem. Are the mind and the brain the same thing (monism) or are they separate (dualism)? Our worldview teaches us that we exist apart from our bodies and that we not only have a separate consciousness but a soul. The naturalists claim that cognition is simply an epiphenomenon, a byproduct, of the electrochemical activity of the brain.

Christian philosopher Alvin Plantinga suggests that when there is an apparent conflict between a disciplinary claim and the Christian worldview, the conflict can be addressed in more than one way. He says there are "three ways in which a scientific theory can be relevantly related to the theological or religious claims characteristic of the theistic religions. First, a scientific theory may be incompatible with those claims; alternatively, it might be such that its probability with respect to those claims is quite different from what it is with respect to a naturalistic world view; thirdly, religious or theological views can help determine what needs explanation."[8] Each of these can give us some insight into how to handle these conflicts.

1. Incompatible Claims. Under the worldview of naturalism, the concept of altruism (selfless commitment to the welfare of others) appears to be evolutionarily counterproductive, since it works against "the probability that one's genes will be widely disseminated in the next and subsequent generation."[9] Recall that one of the pillars of evolutionary theory is differential reproduction — those who leave the most offspring have an advantage over those who leave fewer. Under naturalism, then, there must be something wrong with selfless people who fail to focus on maximum production of offspring. Plantinga cites a naturalistic theory claiming that altruistic people must therefore suffer from the abnormal and dysfunctional characteristics of "docility" and "bounded rationality." If those who focus on serving others were fully rational, this theory claims, then they would not be altruistic. Since they are altruistic, they must be somewhat irrational. As Plantinga says, this theory "is clearly not neutral with respect to Christian commitment; indeed, it is inconsistent with it."[10]

In a case like this, the incompatible theory should be remembered, but not accepted. Notice that in this case we are dealing not with a contest of facts or observations but of interpretations. How is selfless generosity to be explained? Is it the result of the reflection of humanity and the love of God in the human heart, part of the image of God in us, or is it the result of a mental deficiency? The interpretive conflict arises from incompatible views of human nature and the image of God (or lack thereof) in humankind.

2. *Differential Probability.* A second way of relating the apparently conflicting claims of a scientific theory to the claims of the Christian (or other theistic) worldview is to determine whether the claims vary in their coherence or credibility as they are viewed from the different worldviews. That is, a theory may appear to be more credible or probable under naturalism than under the Christian worldview, largely because of the different assumptions of each worldview. The ontological set and the epistemic rules of each worldview may affect the evaluation of the claims. The obvious example would be the theory of evolution. As Plantinga explains, "If you reject theism in favor of naturalism, this evolutionary story is the only game in town, the only visible answer to the question, 'Where did all this enormous variety of flora and fauna come from?'"[11] A worldview that rules out God as creator is therefore *required* to find a theory that explains the creation without reference to

God or a creator. In such a case, evolutionary theory, for all its problems and weaknesses, is the best available explanation. So to someone who subscribes to the worldview of naturalism, evolution has enormous probability. This explains why evolutionists are so often declaring that evolution is a "fact" and getting upset when their claims are not met with agreement.

On the other hand, to a Christian, whose worldview includes not only the natural world but the supernatural world and its Creator God, evolutionary theory falls short because there is a more reasonable and probable alternative. Plantinga says that "the epistemic probability of the whole grand evolutionary story is quite different for the theist and for the naturalist. The probability of this story with respect to the evidence together with the views a *theist* typically holds, is much lower than its probability with respect to the evidence together with the views the *naturalist* typically holds."[12] To the theist, open to the possible explanation that the world was formed by an intelligent designer who is the source of the massive amounts of information we find in the biological world, the alternative explanation that life arose through chance, mutation, and time seems much less credible, much less probable.

Thus, the same explanation (evolution) has differential probability from different worldviews. In a case like this, the integrative act is to recognize that the claim's probability and ultimately its credibility depend on the worldview from which it is considered, and upon what alternatives are permitted by each worldview. This is decision theory at its simplest. A decision is based on an examination of alternatives and criteria. If some alternatives are ruled out of order at the outset (such as any God-based explanation), then the same criteria (such as simplest explanation, most coherent, best match with data) will yield a different choice from among the permitted alternatives. Imagine that you are asked to choose the best tasting, creamiest ice cream, and you are given two bowls, A and B. Based on the criteria of "best tasting" and "creamiest" you choose A. Now suppose the same test, only now the judges have ruled that only ice cream made by company B is truly ice cream, so you are given a choice of B. Based on the criteria of "best tasting" and "creamiest" you must now choose B, since A is no longer a possible option.

3. *Problem Contingency*. The third way of relating the claim of a scientific theory to the Christian worldview is in Plantinga's words, to determine "what needs explanation." In other words, the very question of whether a problem exists may be dependent (contingent) on the worldview from which the data embodying the possible problem is approached. What is a problem for, say, the follower of philosophical naturalism may not be a problem for the Christian or theistic worldview follower.

An analogy may help to clarify this idea. Constructing a worldview is in part an exercise in problem solving. What theory, story, hypothesis explains everything in the best way? Think of a crime scene, where the job of the detective is to construct a story that includes all the clues and organizes them in a coherent way, leading to an understanding of what happened. Usually, no explanation covers absolutely every clue. There are always unexplained items, anomalies, sometimes evidence that actually appears to disconfirm the working hypothesis. Good detectives often create multiple or rival hypotheses, more than one way of explaining the same data, in order to see which one fits the best.

For example, suppose a burglary has been committed. Caught on a security camera is a single shadowy figure leaving the scene. At the scene, investigators find a footprint and two cigarette butts, one with lipstick on it and one without. The detective whose hypothesis (or story) says that the burglar was a woman (based on size of the figure in the video) wearing lipstick does not need to explain the butt with the lipstick as an anomaly, since it is consistent with the general story. But the second butt without the lipstick is a problem for that hypothesis. Similarly, for the detective who thinks the burglar was a man (based on the size of the footprint), the lipsticked butt is a problem that needs to be explained, while the non-lipsticked butt is not.

Plantinga's example of problem contingency is the fine tuning of the universe in cosmology. For the naturalist, the universe is "scientifically problematic"[13] because it is constructed within very small tolerances. If the forces of elementary particles, gravity, electromagnetism, and so on were only minutely different, the universe could not have continued to exist. The problem for the naturalist is how this high degree of exactness just happened to occur all in one place and time. It is beyond probability. And that makes it a substantial problem. One naturalistic explanation is that "there are infinitely many different universes, displaying all possible combinations of initial conditions and values for the fundamental constants" and we just happen to "occupy one of the universes in which these values permit the development of intelligent life."[14] Though this answer does not overcome the improbability issue, it does provide a solution.

To those who have the alternative choice of a universe created by God, however, this explanation may seem almost ridiculous. It is much simpler to approach the problem from the standpoint of a Christian worldview, which posits an intelligent creator. With such an assumption, this fine tuning — exactness, uniqueness, and specification — of the cosmos is not a problem at all, but follows logically from that worldview's presuppositions. We would expect an intelligently designed universe to reflect the appropriate exactness requisite for life and endurance. The universe seems to show features of careful design and intelligence because that's how it was made. The other explanation, that it was all a chance occurrence, but realized only because of an infinite number of other, failed chance occurrences, seems to defy the rule of thumb that the simplest explanation is usually the best.

The methodology of this approach for relating scientific claims and the Christian worldview, then, is to assess the reason the theory or claim exists. What is the basis of the problem and how does the solution or explanation of the problem operate? Do the facts that represent a problem under naturalism also represent a problem in need of explanation under the Christian worldview?

Before we leave the issue of problem explanation, it may have occurred to you to ask, "When the explanation is unclear or unknown, why not just say that we don't have a solution?" To answer this, we can appeal to the most famously misunderstood proverb in the English language, "The exception proves the rule." In the modern sense of *prove*, exceptions don't prove anything. But in the original meaning of *prove*, as in another old proverb, "Fire proves gold, and gold proves a man," or even better, as in the King James Version of 1 Thessalonians 5:21, "Prove all things; hold fast to that which is good," the word *prove* means to test or challenge. Thus, "The exception proves the rule" means that the exception *challenges* the rule, puts pressure on it, calls it into question.

The purpose of this little semantic tour is to emphasize that at the higher level of theory, anomalous problems (problems solved by one theory but not another) put pressure on the theory's supporters to find a solution. After all, science is about problem solving, and the larger theories seek to be unifying, so they must reasonably account for all the facts possible. At the lower level of theory, there may remain the unanswered question, such as in our example above, "But how do you account for the other cigarette butt?" Even there, though, the explanation may be somewhat weakened by the failure to solve this problem.

Note, by the way, that problem contingency occurs in areas outside of scientific theories. An example is the well-known problem of evil. In the Christian worldview, the existence of evil—of pain and suffering, natural disasters, and the like—in a world where a loving and omnipotent God is sovereign is a problem in need of explanation. How can the two facts be reconciled? The answers have been many. Boethius in the *Consolation of Philosophy*, C. S. Lewis in *The Problem of Pain*, and many Christian and other theistic philosophers have addressed this issue.[15] To the naturalist, on the other hand, there is no problem. The naturalist posits an uncaring, random universe where the struggle for survival and natural processes (like tornadoes and earthquakes) are to be expected. And without a sovereign moral being, there is no such thing as evil. All the pain and suffering we witness are merely expected, though unfortunate, events. (The problem for the naturalist is to explain good in the world.)

10.4 Integrative Outcomes

Integration occurs not only when we first deny the separation between secular and sacred truth but when we work intentionally to bring all of our sources of truth together in a coherent and unified picture of reality. Integration, then, is "the teaching of all subjects as a part of the total truth of God thereby enabling the student to see the unity of natural and special revelation."[16] But more than this, it involves the putting together of all our knowledge. William Hasker says,

> Integration is concerned with *integral* relationships between faith and knowledge, the relationships which *inherently exist* between the content of the faith and the subject-matter of this or that discipline; such connections do not have to be invented or manufactured. But they do need to be *ascertained* and *developed*; unless this is done faith and knowledge may appear to be, and for practical purposes may be in fact, alien and unrelated to each other.[17]

The great question, then, is, "What is the relationship of this knowledge claim to Christian truth?" The claim can be an idea, opinion, interpretation, model, interpretive scheme, ideology, theory or other idea. And the second question is, "What is the meaning of this relationship?" When faith-knowledge interacts with disciplinary knowledge, and the two become integrated, several outcomes are possible.

Christian knowledge affirms disciplinary knowledge. The idea or knowledge claim from the discipline is supported by the Christian worldview and its revealed truth. Shared assumptions, methods, facts, observations, and even interpretations show a harmony between the two. The Christian worldview supports the use of reason, the goal of objective investigation, and the method of experiment in science, for example.

Christian knowledge supplements disciplinary knowledge. Knowledge of the fall, sin, the unchanging character of human nature, the need for God, spiritual striving, and many other theological truths offer enormous contributions to understanding how and why people behave the way they do, and what solutions should be chosen from among the options.

Such supplemental knowledge has enormous implications in law, economics, the social sciences, history, and other fields.

Modernism and postmodernism both feature limited and distorted views of reality, omitting or denying spiritual and supernatural dimensions, and do poorly on moral, ethical, aesthetic, and philosophical areas. Disciplinary knowledge from these worldviews needs to be supplemented by Christian knowledge.

Christian knowledge challenges the disciplinary claim. The knowledge claim conflicts with what we have reason to believe from the Christian worldview. For example, our belief in truth, reason, and the objective nature of Scripture challenges many of the assumptions and specific claims of arising from the postmodernist worldview. We believe in the "authorial intention" behind Scripture and that God had a specific meaning for us to gain from his words. The postmodern belief in an unlimited number of meanings for a text is in conflict with this.

In this integrative outcome, the Christian worldview and Biblical revelation change our understanding and knowledge from the discipline, correcting and transforming its biases and errors. Examples would include Margaret Mead's claim that free love is a cure for the stress of adolescence, the behaviorist school in psychology, and the reigning dogma of cultural relativism.

Disciplinary knowledge affirms Christian knowledge. Because we believe that Christian knowledge as revealed through Scripture represents the truth, we should not be surprised when scientific or other scholarly findings support that truth. Caution is advised here, however, because of the nature of science and scholarly knowledge. As C. S. Lewis reminds us,

> Science is in continual change and we must try to keep abreast of *it*. For the same reason, we must be very cautious of snatching at any scientific theory which, for the moment, seems to be in our favour. . . . If we try to base our apologetic on some recent development in science, we shall usually find that just as we have put the finishing touches to our ar-

gument science has changed its mind and quietly withdrawn
the theory. . . .[18]

Lewis says we should merely comment on such supportive
findings as "interesting." In that spirit, then, an interesting example of disciplinary knowledge harmonizing with Biblical
teaching is a report from the Heritage Center for Data Analysis, revealing that "teenage boys and girls who are sexually
active are significantly less likely to be happy and more likely
to feel depressed," and that they "are significantly more likely
to attempt suicide."[19] Further, the analysis found that "a majority of sexually active boys and nearly three-quarters of
sexually active girls regard their own initial sexual experience
unfavorably — as an event they wish they had avoided."[20]

The findings of this analysis support the Christian view of
sexual morality and remind us that regardless of the current
trends in mores or the depiction of youthful sex by Hollywood, God's teaching fits much better with his creatures, for
he made us and knows what is good (or bad) for us. If I may
sermonize a moment, Biblical morality was not created as a
means to oppress us or to keep us from having fun; it is designed for our happiness by the God who loves us and wants
the best for us.

**Disciplinary knowledge supplements Christian knowl-
edge.** A theory or finding in the discipline clarifies, elaborates,
underlines, and supports the Christian worldview and its
knowledge. The beauty of the creation and the intelligence of
the Creator are known to us by revelation, and supplemented
by the deeper investigation into the complexities of, say, the
blood coagulation cascade, metamorphosis, or particle physics. As the saying is, "God is as deep as you want to go."

**Disciplinary knowledge challenges Christian knowl-
edge.** In this outcome, there is a rational claim or a fact in evidence that appears to conflict with Christian knowledge. In
such a case, we need to determine why.

1. Is the claim accurate or true? Is the claim a substantiated
fact or is it a matter of interpretation? Recall that there is a
world of difference between a fact and the meaning of a fact.
Sometimes there is even disagreement over whether some

claim is indeed a fact. Two major problems with knowledge claims are (a) the failure to distinguish between an observed fact and the interpretive conclusion regarding that fact (the meaning, significance, or implications) and (b) the failure to distinguish between an observation or set of observations and the inductive generalization derived from the observation. (Remember that all inductive generalizations exist on a probability continuum; they are not unimpeachable facts.) In earlier chapters we have seen the widespread acceptance of ideas that later were exposed as false or problematic. Many findings are not presented as theories or possible truths, but instead are declared to be the way things are. "We now know" is a favorite catchphrase for those insisting on the truth of a theory (that may later turn out to be other than completely true).

The more you learn about information—misinformation, disinformation, hoaxes, fabrications, misinterpretations, distortions, and so on—the more cautious you will become when you encounter an idea that appears to contradict Biblical truth. You may have to file away the idea and wait awhile. Several years ago, there was an idea in psychology that encouraged people to vent their anger, to let it all out, to reveal their anger with others. The idea was that such actions would produce a cathartic experience. Yet this idea seemed to conflict with Biblical teaching about not stirring up anger (Proverbs 30:33) and not letting anger last (Ephesians 4:26). More recently, this idea has been discredited by the observation that people who express their anger become more angry than ever, not less. So, the current idea seems to harmonize with Scripture.

Philosopher Norman Geisler reminds us, "Since science is limited and progressive, we should not expect complete agreement in every detail with the Biblical presentation."[21] Conflicts are to be expected, first because empirical knowledge is always under development, seeing the world dimly in a mirror, and second because some scholars have tendentious agendas whose aim is to attack competing worldviews like Christianity. They want to discover or interpret evidence that will discredit Christianity.

2. *Is the relevant part of your Christian worldview accurate?* It is possible that some interpretation of Christian truth may

need to be adjusted in light of a disciplinary finding. Developing a Christian worldview is an ongoing, life-long process, just as integration is. Obviously, any clear fundamental of our worldview, such as the existence and sovereignty of God, his role as creator, fallen human nature, and the like, will not be subject to change, so that a knowledge claim that denies such a fundamental must be considered in error. However, there may be points of interpretation or understanding that need to be reexamined. For example, in the King James version of the Bible, the Hebrew word for *wild ox* was translated (through a Hebrew-to-Greek-to-English error in translation) as *unicorn* in half a dozen places, such as Job 39:9-10. Until this translation error was identified, many people were led to believe that unicorns must have been real.

Be careful here. Adjusting your world view in light of a new knowledge claim is the most risky strategy of integration, because it creates the temptation to compromise Christian teaching in order to make it fit current scholarship. The disciplinary claim may be far from tentatively expressed, but may be presented as incontrovertible fact. (It's amazing how many of those have been shot out of the air over the years.) You want to be careful to avoid mere accommodationism, the idea that you must "compromise to harmonize." Nevertheless, you must expect that in some areas your understanding of Scripture or the Biblical framework might be inaccurate. Look carefully to discover whether you are faced with a problematic fact or merely an interpretation (even if that interpretation is presented in the guise of a fact). And continue to develop your own hermeneutics of integration (see Chapter 8).

3. *What do other Christian scholars say?* Remember that integration is both a personal and a communal activity. You do not have to do all the mental work yourself. Fellow believers face the same integrative issues you do, and many of them are practiced at working out problems and thinking things through. There is expertise from many disciplines to aid in this work. How blessed we are to live in the age of the Internet, where hundreds of Web sites offer instantly available discussions. Explore some of these sites when you have the opportunity. See the Appendix for some places to start.

4. *Should this conflict be put on the shelf for awhile?* It's okay to say, "I don't know what to do with that yet." Just remember the information without committing to it pro or con and wait until more information or understanding becomes available. We can be heartened by the fact that historically, many ideas that were in conflict with Christian belief turned out to be false. The surprising number of cases like this makes us think that some other (current) problems will also be resolved in the same way. Here again is a reason for studying the history of ideas and the history of theories in your own major or discipline.

10.5 A Hint About Christian Scholarship

Because so many knowledge claims in the disciplines come from hostile worldviews, integration with them will remain a challenge as the Christian worldview interacts with conflicts, incompatible assumptions, underlying interpretive frameworks, and evaluative paradigms, while at the same time finding areas of agreement and compatibility.

Another way to think about integration is not simply as engagement of disciplinary knowledge with Christian truth in order to develop and elaborate a holistic view of truth and reality, but as the practice of developing specifically Christian disciplinary knowledge. That is, instead of viewing integration as largely a reactive process of bringing the faith to the discipline, integration should become proactive, working to shape the discipline itself or at least to pursue disciplinary learning (the creation of new knowledge and interpretations) from a Christian perspective.

At a minimum, then, Christian scholarship should be informed by Christian principles. In his article, "The Use of the Bible in Christian Scholarship," Stanley Greidanus offers some exemplary ideas about how Biblical norms might apply to particular disciplines. To make this lengthy quotation easier to negotiate, I have broken it up into bullet points by subject.

- In the discipline of ethics, for example, one can draw on the biblically revealed norms for right conduct. Of central importance here is the love commandment, but the significance of other biblical passages should not be overlooked. Biblical laws relating to the protection of life, the concern for the poor, the care for animals, trees, and land—all these and more give us insights into the divine norms for justice and stewardship.

- In political science one would be guided by such biblical themes as the sovereignty of God, the God-given authority of government, the task of government to promote (the biblical norms of) justice, liberty, and peace, and the required obedience of citizens.
- In sociology one would take into account the biblical norms for marriage, family, and other societal structures.
- In psychology one would view man not as an animal that can be conditioned, nor as a machine that can be programmed, but as a creature of exceptional worth because man alone is made in the image of God. One would be guided by biblical insights into the essence of man (his relationship with God) and the fundamental unity of man ("a living soul," "heart").
- In the discipline of history, one would be guided by the biblical theme that God acts in history, that he is bringing his Kingdom into the world, and by biblical insights concerning humanity's origin, purpose, and destiny, the cultural mandate, and the antithesis between believers and unbelievers.
- In economics one would want to take into account the biblical ideas of justice and stewardship, of ownership, of work and play.[22]

Greidanus concludes:

The point is that Christian scholars can make more specific use of the Bible than the general (often rather vague) notions of "my faith" and "the biblical framework." It will be clear, however, that by this more specific use we do not mean some kind of prooftext method but the uncovering and use of genuinely biblical themes that have developed progressively in the history of revelation.[23]

This raises the great question: Is there a Christian psychology, history, sociology, literature, or business that is somehow distinct from what is ordinarily taught in a non-Christian environment? If not, can there be? This question often raises the temperature of some Christian professors, who perhaps fear being laughed at by their secular colleagues for departing from traditionally—or currently—accepted disciplinary content. But let's think about this for just a few moments.

In literary studies, there have been many schools of theory and interpretation. Currently, several schools are popular in the academy, nearly all representing some flavor of or compatibility with postmodernist ideas: Marxist, feminist, deconstructionist and similar interpretive patterns. While it may be important for the Christian to learn about these, could not—should not—Christians develop a deliberately Christian literary interpretation? It might be similar to the old so-called moral school of interpretation, where it was all right to ask if an idea was good or true, whether a character had moral flaws or strengths, and to examine how a character's values helped determine the outcome of his or her activities. What role does sin or the pursuit of righteousness or faith or pride or greed play in Shakespeare? It seems that the possibilities are endless, and the answers to some of these questions may be more practically useful for building wisdom and a richer life than the question of whether Shakespeare has trapped himself in a set of self-contradictory verbal evasions. In literature that is distinctively Christian, such as Spenser's *Faerie Queene*, Christian literature professors ought to have much to say. And in literature that is entirely worldly, a Christian contextualizing could prove very profitable as well.

The Christian worldview has much to add to psychology, by considering the nature of sin, spiritual striving, the possibility of redemption (both in a spiritual way and in an emotional way, where people can discover the possibility of turning around from self destructive behavior).

There may even be something to do in Christian theories of business. Perhaps the concept of profit maximization needs to be adjusted by taking into account human benefit maximization. For example, assuming that the elasticity of demand is such that you could make $100 by selling ten ballpoint pens at $10 each or $100 by selling 100 pens at a dollar each, which should you do? The efficiency model may dictate selling the 10 pens at the higher price, but by selling 100 pens cheaply you would create a larger benefit to the consumer. And there is the question of the privilege (I don't say duty) of business to act for humanity. The first publisher of J. R. R. Tolkein expected to lose money on *Lord of the Rings*, but thought the book deserved to be published because of its merits. Businesses, of course, do not exist to lose money, but there is a lot of flexibility in what they do. As another example, Target stores will not sell cigarettes, even though that "doesn't make economic sense" because of the revenue they do not receive as a result. How might such acts fit in with or derive from a formal, Christian theory of business practices?

By producing Christian scholarship, which may or may not be unique to the faith, Christian scholars would have ideas to contribute to their disciplines, material to integrate in one of the ways described above. New theoretical and interpretive schools and movements are always arising in the academy. Why shouldn't some of those be distinctively Christian ones? Why wait to react to still another Freudian psychological theory or another Marxist view of history?

10.6 Implications for Integration

Let me emphasize once again the two-way street of integration. The Christian worldview serves as a test of disciplinary knowledge claims, and it uses disciplinary knowledge to help construct a more complete and richer view of reality. William Hasker says that an important question to keep present is

> what specific contribution does this discipline make to the Christian vision of reality? How does it enable us to understand God, and his world, and our fellow human beings differently than if the insights of the discipline were not available? What insights, projects, and activities does the discipline make possible? In short, what difference does the discipline make for Christians who are not its students or practitioners?[24]

So-called secular learning has an enormous contribution to make to the development of the Christian worldview and an understanding of total reality.

Driving in the other direction, we must assert that integration should not be merely a Christian response to secular learning and knowledge claims, not merely an evaluating and choosing, a dividing the truth from the falsehood, but a Christian contribution to the knowledge of the world and ourselves. Christian philosopher Alvin Plantinga says that "we are all, theist and non-theist alike, engaged in the common human project of understanding ourselves and the world in which we find ourselves."[25] Christians have knowledge and insights to bring to the marketplace of ideas, and faith-based learning can contribute to the rest of human learning, to fill in, correct, supplement, or challenge what is thought and taught. The Christian scholarly community can contribute to the building of an interconnected realm of reality, transcending but including the physical world and traditional disciplinary knowledge, making the external world, the senses, the heart, the mind, experience, all make sense to a thoughtful, reasonable person.

Summary

This chapter provides several approaches, methods, and examples of how the integrative process can be performed. The Christian worldview has much to learn and much to contribute in the understanding of the world.

Questions for Thought and Discussion

1. Find a specific example of a disciplinary knowledge claim you have in the past found to be problematic in relation to your faith, and discuss how it might now be located in the integrative approaches outlined in this chapter.

2. Give an example of Christian knowledge informing, qualifying, or correcting a disciplinary knowledge claim.

3. Give an example of disciplinary knowledge extending your Christian worldview.

4. Can true knowledge come from wrong theories or assumptions? If so, what are the implications for integrative activity?

---

[1] J. P. Moreland and William Lane Craig, *Philosophical Foundations for a Christian Worldview* (Downers Grove, IL: InterVarsity, 2003), p. 17.

[2] Jeff Childers, Chapter 5 Summary, "Christian Scholarship Symposium at ACU on *The Outrageous Idea of Christian Scholarship* by George Marsden," Abilene Christian University, Feb. 1999. Retrieved from http://www.acu.edu/academics/adamscenter/resources/faithlearning/christianschol.html.

[3] Allan Sandage, "A Scientist Reflects on Religious Belief," *Truth Journal*. Retrieved from http://www.leaderu.com/truth/1truth15.html.

[4] Hasker, op. cit.

[5] This section is indebted to J. P. Moreland and William Lane Craig, *Philosophical Foundations for a Christian Worldview* (Downers Grove, IL: InterVarsity Press, 2003), pp. 20-21 and 350-352.

[6] Moreland and Craig, p. 21.

[7] Moreland and Craig, p. 21.

[8] Alvin Plantinga, "Methodological Naturalism? Part One: Is Science Religiously Neutral? Three Examples," The Faculty-Staff Christian Forum at the University of California Santa Barbara, retrieved from http://id-www.ucsb.edu/fscf/library/plantinga/mn/MN1.html.

[9] Ibid.

[10] Ibid.

[11] Ibid.

[12] Ibid.

[13] Stanley L. Jaki, "From Scientific Cosmology to a Created Universe," in Roy Abraham Varghese, ed., *The Intellectuals Speak Out About God* (Chicago: Regnery, 1984), p. 62.

[14] Plantinga, "Methodological Naturalism, Part One."

[15] This isn't a book about apologetics, but footnote readers need some reward, so here in a tiny nutshell are some of the reasons offered for the existence of evil: God created mankind with free will, and the ability to choose means that some will choose evil and cause others or themselves pain. The existence of sin in the world, since the fall, requires punishment to bring about cosmic justice. The earth is under a curse since the fall and suffers together with mankind. Good comes from evil (punishment for rehabilitation), and the human soul is shaped, and this shaping is the true purpose of life on earth—a preparation for the next life. Evil may be necessary to prevent a worse evil: A limited evil may produce a greater good. Some evil is a mystery to our limited understanding, but we trust that God, being perfect, has a good reason to allow any evil that occurs. The problem of evil is a fas-

cinating and crucially important subject in philosophy and theology, partly because it is used by atheists to attack theism.

[16] Kenneth O. Gangel, "Integrating Faith and Learning: Principles and Process," *Bibliotheca Sacra* (April-June 1978), p. 100. Retrieved from http://www.ici.edu/journals/bibsac/7584/78b1.htm.

[17] William Hasker, "Faith-Learning Integration: An Overview," *Christian Scholars Review* 21:3 (March 1992), 231-248. Retrieved from http://www.gospelcom.net/cccu/journals/csr/hasker.html.

[18] Quoted in Kenneth D. Boa and Robert M. Bowman, Jr., *Faith Has Its Reasons: An Integrative Approach to Defending Christianity* (Colorado Springs: NavPress, 2001), p. 99.

[19] Robert E. Rector, Kirk A. Johnson, and Lauren R Noyes, "Sexually Active Teenagers Are More Likely to Be Depressed and to Attempt Suicide," A Report of the Heritage Center for Data Analysis, The Heritage Foundation, June 2, 2003, p. 1. Retrieved from http://www.heritage.org/Research/Family/cda0304.cfm.

[20] Ibid., p. 5.

[21] Quoted in Boa and Bowman, *Faith Has Its Reasons*, p. 100.

[22] Stanley Greidanus, "The Use of the Bible in Christian Scholarship," *Christian Scholar's Review* 11:2 (March 1982), pp. 138-147, reprinted in *Discipleship and the Disciplines: Enhancing Faith-Learning Integration*, Coalition for Christian Colleges and Universities, 1996. Unit 4, p. 22.

[23] Ibid., p. 22.

[24] Hasker, op. cit.

[25] Alvin Plantinga, "Advice to Christian Philosophers," *Truth Journal*. Retrieved from http://www.leaderu.com/truth/1truth10.html.

Chapter 11
A Taxonomy for Worldview Integration

[I]t is time for Christian scholars and thinkers seeking to pene-
trate and transform culture to formulate incisive critiques of
assumptions that are accepted in their fields and to treat im-
portant subjects in ways that are informed by a decidedly
Christian understanding.
　　　　　— Michael Peterson[1]

The philosophy of these respective disciplines is not theologi-
cally neutral. Adoption of presuppositions consonant with or
inimical to orthodox Christian theism will have a significant
leavening effect throughout that discipline which will, in turn,
dispose its practitioners for or against the Christian faith.
　　　　　— J. P. Moreland and William Lane Craig[2]

11.1 The Integrative Challenge

The purpose of this chapter is to provide you with some
guidelines for understanding knowledge claims in their theoretical and philosophical context so that you will be able to
compare their ontological and epistemological foundations
with those of the Christian worldview. By asking about the
purpose of various knowledge claims and by discovering how
those claims are expressive of a worldview or attitude, you
will be better able to evaluate them for important qualities like
credibility, accuracy, reasonableness, and fairness.

The process of integration is made much less difficult once
you learn to hold new ideas at arm's length and examine them
before deciding to incorporate them into your own understanding of truth. The discussion in this chapter offers some
strategies that will enable you to do the following:

- **Contextualize the knowledge claim** to get a larger picture about where the claim (fact claim, theory, principle, conclusion) is coming from, and what philosophical or ideological context it belongs to. There is no better aid to understanding than the ability to stand back and see how an idea fits into the "big picture." (That's why a knowledge of various worldviews is so important.)

- **Identify the foundations underlying the claim.** These foundations include disciplinary assumptions, personal biases, pre-theoretical commitments (such as metaphysical preferences), axioms, even, as Francis Bacon called them, "idols of the tribe": the influence of human nature, psychology, and sociological factors on what and how we believe.[3]

- **Seek alternate approaches, interpretations, and claims.** Live the controversy! Find out who supports and who opposes a given idea or theory or claim, and what the reasons and evidence show. Do some research beyond the reading list for the course and see what other books, articles, Web sites, and other information sources address this issue. The operative wisdom here is Proverbs 18:17: "The first to plead his case seems right, until another comes and examines him."

Fact and Interpretation. In his article, "Faith-Learning Integration: An Overview," William Hasker says that the process of integration may include different questions and issues for different disciplines, depending on whether the discipline is a theoretical one (such as literature, history, political science, and philosophy) or an applied one (such as chemistry, physics, engineering, and medicine).[4] This distinction is useful, since the more theoretical the work in a disciplinary area, the more the likelihood that worldview assumptions will color the disciplinary content. However, remember that many, if not most, disciplines combine both theoretical and applied features. Especially in the social sciences (sociology, psychology, anthropology) theoretical concerns combine with practical experiments to shape area content. It is not usually the practical side of the discipline that proves problematic. As George Marsden notes, Christian scholars recognize that their unique perspective "will not be apparent in the technical dimensions of their work, but . . . the implications of the faith may sometimes have an important bearing on their theories and interpretations."[5] Elsewhere Marsden states,

> In the corridors of the pragmatic academy Christians and non-Christians can readily share basic standards of evidence and argument. These standards work in separating good arguments from bad, and on many topics they can establish a sort of "public knowledge" that persons from many ideological sub-communities can agree on and which are not simply matters of opinion.[6]

That said, caution is still in order when you are faced with what are purported to be plain facts. Shared standards do not necessarily mean shared agreement, even over what a fact is. Do the propositions or knowledge claims you are presented with represent real history or sociology or science, or are they philosophical statements *about* history or sociology or science?

Submerged Assumptions. A further complication facing the contextualizer is that the assumptions, beliefs, and values behind a knowledge claim or even an entire theory are often not explicitly articulated, either because they are unrecognized as assumptions (rather than, say, established facts), or because they are considered axiomatic. If you ask about the underlying presuppositions, those advancing the idea may even feel threatened because your question will imply that you do not share the same set of beliefs. There is a large amount of what Alvin Plantinga has called "as-we-now-knowism,"[7] the pronouncement of conclusions, interpretations, sometimes even wishful thinking as if they were facts so well established that "we all now know" their truth and cogency. There is often an attitude of "everyone thinks this or agrees with this. It isn't a 'view.' It's reality." It follows then that anyone who dares to disagree is somehow irrational or impervious to knowledge. And yet, the questioning of assumptions is supposed to be one of the foundational principles of better investigation and closer reasoning.

Integration as a Moving Target. A substantial challenge facing those who wish to construct a stable, integrated world-view that includes both faith commitments and disciplinary studies is that disciplinary knowledge (1) is constantly changing as new information and ideas rise to prominence, (2) involves internally conflicting claims or alternative schools of thought, and (3) is subject to methodological and interpretive weaknesses that sometimes produce wrong results. And as we have seen in earlier chapters, sometimes these wrong results are accepted as valid for many years before being rejected. The challenge, then, is not just whether to accept or reject a claim, but when, how, how long, in what part, and so on. The advice given at the beginning of this book, to learn and then file away some types of problematic or confusing information without either accepting or rejecting it, is sometimes the best option.

Selection and Spin. There are about 150,000 books published each year in the United States (and about 130,000 others go out of print). There are more than 8,000 medical journals alone, to say nothing of other subjects. Obviously, someone has to do some selecting of the information you will be learning. So the question is sometimes, "Integration with what?" How full a picture of the discipline are you getting? Should you attempt to interconnect your faith with your professor's latest lecture, with the textbook's claims, with the "sense" of the discipline?

Professors tend to select books that reflect their points of view. There is nothing wrong with that. It becomes a problem only when a limited number of points of view are represented by the faculty (such as half postmodern and half naturalistic or all politically to the left) or when the professor pretends that this point of view is the only one or the only acceptable one. Whatever the current issues on campus, you may be on your own if you want to know what other viewpoints exist. (If your course has five required books, all from the same viewpoint, be careful to find some alternatives, especially if the viewpoint appears to be controversial.)

To help avoid the problem of distortion by selection, you should get a broader and more complete view of the claims presented, especially if they appear to conflict with Biblical knowledge. Search for other interpretations. Find out what has been omitted or neglected or perhaps presented in an unfair way. Search the Web to see what's available. A handy trick is to enter your subject, followed by the word *controversy*, and see what you get. For example, go to Google or your favorite search engine and type in *sapir whorf controversy*. Do a literature search with an online database of professional journal articles. Use the library to find some books related to the issue in question. Take a proactive stand toward information.

Recognizing worldviews and their ideological children will help you with the process of integration also. Is there a Marxist, feminist, postmodern, or antireligious spin to the information? Once you are able to recognize such practices, you'll be on the way to an easier process of knowing just how to interpret and handle those knowledge claims.

The naïve view is that we are all coming from the same place when we make claims about truth or reality or knowledge. Now you have the tools to understand that there is a variety of ontological sets (views of what is real), epistemologies (views of what constitutes knowledge, truth, rationality), social knowledge pressures (group practices and assumptions and methodologies), and political biases or ideologies (political agendas and pre-theoretical commitments) all driving interpretation and belief. And unfortunately, many findings are flawed even by their own methodological and interpretive standards. As books like *False Prophets* and *Studies Show* reveal, poor statistical analyses and poor experimental design are not so rare as we could hope.[8]

The questions in the following sections can be applied to individual studies, knowledge claims, theories, schools of thought, or sometimes entire disciplines. For the sake of efficiency, rather than repeat all of these possibilities over and over, I've usually continued to use the term *knowledge claim* to cover everything, though I sometimes use *theory* or *idea*.

By clarifying these issues, you will be able not only to understand the subject matter better but proceed with the task of integration more effectively.

11.2 Worldview

By now you've come to understand what an important influence one's worldview has on the discovery, belief, and expression of ideas. So an obvious first question to ask of any knowledge claim is, "What is the worldview of the source?" In identifying the worldview of the source of a knowledge claim, there is good news and bad news. The good news is that there are actually a very limited number of worldviews.[9] In fact, nearly everything you will read or hear can be divided into three broad categories: the Christian worldview, philosophical naturalism or materialism, and what philosopher Alvin Plantinga calls "creative anti-realism,"[10] which includes our academic friends the postmodernists, as well as existentialism, relativism, the smorgasbord theology of New Age, and several others. The bad news is that, as Plantinga says,

> These three main perspectives or total ways of looking at man and the world can be found in every conceivable and inconceivable sort of combination and mixture. There are many crosscurrents and eddies and halfway houses; people think and act in accordance with these basic ways of looking at things without being at all clearly aware of them, having at best a sort of dim apprehension of them.[11]

Just as an example, postmodernist influences have become pervasive in the culture, while many people have not been consciously aware of that fact. Statements like, "That may be true for you but not for me," reflect the postmodernist belief in the relativity of truth. Even some Christians have embraced certain postmodernist ideas, such as the rejection of reason and argument in evangelism. Those apologists who still think reason is a valuable tool are accused of being "stuck in the failed project of modernism."

Instead of attempting to pigeonhole a professor or a knowledge claim or even a discipline as naturalist or postmodernist (or Christian if you attend a Christian university), look for influences, aspects, and tendencies that may be significant if they skew the interpretation or claim. And remember too, that many professors are faddish and like to pick up ideas and vocabulary[12] that they perceive to be on the cutting edge. So you may find a professor using the vocabulary of an ideology without necessarily embracing its entire philosophy.

11.3 Purpose and Focus

What is the purpose for making this knowledge claim? Does it solve a problem? Why was this particular problem identified (1) as a problem and (2) as important enough to address? Problems are selected from an almost infinite number of possible ones. Pay attention to problem selection. Why just this one rather than another? Are there worldview implications behind this? And what about solutions? Is the set of possible or acceptable solutions constrained in some way (by ideology, theory, politics, bias)? Are some solutions ruled out from the start?

Is the selection limited? Mere selection of a problem because one finds it interesting is normal and is done by everyone. A distortion can occur, however, if most of the practitioners in the field (or department) have the same or similar interests and philosophies because then some areas get ignored. Remember the social influences on practices. What gets researched and the conclusions that are permitted can be influenced by the scholarly community, local or general. If everyone in the economics department is interested in showing the evils of globalization or the benefits of globalization, then important knowledge will be ignored, downplayed, or not discovered. The danger of distortion forms another argument for true diversity at the university — diversity of political, philosophical, and theological commitments.

Is there an agenda? A more serious risk to true knowledge occurs when the singularity of purpose turns into tendentiousness, or "agenda scholarship" (an oxymoron if there ever was one). Agenda scholarship occurs when knowledge claims are made, accepted, or rejected based on ideological concerns. As we have seen in the discussion of political correctness, there is a predefined right answer rather than an open search for the truth wherever it may lead.

The question to ask then, is "Does the purpose of the scholarship appear to be reasonable and objective or is there an agenda behind it?" An agenda might be one of self interest, such as a tobacco company funding a study that will show that smoking is not harmful, or it might be ideological, such as the desire to prove or disprove something with moral implications. Is there a difference between the stated purpose and actual practice?

Phillip Johnson offers an example of the effect of ideology on science. In June of 2000, President Clinton made an announcement regarding a milestone in the human genome project, saying that "today, we are learning the language in which God created life." Several scientists rejected this reference to God, one of them saying that such comments would "give more ammunition to creationists to further their destructive social and political agenda." Phillip Johnson observes:

> The scientist did not say what that destructive agenda is, but by raising this objection he implied the possibility that biologists may reject the concept of design in biology because they dislike the possible religious, political, or moral implications rather than because their data compel that conclusion. In that case, the rest of us may wonder where biologists got the idea that they should have authority over religion, politics, and morality. . . .[13]

Agenda scholarship can be combined with the postmodern lack of respect for truth and accuracy, sometimes devolving into the use of questionable knowledge claims as morality tales. These tales continue to be repeated because they reinforce preferred beliefs or values. A striking example is the claim that in the United States, "about 150,000 females die of anorexia each year."[14] This shocking statistic makes a great morality tale, because these girls are, according to Naomi Wolf, "starved not by nature but by men." Professor Joan Brumberg states that "these disorders are an inevitable consequence of a misogynistic society that demeans women. . . ." The figure has been quoted by everyone from Ann Landers to college textbooks, because as Carol Iannone remarks about the general atmosphere of women as victims, "It is almost as if feminism had finally discovered a problem that can unite all women across all barriers: the existence of men."[15]

Philosophy professor Christina Hoff Sommers investigated this claim and learned that the American Anorexia and Bulimia Association had said that an estimated 150,000 people *suffer from* anorexia. The annual number of fatalities in the United States is about 100. A hundred deaths is not good news, but it fails to offer the same shock value to use in connection with the anti-men philosophy that the much larger number does.

(In passing, we should note how often incorrect facts get transferred from source to source and textbook to textbook. We've already seen some of this, such as the peppered moth story, in science. Jonathan Wells' book *Icons of Evolution* discusses how ten common false or distorted ideas have passed from text to text in the area of evolutionary theory. This failure to check facts and sources makes the testing of knowledge claims all the more difficult. Corroboration is one of the tests of truth, but how can we apply this test when several sources may contain the same error?)

The extent of agenda scholarship in this anti-male area can be seen by other, similar false stories that have rapidly made the rounds. The claim that "domestic violence is the leading cause of birth defects" passed through many media outlets. But the claim was simply not true. The original source had said that at the March of Dimes, many more women are screened for birth defects than are screened for domestic battery. The two were not connected in any way, other than being in the same sentence.[16] Similarly false is the highly popularized claim that the expression *rule of thumb* "originated from English common law, which allowed a husband to beat his wife with a whip or stick no bigger in diameter that his thumb."[17] As a quick trip to a phrase dictionary or the Oxford English Dictionary will show, *rule of thumb* actually refers exactly to what you would guess, the use of the thumb as a rough and ready measure, either of length or of temperature (brewers tested the brew while it cooked by dipping in their thumbs), or as a metaphorical rule, as in "As a rule of thumb, we use six parts sand to one part cement."

Agenda scholarship, then, can distort or even invent knowledge claims in order to advance an ideology. Claims that seem especially outrageous should be viewed with skepticism and investigated thoroughly.

11.4 Assumptions

What are the pre-theoretical commitments, the basic beliefs, values, and assumptions behind the theory or research or the commitment to the theory? Discovering assumptions can be difficult for two reasons. First, as mentioned above, much of the time assumptions are not expressed. The nature of assumptions is to leave them in the background: agreement with the assumptions is often seen as a given. The elaborate sets of assumptions behind worldviews such as naturalism and postmodernism are often understood as simply part of reality. After all, no one begins the discussion of information by saying, "Now, what follows assumes that the external world is real, that you actually exist independent of me, that your reason is capable of drawing reliable inferences . . ." and so on. Assumptions, by their very nature of being taken for granted, are usually not expressed. And in most cases many of the assumptions made by those making knowledge claims are shared by their audience. The difficulty arises when some of those assumptions are controversial or not shared by members of the audience. The assumptions, perhaps thought to be universal, are accepted by only a certain school of thought or by a particular worldview.

A second factor that makes the identification of assumptions difficult is that those who come to the table with new knowledge claims may themselves not be aware of (all of) the assumptions behind their work and conclusions. As George Marsden notes, "Many scholars are oblivious to the first principles that they take for granted when they are initiated into contemporary scholarly communities."[18] The assumptions have become part of the methodology and interpretive structure of their work, unnoticed in the background. In such a case, should you ask the presenter to identify his or her assumptions, you may get only a partial list. If you ask, "But aren't you assuming that X is the case?" you may receive a blank look or a negative answer, though you may be correct after all. If the underlying assumptions conflict with Biblical truth, then the conclusion based on those assumptions will be in doubt. It is possible to derive correct conclusions from incorrect assumptions, but less likely than if the assumptions are correct.

Assumptions are so powerful because by being left unstated, they remain unexamined while at the same time they control to some extent the direction and outcome of research.

Assumptions about the realm of knowledge. First, how does the discipline define knowledge and thus circumscribe or limit it? Recall the early questions we asked, such as, "Who gets to say what knowledge is important?" More pointedly, "Who gets to say what knowledge *is*?" A common way to support one claim is to rule others off the table, to deny their status as genuine or possible knowledge.

Second, what is being assumed about the sources of knowledge? Which sources are endorsed as producers of knowledge and which are denied approval? Another way to phrase this is to ask, "What is the controlling epistemology here?" Here your knowledge of epistemology comes into play. Is the identification of some claim as knowledge being controlled by a particular methodology? Is that methodology appropriate?

Assumptions about the definition of truth. Does the knowledge claim assume that truth exists in an objective way? Is the claim intended to be taken as true in a relative, local, or universal way? A question to ask might be, "Would you describe that claim as true, and if so, could you define your idea of truth for me?" Answers such as, "Truth comes from scientific proof," or "Truth is culture bound," will let you know the epistemological assumptions being made about the source of truth.

Is truth an ideal or merely a product of power? Do the writers put sneer quotes around the word?

Related to the definition of truth is the attitude toward it or its ultimate value. Is truth the highest value, or can truth be subordinated to more important concerns (such as persuasion, a morality tale, an agenda, or political correctness)?

Assumptions about the view of human nature. What assumptions about human nature seem to underlie the knowledge claim? Is mankind basically good, evil, deterministic, socially constructed? Does the claim imply that human nature can change, that mankind is perfectible, or that we are fallen, sinful creatures in need of supernatural redemption? What are the assumptions relating to free will versus determinism? Is there an assumed purpose in life or does the claim rest on an assumption of meaninglessness?

How does the particular assumption about humankind affect the interpretations and conclusions of the source? Especially in the humanities and social sciences, the issue of the "nature of human nature" is crucial for understanding the studies, arguments, and analyses you will encounter. But in the sciences also, the source of the reigning belief that human beings are simply accidentally developed mechanistic beings, the idea that life lacks transcendence or higher meaning informs the ideas and interpretations of data. As we saw in earlier chapters, the desire to believe in life as merely material and accidental is almost an agenda among many scientists.

Therefore, *if there is a single key to the whole enterprise of integration, it is the question, "What is mankind?"* What does it mean to be human? For in the answer to this question, all other questions are included: the existence of God; the possibility of sin; the need for salvation; our responsibility to our creator; the source of supreme authority; the kinds of solutions that are acceptable—or even workable—for treating crime, poverty, and other social ills; and so on. Find out how the professor, textbook, discipline, paper, or study views human beings and human nature, and you will have the key insight you need. This is true for any worldview.

Assumptions about good and evil, morals and values. What is the view about the source and objectivity of moral rules? Are the concepts of good and evil criticized as naïve or dated in light of relativism or determinism? Are values and behavioral standards seen as local and temporary or even meaningless?

The followers of the antimetaphysical worldviews of naturalism and postmodernism might be thought to lack moral principles because they deny a transcendent reality and a theological basis for values. However, anyone familiar with such folks knows how angrily moralistic they can be. Thomas Sowell even refers to some of them as sanctimonious,[19] because they seem to have a strong sense of moral superiority. At any rate, professors often have a strong sense about what is right and wrong—or better, just and unjust—and are constantly on the lookout for what they believe are signs of oppression, intolerance, and the like. The problem, of course, is that neither the naturalist nor the postmodernist has a stable grounding for such beliefs. If we have evolved by random mutations and our very thoughts are determined by our brain chemistry, or if we are socially constructed slaves to our own cultures, then there is no foundation for objective moral claims. Morality can be based only on consensus, utility, or power.

When I was a graduate student, some books began to disappear from the department library, so the faculty decided to take away the graduate students' keys. We naturally protested that we were all being convicted without evidence, and I wrote an open letter to the faculty saying that the new policy punished graduate students "while allowing the faculty to sin on." Using the word *sin* in a secular university caused quite an uproar, because it implied divine accountability. Similarly, a friend of mine, in a secular law school, once made the comment in class that a prison term for a certain person was "just punishment for his evil deeds." The resulting uproar was not over my friend's agreement with the punishment, but with his use of the word *evil*.

The question, then, is not whether the ideas concur with our theological concepts of good and evil, but what the source of moral judgments is. How is the idea morally informed? What is the basis for moral pronouncements or claims about justice and injustice? Whenever there is an expressed or implied sense of injustice, justice, right, wrong, or the support of morally based ideals like tolerance, kindness, empathy, etc. there is some moral appeal. The question then arises, what is the basis for this appeal? What is the standard? How does that standard compare with Biblical standards? What are the moral and spiritual consequences of the idea or practice or method?

While it may be true that discussions about values or implying values are more common in the humanities and social sciences, they are present in the sciences as well. The claim that science has separated fact from values is simply not true, either in actual practice (where values inform judgments about what to study or the meaning of data, for example), or in issues related to practice. As George Marsden says, "On the larger questions of life, empirical science is not competent to provide definitive answers, so academia is ruled largely by secular sects motivated by political interests. The idea that reliance on empirical scientific models will eliminate sectarianism is simply false."[20] A politico-secular value system is still a value system.

11.5 Methods

How is the discipline (or the individual study, book, or idea) conducted? What are the methodological rules for discovering new knowledge or for interpreting the discovered knowledge? How do these methodological constraints affect the outcomes of the process?

The Rules of Interpretation and Evidence. As we have seen, it is not the facts but the interpretation of the facts (and sometimes the judgment about what really is a fact) that lies at the heart of the integrative challenge. The facts do not interpret themselves, but are subject to worldview orientations, social factors, consensus and power relationship issues, and sometimes even political correctness. The question, "Where is the evidence permitted to lead?" upsets some people, but if you look closely, you'll see that sometimes politics or ideology trumps the pursuit of truth for its own sake.

For example, journalist Clifford May writes that "when I was a *New York Times* correspondent in Africa in the mid-1980s, it was politically incorrect even to suggest" that Africa was failing, because those "in American universities and liberal think tanks" insisted the African nations were "making progress, and that it bordered on the racist to suggest otherwise."[21] The problems, of course, had nothing to do with race but were, May says, the result of "the legacy of socialism," but that, too, is a politically incorrect claim, especially because it was some of the same people in the universities and think tanks who had recommended socialism over capitalism to the post-independence African leaders.[22] So the reporting was either that there were no problems of note or that what problems did exist were the result of "the legacy of colonialism," a more acceptable (more politically correct) interpretation.

The Role of Authority. Enormous insight into the mindset of both contemporary scholarship and popular culture can be gained by studying the attitudes toward and the perceived role of authority. To some extent, we all still live in an environment shaped by the nineteenth-century romantic rebellion against authority, and its subsequent exaltation of the individual. Rebellion against rules, norms, and values and the embracing of narcissism are only one result. In the academy, the influence of nineteenth and twentieth century French intellectuals, whose favorite pastime has been attacking symbols of restraint and authority (the state, the bourgeoisie, God) has been substantial, especially in the humanities and social sciences. And don't forget that Marx's original claim about the success of communism was that the government would wither away, leaving an anarchic utopia.

A first question here, then, is, "Is there an anti-authority bias at the bottom of this knowledge claim?" One clue to the answer might be the confusion—or deliberate equation—by the writer or speaker between authority and authoritarianism. It is popular among some academics now to label any suggestion of moral restraint as fascist. Any hint of authority is immediately decried as authoritarian, oppressive, dictatorial, even totalitarian.

A second point to be made about the authority issue is that even though there may be a general hostility toward the idea of authority in the academy, most scholars have clear allegiances to authority figures in their own discipline. We have already mentioned how the famous names in postmodernist literary theory are cited and fawned over. There is a definite pecking order among scholars, institutions, and journals, reflecting a marked deference to those identified as authorities. Moreover, many academics are quite willing to use their own authority or power to advance their own agendas and inhibit the agendas of those they oppose. And many of these same academics favor coercive government programs in areas of social engineering that they approve.

A final question here, then, is, "Who or what has the authority to make pronouncements about what is true in this area?" That is, are some ideas ignored or rejected based on an appeal to authority rather than an appeal to evidence?

The Attitude Toward Inference and Reason. There is a debate among Christians about the role and power of reason. Take a look at any good book on apologetics and you'll see that some approaches view reason as more powerful or more limited than others.[23] In general, though, the Christian worldview supports the use of reason as a useful tool, and shares that attitude with the adherents of naturalism. Postmodernists, as we have seen, usually view reason as a language game.

A first question to ask about the school of thought or knowledge claim is, "What attitude toward inference and reason does it reflect?" Is it admittedly arbitrary and subjective, or does it attempt to use reason to find a justified position? Is reason viewed as a shameful perpetuation of male oppression which has no role in legitimate discourse, or is it viewed as only one of many forms of thinking? Is reason exalted as the only way to truth?

If reason is denied epistemological value, then the knowledge claim arising from such a philosophical environment must be questioned, because admittedly subjective or emotional claims remain matters of opinion or feeling. If reason is supported as a tool in the pursuit of truth, the second question that must be asked is, "What is a rational conclusion?" In other words, what does the source believe about the nature of reason and rationality? Because our standard of measurement is Biblical rationality, claims must be assessed according to that standard in order to determine their coherence with the Christian worldview.

11.6 Origins

For the subject matter in your major, take the time to look into the sources of the current and historical development of the discipline. Disciplinary knowledge is not tested or judged on the basis of its origins or sources, for it is judged on its correspondence to reality and Biblical truth. At the same time, an understanding of the origins of a discipline can provide context and understanding of the movements, motives, directions, conflicts, varied schools and claims, how issues were resolved, and so forth. All this knowledge will enable you to gain a wider perspective of the discipline.

Beginning. Where did the discipline come from? Did it branch off another discipline? If so, why? Were its origins the result of knowledge seeking or a philosophical dispute of some sort? Were there early agendas revealed in the beginning of the discipline? Have these affected its development? Who were the discipline's founders? Was there more than one early thread? Did those threads combine or were some cut off? Which ideas that were prominent at the beginning still continue and which are now forgotten or ignored?

History. What theories replaced others during the development of the discipline's ideas and why? Were the replacements the result of compelling evidence and argument or the outcome of political battles and power struggles? Don't always accept a textbook's account of the history of the discipline, for it may have been sanitized and normalized. Find out what the controversies were and how disagreements were negotiated.

A minor example is the discovery of the Kanam jaw, a bone fossil found by Louis Leakey in 1932. While it is now considered "probably human" or "enigmatic," over the years of controversy surrounding it "scientists have attributed the Kanam jaw to almost every known hominid (*Australopithecus, Australopithecus boisei, Homo habilis*, Neanderthal man, early *Homo sapiens*, and anatomically modern *Homo sapiens*)" thus showing "the difficulties involved in properly classifying hominid fossil remains."[24]

Often, once consensus is reached, the losing schools of thought are omitted or depreciated (as the saying is, "History is written by the victors"). Find out what happened during the development of the discipline.

Biography. Study the biography and worldview of the important figures in the discipline. What are their philosophical commitments, their attitudes (toward, say, truth, God, human nature, etc.)? Remember that one's philosophical commitments can have a profound influence on one's intellectual endeavors. Find out what philosophy guided John Dewey or Max Weber or Alfred Kinsey or Michel Foucault.

Note. It would be wrong to criticize or reject an idea because of its origin. To do so would be to commit a logical fallacy known as the genetic error. Atheists and evil people can have good ideas or discover truth just as others can. The point of learning about the advocates of various theories is not to reject the theory on the basis of an unseemly biography, but to give you insight into their worldview, to illuminate and explain why they may have preferred to develop certain ideas rather than others, and to discover the reasons behind their emphases. You may also conclude that their philosophical commitments did indeed distort their conclusions, or at least that their ideas are built on a worldview hostile to Christianity.

At least as important as studying the biographies of disciplinary practitioners who were antagonistic to Christianity is the question of early and even current practitioners who share Christian faith. Reading the works of Christian scholars in your area (even if they date back awhile) can give you ideas and alternative approaches that will help you with your own process of integration. Learn how they integrated their faith with their discipline. Many of the currently respected figures in many disciplines thought and wrote in the nineteenth or even eighteenth century, so don't be shy about locating some early figures who, while they may now be ignored, contributed some profitable ideas before they were marginalized by the current outlook. What current Christian scholars are writing in your area? How do they integrate faith and discipline?

11.7 Implications for Integration

If you look back over the taxonomy presented in this chapter, with its discussion of worldview, purpose and focus, assumptions, the role of authority, etc., you'll see that the heart of integration is not the matching or contrasting a particular Biblical passage with a particular fact claim. The heart of integration, says Sidney Greidanus, involves making "the connection between the Bible and scholarship . . . in terms of *the biblical framework of reality*."[25] The so-called culture wars are also scholarship wars, where values are in conflict and where these conflicts are frequently expressed in scholarly pursuits. The culture wars are values wars, with theological overtones.

For this reason, it is all the more important for Christians to apply a holistic approach to faith and knowledge, using faith to inform every aspect of the "framework of reality." We criticize the reductionism of the naturalists, yet if we do not take the steps to extend faith to all of life, we too are being reductionists of a different sort, a sort that is likely also lead to wrong belief. William Hasker says,

> To compartmentalize one's faith in one part of one's mind, one's scholarly discipline in another part, and to put one's business and civic concerns in yet other compartments is in effect to deny God's lordship over all of life. To do this brings several very real dangers. At a minimum, the failure to integrate means that one will lack the enrichment of an overall, unifying perspective by which to connect, unify, and comprehend all of what is known and experienced. It is also likely to mean that, in various respects, one will accept without question positions, viewpoints, and methods which are in serious tension or outright conflict with one's faith. The divided thinking which results can be a source of considerable discomfort for a reflective individual, and in some cases may even undermine one's faith. It also contributes to the impression, which in our day is extremely widespread, that Christian faith is essentially a purely private matter which has no bearing on the day-to-day business of life. To love God with all our minds requires that we try to think in a single, unified pattern all the truth he has enabled us to grasp.[26]

Finally, a word of encouragement. In spite of the use of knowledge as a weapon and of many scholars with agendas of various kinds (some of them deliberately anti-Christian), and in spite of the spiritual warfare we must fight against the forces of falsehood, we nevertheless have much in common with the adherents of philosophical naturalism (as we saw in the discussion of ontology) and with the practical lives of postmodernists, who are sometimes interested in reason far beyond their philosophical stands. Even where they err, we have much to learn from them. While one of the goals of these chapters is to make you cautious about knowledge claims, you should not become paralyzingly skeptical and reject everything. Learn even what you cannot assent to as true or correct. And make the effort to test the claims where you can.

Summary

There are several methods for approaching the backgrounds and sources of knowledge claims, both philosophically and historically, in order to help you determine their credibility or test their factual content. Whether stemming from agenda scholarship or simply a worldview preference, knowledge claims are often not neutral in their construction or intended effect.

Questions for Thought and Discussion

1. How does the issue of "the nature of human nature" impact the content of your own major or discipline? What is the prominent view of human nature in your field?

2. What are the moral values supported by your discipline and what is their basis? (An example of a moral value would be tolerance or justice.) Are there any traditional (or Judeo-Christian) moral values that are criticized by your discipline or some of its practitioners? Does the choice of values influence scholarship in this area? If so, how?

3. What "basic standards of evidence and argument" do you share with your major or discipline? Are there any other standards that conflict with your Christian worldview?

4. Which areas of your major or discipline to do you find the easiest to integrate with your faith and which do you find most problematic? Explain why.

---

[1] Michael L. Peterson, *With All Your Mind* (Notre Dame: University of Notre Dame Press, 2001), p. 218.

[2] J. P. Moreland and William Lane Craig, *Philosophical Foundations for a Christian Worldview* (Downers Grove, IL: InterVarsity Press, 2003), p. 3.

[3] See Francis Bacon, *The New Organon* (1620; rpt., Indianapolis: Bobbs-Merrill, 1960), pp. 48ff.

[4] William Hasker, "Faith-Learning Integration: An Overview," *Christian Scholars Review* 21:3 (March 1992), pp. 231-248. Retrieved from http://www.gospelcom.net/cccu/journals/csr/hasker.html.

[5] George Marsden, *The Outrageous Idea of Christian Scholarship* (New York: Oxford University Press, 1997), p. 61.

[6] Marsden, p. 47.

[7] Alvin Plantinga, "On Christian Scholarship," The Faculty-Staff Christian Forum at the University of California Santa Barbara, retrieved from http://www.id.ucsb.edu/fscf/library/plantinga/OCS.html.

[8] See especially the discussion of the reliability of published studies in Alexander Kohn, *False Prophets*, rev. ed. New York: Barnes & Noble, 1988), pp. 8-9 and John H. Fennick, *Studies Show: A Popular Guide to Understanding Scientific Studies* (New York: Prometheus Books, 1997).

[9] For a helpful discussion, see Kenneth D. Boa and Robert M. Bowman, Jr., *Faith Has Its Reasons: An Integrative Approach to Defending Christianity* (Colorado Springs: NavPress, 2001), pp. 111-114.

[10] Plantinga, op. cit.

[11] Ibid.

[12] Vocabulary is very faddish. In the 1970's, my professors were always talking about *relevant* and *viable* ideas. In the 1980's, they were always concerned with *bifurcation*. In the 1990's, meaning was always being *unpacked*. And of course, the virtual mantra of *race, class, and gender* pops up like weeds all over the landscape today.

[13] Phillip Johnson, *The Right Questions* (Downers Grove, IL: InterVarsity, 2002), pp. 37, 39.

[14] This and subsequent quotations about this statistic all come from Christina Hoff Sommers, *Who Stole Feminism?* (New York: Simon and Schuster, 1994), pp. 11-13.

[15] Carol Iannone, "Sex and the Feminists," *Commentary* 96:3 (Sept. 1993), p. 52.

[16] Sommers, op. cit., pp. 13-14.

[17] Quoted in Sommers, p. 203. See pp. 203-208 for a full discussion and refutation of the claim.

[18] Marsden, p. 72.

[19] Thomas Sowell, "Morality Vs. Sanctimoniousness," retrieved from http://www.tsowell.com/spmorali.html.
[20] George Marsden, *The Outrageous Idea of Christian Scholarship* (New York: Oxford University Press, 1997), p. 28.
[21] Clifford D. May, "Chaos, Opportunity . . . and Caution in Africa," *Washington Times*, July 6 2003. Retrieved from http://washingtontimes.com/commentary/20030705-111504-3974r.htm.
[22] Ibid.
[23] See, for example, Boa and Bowman, op. cit.
[24] Michael A. Cremo and Richard L. Thompson, *Forbidden Archeology: The Hidden History of the Human Race*, rev. ed., (Los Angeles: Bhaktivedanta Book Publishing, 1998), p. 656.
[25] Sidney Greidanus, "The Use of the Bible in Christian Scholarship," *Christian Scholar's Review* 11:2 (March 1982), pp. 138-147, reprinted in *Discipleship and the Disciplines: Enhancing Faith-Learning Integration*, Coalition for Christian Colleges and Universities, 1996, Unit 4, p. 20.
[26] Hasker, op. cit.

Chapter 12
The Christian Touchstone

*So the central argument here is simplicity itself: as Christians
we need and want answers to the sorts of questions that arise
in the theoretical and interpretative disciplines; in an enormous number of such cases, what we know as Christians is
crucially relevant to coming to a proper understanding; therefore we Christians should pursue these disciplines from a specifically Christian perspective.*
                                    — Alvin Plantinga[1]

*God has given enough evidence of the truth of Christianity
that those who want to know the truth will see it, but He has
not shown Himself in a way that would compel faith in those
who don't care or don't want to believe.*
                    — Kenneth Boa and Robert Bowman, Jr.[2]

12.1 The Dynamics of Integration

Challenge. If you should mention to a non-Christian (professor or student) that one of the goals of your educational life
is to integrate your faith and the learning of the university, the
non-Christian is likely to smile condescendingly and perhaps
call you naïve. And yet, as mentioned at the very beginning of
this book, there is nothing quaint or bizarre or even unusual
about the process of integration itself. Every person is faced
with the task of integrating new ideas and knowledge claims
with currently held knowledge. Knowledge claims that do not
fit in well with currently held knowledge are a challenge for
everyone. Naturalists must integrate the appearance of design
in nature into their worldview committed to an undesigned
world; postmodernists must integrate their often strong moral
stands into a worldview that sees morality as localized and

subjective. Nearly all of us practice a kind of correspondence theory of truth, attempting to match the new information with what we think is already true. Inconsistency, conflict, or incompatibility causes us to work to harmonize or at least understand the problem.

The reason you will be thought naive is that you are attempting to integrate knowledge claims that are new to you with the Christian worldview you are developing rather than with the worldview of the other person. The only way to keep from being criticized is to agree with the worldview of the other person. The scorn of those with differing philosophical foundations is not limited to Christians, by the way. If you want to try an experiment, tell a philosophical naturalist (such as a biology professor) that one of the goals of your education is to integrate his teaching with your postmodernist worldview. Or tell your deconstructionist literature professor that "postmodernism is unscientific." You're likely to get the same response, a "Tsk!" or a critical laugh. But the laugh may not be quite as great as what you'll get if you identify your worldview as Christian.

Thus, a challenge for integration, especially at a secular university, is that you cannot count on the support or guidance of professors with differing worldviews. (Even some Christian professors at Christian universities resist the kind of integrative processes described in this book, preferring such approaches as the "two realms" view.) Instead of support, you may meet resistance.

Ridicule is a very powerful weapon. None of us wants to be made to feel foolish or stupid or both. Ridicule of an opposing or competing idea is a violation of the ideals of a free academy in pursuit of truth, where ideas should stand or fall on the basis of their merit, as discovered through respectful argument and analysis. It is all the more unfortunate, then, to see how commonly this ploy is used to attack opponents. It is designed to amplify the fear of inadequacy felt by those who disagree with an idea or knowledge claim. The purpose is to isolate, demonize, and cut off anyone who does not accept the "correct" view. And ridicule, which involves belittling or diminishment, is intended to render opponents, at least in the eyes of the scorner, as not worthy of serious consideration. An idea you don't have to think about is an idea you don't have to worry about. It's not a threat to your belief system.

If, therefore, you attempt to work out integrative issues in your academic papers or by questions asked in class, expect not just disagreement, but something more emotional.

But don't take the ridicule too personally. Part of the conflict is philosophical and theological, but part of it also comes from the history and nature of scholarship and its practitioners. Those who have built entire careers by promoting a particular theory (and receiving grants to do so, perhaps) are usually loath to view a new, upstart, rival theory with favor.

If you study the history of science or the history of philosophy or literary criticism or any other field, you'll find that one of the constants is the resistance to new ideas. This resistance reflects the difficulty of integration and the tendency humans have to become set in their ways. If a new finding is not automatically compatible with current ideas, then it is usually greeted with hostility. Scientists, who know that science is always in transition and subject to change, should exhibit this phenomenon the least, and yet they often are the most hostile toward threats to the status quo.

Support. At the same time you meet hostility to your integrative project, you should be able to find support in your endeavors among like-minded students, some faculty who will help mentor you, published resources (books, articles, Web sites), pastors, youth leaders, and so on. The pursuit of truth has always been a social endeavor, where ideas are tested and refined in community. Integration as an aspect of the pursuit of truth is the same. Sharing ideas and questions and answers, seeking a better understanding of Scripture, finding alternative arguments and interpretations, integrating new knowledge into your worldview—all of these activities are often better processed in community than individually. Individual reading and thinking are crucial, of course, but they should be supplemented. The basic philosophical (and spiritual) battleground is not new, and many wise and helpful thinkers have trod the same ground before you.

Just in the last twenty or thirty years, there has been an enormous amount of excellent work developing the Christian worldview along many lines. And with the Web, much of that material is at your fingertips. Whether your area of interest is philosophy, apologetics, science, art, literature, or a specific discipline, you'll find resources to help you in building your own worldview.

Response to error. Successful integration poses a problem when you are taking a class presented from an opposing, and in your view, incomplete or incorrect worldview. Now that you have arrived at what you think is at least a tentative, genuine understanding of the truth, how do you approach the conflict this creates with some of the course material itself? That is, do you raise your hand or write in your paper that some of the assumptions behind the data are objectionable, or that some of the interpretations are biased? Or do you "tell the professor what he wants to hear" so that you will not be penalized, either by a lowered brow or a lowered grade? Should you ask those provocative questions listed in Chapter 9, Section 9.6?

I cannot answer this question for you. The answer may depend on your own personality (do you like a lively discussion?) or on the nature of the course. But here are a few questions to help you with your thinking.

- *How willing is the professor to listen to and discuss conflicting theories or alternative ideas, especially those from another worldview?*
- *What do you hope to accomplish if you speak up?* Providing alternative ideas in class and representing the Christian worldview may be helpful for other students who have never heard these things or never heard them clearly and intelligently articulated. On the other hand, putting your criticisms and alternatives in a paper will limit their audience to the professor or the teaching assistant doing the grading.

Based on my own experience traveling through secular universities and observing many professors since then, I'd say that your chance of changing a professor's mind about his or her theoretical (or political!) stand (to say nothing of the underlying ontology and epistemology) is extremely slim. In what may be a realistic assessment, Professor John G. West, Jr. says, "Old errors die hard, and many in the humanities and social sciences will likely cling to their materialist superstitions rather than face the shock of reinventing their disciplines."[3] I think the same could be said for some of the theoretical aspects of the natural sciences.

I would encourage you, however, to be forthright and articulate outside of class — with roommates, fellow students in study groups, in campus publications, in informal interactions. Christian truth has been marginalized and *can be scorned* precisely because it has not often enough been presented by thoughtful persons as a strong, rational, sturdy alternative — a superior alternative — to the tendentious knowledge and agenda scholarship that is presented *as if* there is no reasonable alternative or *as if* disagreement is somehow immoral (or racist, sexist, intolerant, etc.). Christians have for too long been too polite or shy or afraid to present the truth, not in hectoring threats of hellfire or appeals to Scripture (which bears no weight with nonbelievers) but in a calm, reasoned, informed, respectful laying out of the reasons and evidence, at a level and from a perspective that the hearers can work with.

Don't expect instant assent. The stories are myriad of people who responded to "the Christian perspective" with laughter or shouting and anger or a dismissing wave of the hand, but who could not get the cogency of the arguments out of their heads. Words can burn in the heart (the Holy Spirit has quite a blow torch) and bring about change months or even years later. Remember to take the long view. Forget the desire for instant gratification that our culture keeps forcing on us. Plant the seeds and pray hopefully.

Patience. As you work to connect what you are learning with your faith, don't worry about getting every detail correct right from the start or about having an answer to every problem. Feel free to say or think, "I don't know about that yet." Remember that the most important aspect of the integrative process is maintaining a Biblical framework of reality, a standpoint from which to view and eventually evaluate all other reality and knowledge claims. The shifting details and claims you will be handed may change and change again. Be patient as you entertain new ideas and wonder how they might connect with your growing view of truth.

12.2 Christophobia

Christophobia is an irrational fear and often hatred of Christianity and sometimes of Christians individually. It appears to be on the rise in the Western world and accounts for much of the hostility toward the Christian worldview. Among the secularists, and this includes both philosophical naturalists and postmodernists, Christianity is by some now perceived as not just wrong or foolish, but as harmful, an enemy of progress. History is even being rewritten, for example, to remove the role Christians and the Christian worldview have played in the rise of science and to attempt to blame Christianity for inhibiting science.[4] Christophobia has several dimensions, so we can look at just a few here.

The moral dimension. As we saw in the words of Aldous Huxley in Chapter 5, Christianity is often viewed by many as a threat of restraint on their personal behavior, and thus any attempt to empower it is to be opposed. If the Christian worldview rises in status (or worse, influence), then moral constraints might return. At this level, opposition to Christianity is about sexual freedom. Peter Kreeft says that "we cannot win the culture war unless we win the sex war, because sex is the effective religion of our culture, and religion is the strongest force in the world, the strongest motivation there is."[5]

Sex is indeed an important motivator, as you know if you follow the news, where various groups are always demonstrating for various "rights" involving sexual practices and abortion. Robert Knight in *The Age of Consent* says that one analyst "concluded after looking at public policy crusades during the twentieth century," that their "real goal" is "to 'make the world safe for fornication.'"[6] That's probably an exaggeration, but it makes a point.

A. S. A. Jones, a former atheist, powerfully (and bluntly) sums up the thinking behind this dimension of Christophobia:

When I debated as a skeptic, I had no desire to learn from Christians. My only purpose was to try and show them how illogical and absurd their belief in God was. It didn't matter if their arguments made sense. My arguments made sense, too! I was on a mission to destroy faith in God because I perceived Christianity as a direct threat to my individual rights and freedom. I thought that if enough Christians were elected in our government, it would only be a matter of time before the legal system would make us slaves to the morality of the Judeo-Christian religion. This . . . "god" was going to infringe upon my rights to [have sex] . . . with other consenting adults outside of marriage! It was going to force women to carry their babies to term! It was going to demand that I wake up every Sunday morning and attend church, and if I refused, no respectable business in town would have me as an employee. I wasn't interested in any TRUTH! If there was even the smallest possibility that truth would interfere with my all out war against Jesus Christ & Company, I did not want to hear it. I wanted to destroy the enemy.[7]

The political dimension. Obviously, those who fear that Christians might attempt to impose moral restraints on them are afraid of seeing Christians gain any political power. Marvin Olasky notes that

> some from media and academia in recent years have complained whenever Christians they could label as "fundamentalists" have involved themselves in public issues — as if such participation represented either an innovation or a dire threat. The Williamsburg Charter Survey on Religion and Public Life a decade ago found 92 percent of surveyed academics demanding a "high wall of separation" between church and state. One-third even claimed that evangelicals are "a threat to democracy."[8]

Obviously, though, the media and academic Christophobes cannot come out directly and say they want Christians disenfranchised. Instead, they must attack any incipient Christian involvement in public issues as (1) a violation of church and state, (2) intolerant, or (3) coming from extremists, bigots, "the religious right," "fundamentalists," and the like, to create a knee-jerk reaction against any such activity. Questions have been raised about whether Catholics are being blocked from appointment to judicial posts because they oppose abortion.[9] And in the view of one Christian apologist, Christianity is now being "dismissed because of its supposed support of racism, sexism, environmental degradation, and imperialism."[10] As you can see, Christians have a huge public relations problem.

In *Persecution*, a book-length examination of the depth and intensity of Christophobia, David Limbaugh provides many examples of the concerted effort to get Christianity out of the public schools (where Christianity is seen as "intolerably offensive"[11] and the Ten Commandments are called "hate speech"[12]) as well as out of the arena of public discourse and the arts (television, film, music). Limbaugh notes that "secular forces are engaged in a war not to preserve a wall of separation, but rather to radically secularize our society."[13] The kinds of blatant discrimination and intolerance he cites over and over are much more serious than merely renaming Christmas trees to "holiday trees."

And Kenneth Minogue, also commenting on Christophobia, argues that the intellectual elite of the West are engaged in a program he calls Olympianism, the goal of which is to extend rationalism and "appropriate human rights" to non-Western nations. To do so, he says, the West must repudiate Christianity: "The basis of much of the visceral hatred of Christianity today is that it contradicts the ambition to present the West as the source of pure reason and compassion."[14] This is a modernist rather than a postmodernist project, of course, but according to Minogue, it has replaced communism as a new ideal for a world order.

The emotional dimension. Another source of Christophobia is emotional distaste. Christianity complicates our lives with ideas like sin and guilt and the need for repentance. To many moderns and postmoderns, these concepts are "antagonistic to self-esteem."[15] Those who reject Christianity, and particularly Americans who reject Christianity, do so from within a culture steeped in narcissism and extreme individualism, where pride and even arrogance are held up by the entertainment media as model behavior. "I did it my way," sings Frank Sinatra. "You deserve this product," the advertisers tell us,

and then go on to say we should observe "No limits" and "i.
boundaries."

The idea of accountability to God in our anti-authority culture seems repellent. Indeed, I've come to the conclusion that in the face of all the ostensible objections to Christianity—the existence of evil, the harm from the Crusades, the supposed lack of evidence for God, whatever—the true and most fundamental objection lies elsewhere. To my mind, the most challenging requirement, the biggest stumbling block to entering into the Christian worldview for many in the academy is not overcoming these ancient objections. It is not even the problem of belief in God, not belief in the virgin birth, not belief in the deity of Christ, not belief in miracles, not belief in the resurrection. It's that little verse in James: "Humble yourselves in the presence of the Lord, and He will exalt you" (James 4:10). The call to humility is simply sand in the teeth to many people, intellectuals especially.

Apologist John A. Bloom says that "because men may distort data to their seeming advantage, they will tend to obscure any evidence which hints that there is an authority or power greater than themselves, especially one which they cannot control and to which they should be subject."[16] It is only in the rejection of Christianity and its claims of a sovereign God that personal autonomy can be extended to its ultimate limits. Denying God (atheism), ignoring God (agnosticism), being part of the divine (pantheism), or seeking personal spiritual fulfillment (some varieties of Hinduism, Buddhism) are all "better" alternatives to those who want to maintain self-referential spiritual and emotional dimensions to their lives. Here, Christophobia is an emotional reaction to the thought of having to face a personal God.

12.3 The Needed Renaissance

Building a Christian worldview that reflects Biblical authority and a proper understanding of academic subject matter (especially in light of the challenges presented by competing worldviews) has been the focus of this book. But as I hinted in Chapter 10, Section 10.5, we—that is, you and I both—need to go beyond our concerns about personal worldview development and become contributors to the great conversation. We need to take our place in the world of ideas, presenting Christian truth, solutions, values, and meaning to the world as better alternatives than those now being held up for acceptance. To do this task, we need a renewal in Christian intellectual life and scholarship.

Our reticence. Right now, as we have seen, Christian thought lies on the periphery of academic life. And it's partly our fault. J. P. Moreland calls us to action this way:

> Our marginalization and ingrown texture are the result of several decades of academic bullying from the outside and intellectual cowardice or indifference on the inside. . . . [W]e need a renaissance of evangelical statements of and defenses for what we believe about the broad issues being debated in the academy and the broader culture.[17]

In the past, too many of us have failed to connect our faith with our lives and our thinking, and we have inadvertently gone along with worldly patterns. David Fraser says that we have become culturally and intellectually secular:

> More subtle has been ideological secularization: the excluding, ignoring or bracketing out of God's truth and reality in the conduct of thought and life. The real problem here is not a godless congress or faculty, but with intellectually secular Christians (who read their Bibles and say their prayers and then work and live in a way exactly given by their surrounding world).[18]

Moreover, too many Christian professors have pursued essentially secular understandings of their own disciplines, rather than making the attempt to develop Christian approaches. Whether from the effects of graduate school or the desire to be accepted by one's secular colleagues, many Christian professors have not just taught, but adopted as their own, existing models rather than worked to develop new ones. George Marsden, in his *The Outrageous Idea of Christian Scholarship*, points out that "among so many academics who are professing Christians, all but a tiny minority keep quiet about the intellectual implications of their faith." He then asks, "Why are there in mainstream academia almost no identifiable Christian schools of thought to compare with various Marxist, feminist, gay, post-modern, African-American, conservative, or liberal schools of thought?"[19]

Whether the problem is philosophical syncretism (the process of blending ultimately incompatible beliefs) or the intellectual version of the Stockholm syndrome (where the victims bond with their captors to make life psychologically endurable), the first step is to recognize that we have been too hesitant in the past to develop our own worldview and work from its foundation.

Our role. The question, then, is this. If Christianity holds the truth about God as creator, about human nature, about spiritual strivings, and values—areas that deeply impact all scholarship and knowledge—then why have we considered it so little in our academic work? If the Biblical framework of reality does provide the most accurate and truthful picture of the world, why do we not live our intellectual lives as if we really thought so? Why have we allowed ourselves to be intimidated by competing ideas and to do scholarly work that too often mimics that of our secular counterparts?

Nicholas Wolterstorff admonishes us:

> We evangelicals are finally beginning to get it through our heads that we in America do not live in a Christian society. We live in a mixed, pluralistic society in which the body of those committed to Jesus Christ is just one of the components in the pluralism. But at the same time—thank the Lord—we are beginning to get it through our heads that it is unworthy and disobedient for the church in this mixed society to cower in timid silence. It is beginning to recognize that it has a liberating word to speak to that society and a healing hand to extend to it. It may not withhold that word and that hand.[20]

In academic terms, this means that we need to develop, refine, argue for, and apply the Christian worldview in our scholarly pursuits as part of our Christian witness. We are to be proactive and creative in our work, not merely participatory or reactive. As George Marsden puts it, "Scholars who have religious faith should be reflecting on the intellectual implications of that faith and bringing those reflections into the mainstream of intellectual life."[21] Rather than Xeroxing knowledge as found and handing out copies to our community, we should develop "a Christian worldview in contrast to the prevailing outlooks of our day."[22]

And our role is not always to critique or contrast our knowledge of the truth with the claims and ideologies of the day. There are many emerging areas of knowledge and activity that lack a theoretical or philosophical analysis from any worldview. As David Fraser says, "The vast numbers of new specializations bring new questions and problems and lack traditions of humane, ethical or Christian values. Far from confronting an aggressive secularist tradition of thinking, one is likely to encounter bewildering novelty with no interpretive framework whatever."[23] In spite of our culture's fierce individualism and resistance to authority, most people feel a need for some kind of philosophical structure with which they can make sense of the world. In emerging areas like genetic engineering of crops, animal and human cloning, and stem cell research, distinctively Christian thinking needs to be done. And in existing areas like the definition of death, animal rights, and the tension between individual rights and the rights of the community (and individual versus community responsibility), there is much room for a Christian contribution.

12.4 Implications for Integration

As you are probably aware, a touchstone was a hard, dark piece of stone, usually basalt or jasper, that was used to test the purity of precious metals, especially gold. The tester would rub a streak of metal of known purity along the stone and then rub a streak of the metal in question next to it. By comparing the color of the two streaks, the tester could determine whether the unknown metal was really pure or had been debased. This book is a reminder that we need to use our touchstone to test the metals of knowledge that are presented to us.

We must test not only the knowledge claims of others but our own beliefs and the ideas from others in Christendom. As David Fraser reminds us, "We do not a priori possess all truth. Often enough we are ignorant and wrong (non-Christians are themselves characterized by truth and error in their thinking as well)."[24] The route to knowledge and to integration of that knowledge with our faith is the highway of labor. Michael Peterson says, "There is no shortcut to truth. We need to study diligently to refine and modify our findings and to engage in critical dialogue on the truths that we think we have found. It is not easy: the principle of commitment to truth must find its expression in rigorous intellectual activity."[25]

In his "Satire III" about the search for truth, seventeenth century poet John Donne puts it this way:

> . . . on a huge hill,
> Cragg'd and steep, Truth stands, and he that will
> Reach her, about must, and about must go;
> And what the hill's suddenness resists, win so. . . .

In calling for a revitalization of the connection between faith and intellect, the use of the mind as a needed partner in the Christian enterprise, I am certainly not arguing for a purely rationalistic Christianity. I embrace the full nature of our faith: rational, revelational, and relational. I understand the emotional and experiential qualities. As I hope I have made clear in the book, though, we must not neglect the intellectual side of the faith and its encounter with the marketplace of ideas. J. Gresham Machen once noted:

> False ideas are the greatest obstacles to the reception of the gospel. We may preach with all the fervour of a reformer and yet succeed only in winning a straggler here and there, if we permit the whole collective thought of the nation or of the world to be controlled by ideas which, by the resistless force of logic, prevent Christianity from being regarded as anything more than a harmless delusion.[26]

Today, when many view Christianity not as a *harmless* delusion but as a *harmful* one, it is more important than ever to present the redemptive, transformational power of the Christian worldview to a suffering world.

I'm optimistic and hopeful about the possibilities in Christian intellectual life. The process of integration can be highly successful. Our touchstone will enable us to find the valuable ideas from within otherwise limited or erroneous worldviews, and our Biblical framework will enable us to supplement or extend truncated worldviews. Irrational worldviews can be countered with wisdom and intelligence, and ideological views can be exposed. When more and more of the faithful take up the charge of transforming culture and the world of learning, demonstrating that Christianity is more than competitive in the arena of thought, then even those who are now content to dismiss us will be forced to pay attention to our position. And many of those who are open to ideas — ideas and choices they have not heard before, or not heard so well articulated — will come to a knowledge of the one who is truth.

Summary

Especially if you attend a secular university, your work to integrate faith and learning will probably be met with opposition. Even at a Christian university, you may find some resistance. But more and more Christians are coming to understand worldview and integrative issues, and you will find growing support for your efforts. I encourage you to become a seeker and a lover of the truth, in every dimension of life. "God is as deep as you want to go."

Questions for Thought and Discussion

1. Outline the steps you want to take for your future integrative work. That is, what strategy or plan would you like to adopt that will help you as you continue to integrate faith and learning in the coming year(s)? What practical methods seem to appeal the most?

2. In Chapter 2, I half jokingly said, "If you read this book in the way I intend it, you will finish it by committing yourself to getting at least a Ph.D." Has this book influenced your commitment to higher education or your learning goals? If so, in what way? Have you decided to become a member of the Christian intelligentsia? Why or why not?

3. Identify or develop a knowledge contribution you can make to your discipline or major based on your Christian worldview. Depending on your area, this could be an interpretive framework, an experiment, a research topic, a review of the literature, or a theoretical model.

4. Analyze an article, finding, book, or study in your major or discipline from the point of view of worldview identification. Discuss the findings in terms of the Christian worldview. That is, how do the author's assumptions and interpretations interact with the Christian worldview?

---

[1] Alvin Plantinga, "On Christian Scholarship," Retrieved May 7, 2003 from Faculty-Staff Christian Forum at the University of California, Santa Barbara, http://www.id.ucsb.edu/fscf/library/planginga/OCS.html

[2] Kenneth D. Boa and Robert M. Bowman, Jr., *Faith Has Its Reasons: An Integrative Approach to Defending Christianity* (Colorado Springs: NavPress, 2001), p. 37.

[3] John G. West, Jr., "The Death of Materialism and the Renewal of Culture," *Intercollegiate Review* 31:2 (Spring 1996), p. 5.

[4] See "Christophobia," online at http://home.infostations.com/quietsun/athart6.htm.

[5] Peter Kreeft, *How to Win the Culture War* (Downers Grove, IL: InterVarsity Press, 2002), p. 95.

[6] Robert H. Knight, *The Age of Consent: The Rise of Relativism and the Corruption of Popular Culture* (Dallas: Spence Publishing, 1998), pp. 35-36.

[7] A. S. A. Jones, "The Games Skeptics Play," Ex-Atheist.com, retrieved from http://www.ex-atheist.com/7.html.

[8] Marvin Olasky, "Media Christophobia," *World* 17:16 (April 27, 2002). Retrieved from http://www.worldmag.com/world/issue/04-27-02/cover_3.asp.

[9] "Ads Accuse Democrats of Barring Catholics from Bench," *Orange County Register*, July 24, 2003, News 9.

[10] Douglas Groothuis, "Defenders of the Faith," *Books and Culture*, July-August 2003, p. 12.

[11] David Limbaugh, *Persecution* (Washington, D.C.: Regnery, 2003), p. 29.

[12] Ibid., p. 45.

[13] Ibid., p. 234.

[14] Kenneth Minogue, "'Christophobia' and the West," *New Criterion* 21:10 (June 2003), p. 11.

[15] Gary DeLashmutt and Roger Braund, "Postmodern Impact: Education," in Dennis McCallum, ed., *The Death of Truth* (Minneapolis: Bethany House, 1996), p. 119.

[16] Quoted in Kenneth Boa and Robert Bowman, Jr., *Faith Has Its Reasons* (Colorado Springs: NavPress, 2001), p. 186.

[17] J. P. Moreland, "Philosophical Apologetics, the Church, and Contemporary Culture," *Premise* 3:4 (April 29, 1996), p. 6. Retrieved from http://capo.org/premist/96/april/p960406.html.

[18] David Fraser, "Book Summary Notes on David Gill, *The Opening of the Christian Mind: Taking Every Thought Captive to Christ*," in *Discipleship and the Disciplines: Enhancing Faith-Learning Integration*, Coalition for Christian Colleges and Universities, 1996, Unit 1, p. 37.

[19] George Marsden, *The Outrageous Idea of Christian Scholarship* (New York: Oxford University Press, 1997), p. 6.

[20] Nicholas Wolterstorff, "The Mission of the Christian College at the End of the 20th Century," *Reformed Journal* 33:6 (June 1983), pp. 14-18. Reprinted in *Discipleship and the Disciplines: Enhancing Faith-Learning Integration*, Coalition for Christian Colleges and Universities, 1996, Unit 1, p. 16.

[21] Marsden, *Outrageous Idea*, pp. 3-4.

[22] Marsden, "State of Evangelical," p. 20.

[23] Fraser, op. cit., p. 3.

[24] Fraser, op. cit., p. 5.

[25] Michael Peterson, *With All Your Mind: A Christian Philosophy of Education* (Notre Dame: University of Notre Dame, 2001), p. 115.

[26] Quoted in J. P. Moreland and William Lane Craig, *Philosophical Foundations for a Christian Worldview* (Downers Grove, IL: InterVarsity, 2003), p. 2.

Appendix
Useful Web Sites

Here is a selection of Web sites you may find useful in your integrative work. Links to these sites and to other articles and materials related to the integration of faith and learning can be found on the author's Web site: www.virtualsalt.com/int/.

General Worldview Resources

Christian Leadership Ministries
www.clm.org
Faculty ministry of Campus Crusade for Christ.

Doorway Papers
www.custance.org
Books and papers making "connections between scientific re-search and biblical understanding."

Internet Christian Library
www.iclnet.org
Resource guides, books, articles, links.

Leadership University
www.leaderu.com
Search 8000 articles and other resources.

Xenos Christian Fellowship
www.xenos.org
Apologetics, Bible study, courses, downloads.

Periodicals

Books and Culture
www.christianitytoday.com/books/
Articles and reviews on issues relating to Christianity.

BreakPoint Online
www.breakpoint.org
Christian perspective on the news.

Christianity Today
www.christianitytoday.com
News and commentary on Christian life.

First Things
www.firstthings.com
The Journal of Religion and Public Life.

World
www.worldmag.com
Site of weekly newsmagazine from a Christian perspective.

Science

Access Research Network
www.arn.org
Science site with an emphasis on intelligent design theory.

Answers in Genesis
www.answeringenesis.org
Science site with an emphasis on creation science.

Center for Science and Culture
www.discovery.org/crsc/
Site emphasizing intelligent design theory.

Origins.org
www.origins.org
Site emphasizing intelligent design and philosophical theism.

Apologetics

Apologetics.com
www.apologetics.com

Academy of Christian Apologetics
www.hisdefense.org/home2.html

Apologetics.org
www.apologetics.org

Center for Reformed Theology and Apologetics
www.reformed.org

Apologetics Information Ministries
www.apologeticsinfo.org

Christian Answers Net
www.christiananswers.net

Apologetics Index
www.apologeticsindex.org

Christian Apologetics and Research Ministry
www.carm.org

Atlanta Christian Apologetics
www.atlantaapologist.org

Reasons to Believe
www.reasons.org

Bibliography

Adler, Mortimer and Charles Van Doren. *How to Read a Book*. Rev.
ed. New York: MJF Books, 1972.

"Ads Accuse Democrats of Barring Catholics from Bench." *Orange
County Register*. July 24, 2003, News 9.

Allan, Kenneth and Jonathan H. Turner. "A Formalization of
Postmodern Theory." *Sociological Perspectives* 43:3, pp. 363-385.

Aristotle. *Nicomachean* Ethics. Tr. Martin Ostwald. New York: Bobbs-
Merrill, 1962.

"ASNE Survey: Journalists Say They're Liberal." *The American Editor*.
26 May 1999. American Society of Newspaper Editors.
http://www.asne.org/kiosk/editor/ 97.jan-feb/dennis4.htm.

Bacon, Francis. *The New Organon*. 1620. Reprint Indianapolis: Bobbs-
Merrill, 1960.

Behe, Michael. *Darwin's Black Box: The Biochemical Challenge to
Evolution*. New York: Free Press, 1996.

Bengtsson, Jan Olof. "Left and Right Eclecticism: Roger Kimball's
Cultural Criticism. *Humanitas* 14:1 (2001), pp. 23-46.

Bennett, William J. *The De-Valuing of America: The Fight for Our
Culture and Our Children*. New York: Summit, 1992.

Berlinski, David. "A Scientific Scandal? David Berlinski and Critics."
Commentary. Retrieved from http://www.commentary.org/
berlinski.htm.

Boa, Kenneth D. and Robert M. Bowman. *Faith Has Its Reasons: An
Integrative Approach to Defending Christianity*. Colorado Springs:
NavPress, 2001.

"Book Summary Notes on Nicholas Wolterstorff, *Reason Within the
Bounds of Religion*, 2nd ed. (Grand Rapids: Eerdmans, 1984)." In
*Discipleship and the Disciplines: Enhancing Faith-Learning
Integration*. Coalition for Christian Colleges and Universities,
1996.

Broad, William and Nicholas Wade. *Betrayers of the Truth: Fraud and
Deceit in the Halls of Science*. New York: Simon and Schuster,
1982.

Brother Lawrence. *The Practice of the Presence of God*. Tr. Donald
Atwater. Springfield, IL: Templegate, 1974.

Carr, David. "Husserl and Phenomenology." In Richard H. Popkin,
ed. *The Columbia History of Western Philosophy*. New York: MJF
Books, 1999.

Childers, Jeff. "Chapter 5 Summary, 'Christian Scholarship
Symposium at ACU on *The Outrageous Idea of Christian*

Scholarship by George Marsden.'" Abilene Christian University, Feb. 1999. Retrieved from http://www.acu.edu/academics/ adamscenter/resources/faithlearning/christianschool.html.

"Christophobia." Retrieved from http://home.infostations.com/ quietsun/athart6.htm.

Clark, Thomas W. "Humanism and Postmodernism: A Reconciliation." *The Humanist*, Jan-Feb 1993, pp. 18-23.

Cremo, Michael A. and Richard L. Thompson. *Forbidden Archeology: The Hidden History of the Human Race*. Rev. Ed., Los Angeles: Bhaktivedanta, 1998.

Cremo, Michael. *Forbidden Archeology's Impact*, 2nd. ed. Los Angeles: Bhaktivedanta, 2001.

Crews, Frederick C., ed. *Unauthorized Freud: Doubters Confront a Legend*. New York: Viking, 1998.

Culverwell, Nathaniel. *An Elegant and Learned Discourse of the Light of Nature* [1652]. Ed. Robert A. Greene and Hugh MacCallum. Toronto: University of Toronto, 1971.

Curtler, Hugh Mercer. "The Myopia of the Cultural Relativist." *The Intercollegiate Review* 38:1 (Fall 2002), pp. 35-43.

Custred, Glynn. "The Forbidden Discovery of Kennewick Man." *Academic Questions*. 13:3 (Summer 2000), pp. 12-30.

Darwin, Francis, ed. *The Life and Letters of Charles Darwin*. New York: D. Appleton, 1888.

"Darwinism: A Time for Funerals." *Contrast*. March-April 1983, pp. 4-5.

Davis, Edward B. "Some Comments on the Course, 'Introduction to Christianity and Science.'" Retrieved online at http://www.messiah.edu/pages/facstaff/davis/ course.html.

DeLashmutt, Gary and Roger Braund, "Postmodern Impact: Education." In Dennis McCallum, ed., *The Death of Truth*. Minneapolis: Bethany House, 1996.

Dembski, William. *Intelligent Design: The Bridge Between Science and Theology*. Downers Grove, IL: InterVarsity, 1999.

Dixon, Tom. "Postmodern Method: History." In Dennis McCallum, ed. *The Death of Truth*. Minneapolis: Bethany House, 1996.

D'Souza, Dinesh. *Illiberal Education: The Politics of Race and Sex on Campus*. New York: The Free Press, 1991.

————. *The End of Racism: Principles for a Multiracial Society*. New York: The Free Press, 1995.

Dupre, Louis. "Postmodernity or Late Modernity? Ambiguities in Richard Rorty's Thought. *The Review of Metaphysics* 47:2 (Dec. 1993), pp. 277-296.

Easterbrook, Greg. "Science Sees the Light." *The New Republic* 219:15 (Oct. 12, 1998), pp. 24-30.

Edgerton, Robert B. *Sick Societies: Challenging the Myth of Primitive Harmony.* New York: Free Press, 1992.

Eger, Martin. "A Tale of Two Controversies: Dissonance in the Theory and Practice of Rationality." *Zygon* 23:3 (September 1988), pp. 291-325.

Eliot, T. S. *Christianity and Culture: The Idea of a Christian Society and Notes Towards the Definition of Culture.* New York: Harcourt, 1948.

Ellis, Frank. "Political Correctness and the Ideological Struggle: From Lenin and Mao to Marcuse and Foucault." *Journal of Social, Political, and Economic Studies* 27:4 (Winter 2002), pp. 409-444.

Ellis, John M. *Against Deconstruction.* Princeton, NJ: Princeton University Press, 1989.

Etzioni, Amitai. *The Monochrome Society.* Princeton: Princeton University Press, 2001.

Fennick, John H. *Studies Show: A Popular Guide to Understanding Scientific Studies.* New York: Prometheus Books, 1997.

Feyerabend, Paul. *Against Method.* London: NLB, 1975.

—————. *Paul K. Feyerabend: Knowledge, Science, and Relativism, Philosophical Papers.* Vol. 3. Ed. John Preston. Cambridge: Cambridge University Press, 1999.

Fine, Gary Alan. "The Ten Commandments of Writing." *The American Sociologist* 19:2 (Summer 1998), pp. 152-157.

Fischer, David Hackett. *Historians' Fallacies: Toward a Logic of Historical Thought.* New York: Harper & Row, 1970.

Fonte, John. "Why There Is a Culture War." *Policy Review* 104, (Dec. 2000-Jan. 2001), pp. 15-31.

Fraser, David. "Book Summary Notes on David Gill, *The Opening of the Christian Mind: Taking Every Thought Captive to Christ.*" In *Discipleship and the Disciplines: Enhancing Faith-Learning Integration.* Coalition for Christian Colleges and Universities, 1996.

Freeman, Derek. *The Fateful Hoaxing of Margaret Mead: A Historical Analysis of Her Samoan Research.* Boulder, CO: Westview, 1999.

Gangel, Kenneth O. "Integrating Faith and Learning: Principles and Process." *Bibliotheca Sacra*, April-June, 1978. Retrieved online at http://www.ici.edu/journals/bibsac/7584/78b1.htm.

Genetics: Readings from Scientific American, With Introductions by Cedric I. Davern. San Francisco: W. H. Freeman, 1981.

Gilder, George. "The Materialist Superstition." *Intercollegiate Review* 21:2 (Spring 1996), pp. 6-14.

Gill, David. *The Opening of the Christian Mind: Taking Every Thought Captive to Christ*. Downers Grove, IL: InterVarsity, 1989.

Goldberg, Bernard. *Bias: A CBS Insider Exposes How the Media Distort the News*. Washington, D.C.: Regnery, 2002.

Greidanus, Sidney. "The Use of the Bible in Christian Scholarship." *Christian Scholar's Review* 11:2 (March 1982), pp. 138-147.

Groothuis, Douglas. "Defenders of the Faith." *Books and Culture*, July-August 2003, p. 12.

Harris, Trester S. Patients Are People, Too. *VirtualSalt*. Retrieved from http://www.virtualsalt.com/pp/.

Hasker, William. "Faith-Learning Integration: An Overview." *Christian Scholars Review* 21:3 (March 1992), pp. 231-248. Retrieved online at http://www.gospelcom.net/journals/csr/hasker.html.

——————. *Metaphysics: Constructing a World View*. Downers Grove, IL: InterVarsity, 1983.

Haughness, Norman and Thomas W. Clark. "Postmodern Anti-Foundationalism Examined." *The Humanist* July-Aug 1993, pp. 19-22.

Heath, Peter. *The Philosopher's Alice*. New York: St. Martin's, 1974.

Hecht, Jeff. "F Is for Fake." *New Scientist*. Feb. 19, 2000, p. 12.

Himmelfarb, Gertrude. "The Christian University: A Call to Counterrevolution." *Discipleship and the Disciplines: Enhancing Faith-Learning Integration*. Coalition for Christian Colleges and Universities, 1996.

——————. *Darwin and the Darwinian Revolution*. New York: W. W. Norton, 1962.

Hoffmann, Roald. "Why Buy That Theory?" *American Scientist* 91:1 (Jan-Feb 2003), pp. 9-11.

Hollander, Paul. "Marxism and Western Intellectuals in the Post-Communist Era." *Society* 37:2 (Jan-Feb 2000), pp. 22-28.

Hooper, Judith. *Of Moths and Men: The Untold Story of Science and the Peppered Moth*. New York: W. W. Norton, 2002.

Hoots, Rita. "Hooper, Judith. Of Moths and Men: An Evolutionary Tale." *Library Journal*, August 2002, p. 136.

Horowitz, David. "Missing Diversity on America's Campuses." *FrontPageMagazine.com*, Sept. 3, 2002. Retrieved from http://www.frontpagemag.com/articles/Printable.asp?ID=1003.

Huck, Schuyler W. and Howard M. Sandler. *Rival Hypotheses: Alternative Interpretations of Data Based Conclusions*. New York: Harper, 1979.

Huxley, Aldous. *Ends and Means: An Inquiry into the Nature of Ideals and into the Methods Employed for Their Realization.* New York: Harper, 1937.

Iannone, Carol. "PC with a Human Face." *Commentary* 96:6 (June 1993), pp. 44-48.

——————. "Sex and the Feminists." *Commentary* 96:3 (September 1993), pp. 51-54.

Ingram, David. "Continental Philosophy: Neo-Marxism." In Richard H. Popkin, ed. *The Columbia History of Western Philosophy.* New York: MJF Books, 1999.

"Industry-Sponsored Research Biased?" Orange County [California] *Register.* January 22, 2003, News 11.

Jaki, Stanley L. "From Scientific Cosmology to a Created Universe." In Roy Abraham Varghese, ed., *The Intellectuals Speak Out About God.* Chicago: Regnery, 1984.

——————. "Science: Western or What?" *Intercollegiate Review* 26:1 (Fall 1990), pp. 3-12.

Johnson, Phillip E. *Darwin on Trial.* Washington, D.C.: Regnery, 1991.

——————. *Objections Sustained: Subversive Essays on Evolution, Law & Culture.* Downers Grove, IL: InterVarsity, 1998.

——————. "The Religion of the Blind Watchmaker." *Christian Leadership Ministries.* Retrieved from http://www.clm.org/real/ri9203/watchmkr.html.

——————. *The Right Questions: Truth, Meaning, and Public Debate.* Downers Grove, IL: InterVarsity, 2002.

——————. *The Wedge of Truth: Splitting the Foundations of Naturalism.* Downers Grove, IL: InterVarsity, 2000.

Johnson, Samuel. "The Vision of Theodore, Hermit of Teneriffe." Retrieved from http://www.virtualsalt.com/lit/theodore.htm.

Jones, A. S. A. "The Games Skeptics Play." *Ex-Atheist.com.* Retrieved from http://www.ex-atheist.com/7.html.

Jones, Roger S. *Physics for the Rest of Us.* 1992. Reprint New York: Barnes and Noble, 1999.

Kearl, Michael. "Sociology of Knowledge." Retrieved from http://www.trinity.edu/~mkearl/knowledge.html.

Keas, Michael and Kerry Magruder. "Unified Studies Natural Science F-2002 Packet." Oklahoma Baptist University, 2002. Retrieved from http://www.okbu.edu/academics/natsci/us/311/pack.pdf.

Kimball, Roger. *Tenured Radicals: How Politics Has Corrupted Our Higher Education.* Chicago: Ivan R. Dee, 1998.

Knight, Robert H. *The Age of Consent: The Rise of Relativism and the Corruption of Popular Culture.* Dallas: Spence, 1998.

Kockelmans, Joseph J. "Continental Philosophy of Science." In Richard H. Popkin, ed. *The Columbia History of Western Philosophy*. New York: MJF Books, 1999.

Kohm, Lynn Marie. "What is a Christian University? or How to Achieve Preeminence as a Graduate Institution." Retrieved online at http://www.regent.edu/admin/cids/christianuniv.pdf.

Kohn, Alexander. *False Prophets*. Rev. ed., New York: Barnes and Noble, 1988.

Kors, Alan Charles and Harvey A. Silverglate. *The Shadow University: The Betrayal of Liberty on American Campuses*. New York: Harper Perennial, 1999.

Kreeft, Peter. *How to Win the Culture War*. Downers Grove, IL: InterVarsity, 2002.

Kuhn, Thomas S. *The Structure of Scientific Revolutions*. 2nd Ed. Chicago: University of Chicago, 1970.

Lawler, Peter Augustine. "Conservative Postmodernism, Postmodern Conservatism." *Intercollegiate Review* 38:1 (Fall 2002), pp. 16-25.

Leo, John. "Gender Wars Redux." *U. S. News & World Report*, Feb. 27, 1999, p. 24.

————. "Nobel Prize for Fiction?" *U. S. News & World Report*, Jan. 25, 1999, p. 17.

Limbaugh, David. *Persecution: How Liberals Are Waging War Against Christianity*. Washington, D.C.: Regnery, 2003.

Lunn, Arnold. *The Revolt Against Reason*. London: Eyre and Spottiswoode, 1950.

Macbeth, Norman. *Darwin Retried: An Appeal to Reason*. Ipswitch, MA: Gambit, 1971.

MacDougall, Curtis D. *Hoaxes*. 2nd Ed., New York: Dover, 1958.

McCallum, Dennis. *Christianity: The Faith that Makes Sense*. Wheaton: Tyndale House, 1992.

————, ed. *The Death of Truth*: Minneapolis: Bethany House, 1996.

McGrath, Alister. "The Christian Scholar in the 21st Century," Christian Leadership Ministries. Retrieved from http://www.clm.org/real/ri0002/mcgrath.html.

Madison, G. B. "Hermeneutics: Gadamer and Ricoeur." In Richard H. Popkin, ed. *The Columbia History of Western Philosophy*. New York: MJF Books, 1999.

Makkreel, Rudolf A. "The Problem of Values in the Late Nineteenth Century." In Richard H. Popkin, ed. *The Columbia History of Western Philosophy*. New York: MJF Books, 1999.

Marsden, George. *The Outrageous Idea of Christian Scholarship*. New York: Oxford University Press, 1997.

————. "The State of Evangelical Christian Scholarship." *Reformed Journal* 37:9 (Sept. 1987), pp. 12-16.

Martin, Jerry L. "Restoring American Cultural Institutions." *Society* 36:2 (Jan-Feb 1999), pp. 35-40.

May, Clifford D. "Chaos, Opportunity . . . and Caution in Africa." *Washington Times*. July 6, 2003.

Meyer, Stephen C. "The Origin of Life and the Death of Materialism." *Intercollegiate Review* 31:2 (Spring 1996), pp. 24-43.

Milton, Richard. "THES and Darwin: The Open Society and Its Enemies." June 26, 2002. http://www.alternativescience.com/thes_and_Richard_dawkins.htm.

Minogue, Kenneth. "'Christophobia' and the West." *New Criterion* 21:10 (June 2003), pp. 4-13.

Moore, Thomas J. *Deadly Medicine: Why Tens of Thousands of Heart Patients Died in America's Worst Drug Disaster*. New York: Simon and Schuster, 1995.

Moreland, J. P. "Academic Integration and the Christian Scholar." *The Real Issue*. Jan/Feb 2000, p. 9.

————. *Love Your God with All Your Mind: The Role of Reason in the Life of the Soul*. Colorado Springs: Navpress, 1997.

————. "Philosophical Apologetics, the Church, and Contemporary Culture." *Premise* 3:4 (April 29, 1996), pp. 6ff. Retrieved from http://capo.org/premise/96/april/p960406.html.

————. and William Lane Craig. *Philosophical Foundations for a Christian Worldview*. Downers Grove, IL: InterVarsity, 2003.

Motluk, Alison. "'Of Moths and Men,' by Judith Hooper." Salon.com Books. Sept. 18, 2002. *Salon.com*. Retrieved from http://www.salon.com/books/review/2002/09/ 18/hooper.

Nash, Ronald H. *Faith and Reason: Searching for a Rational Faith*. Grand Rapids: Zondervan, 1988.

————. *Worldviews in Conflict: Choosing Christianity in a World of Ideas*. Grand Rapids: Zondervan, 1992.

Nenon, Tom. "Martin Heidegger." In Richard H. Popkin, ed. *The Columbia History of Western Philosophy*. New York: MJF Books, 1999.

"Officials See Rise in Lab Fraud," Orange County [California] *Register*. January 22, 2003, News 13.

Olasky, Marvin. "Media Christophobia." *World* 17:16 (April 27, 2002). Retrieved from http://www.worldmag.com/world/issue/04-27-02/cover_3.asp.

Olson, Storrs L. Letter to Dr. Peter Raven. November 1, 1999. Retrieved from http://www.answersingenesis.org/docs/4159.asp?vPrint=1.

Pascal, Blaise. *Pensees*. Tr. Martin Turnell. New York: Harper & Row, 1962.

"Paul Ehrlich." *Overpopulation.com*. Retrieved from http://www.overpopulation.com/faq/people/paul_ehrlich.html.

Peterson, Michael. *With All Your Mind: A Christian Philosophy of Education*. Notre Dame: University of Notre Dame, 2001.

"Piltdown Bird." *EXN.ca* Retrieved from http://exn.ca/Templates/webisode.asp?story_id=2001033054.

Plantinga, Alvin. "Advice to Christian Philosophers." *Truth Journal*. Retrieved from http://www.leaderu.com/truth/1truth10.html.

—————. "Darwin, Mind, and Meaning." Retrieved from UCSB Faculty-Staff Christian Fellowship, http://id-www.ucsb.edu/fscf/library/plantinga/dennett.html.

—————. "Methodological Naturalism? Part One: Is Science Religiously Neutral? Three Examples." The Faculty-Staff Christian Forum at the University of California at Santa Barbara. Retrieved from http://id-www.ucsb.edu/fscf/library/plantinga/mn/MN1.html.

—————. "On Christian Scholarship." The Faculty-Staff Christian Forum at the University of California at Santa Barbara. Retrieved from http://id-www.ucsb.edu/fscf/library/plantinga/OCS.html.

—————. "Theism, Atheism, and Rationality." *Truth Journal*. Retrieved from http://www.leaderu.com/truth/3truth02.html.

"The Press Corps: Liberal, Liberal, Liberal." *Media Reality Check*. August 14, 2001. Media Research Center. http://www.mediaresearch.org/realitycheck/2001/20010814.asp.

Preston, John, ed. *Paul K. Feyerabend: Knowledge, Science and Relativism*. Philsophical Papers, Volume 3. Cambridge: Cambridge University Press, 1999.

Rea, Michael C. *World Without Design: The Ontological Consequences of Naturalism*. New York: Oxford University Press, 2002.

Rector, Robert E., Kirk A. Johnson, and Lauren R. Noyes. "Sexually Active Teenagers Are More Likely to Be Depressed and to attempt Suicide." A Report to the Heritage Center for Data Analysis. *The Heritage Foundation*. June 2, 2002. Retrieved from http://www.heritage.org/Research/Family/cda0304.cfm.

Roberts, J. M. *Twentieth Century: The History of the World, 1901 to 2000*. New York: Viking, 1999.

Rockmore, Tom. "Karl Marx." In Richard H. Popkin, ed. *The Columbia History of Western Philosophy*. New York: MJF Books, 1999.

Romey, William D. "Science as Fiction or Nonfiction?: A Physical Scientist's View from a General Semantics Perspective." *Et Cetera* 37:3 (Fall 1980), pp. 201-207.

Rudel, Thomas K. and Judith M. Gerson. "Postmodernism, Institutional Change, and Academic Workers: A Sociology of Knowledge." *Social Science Quarterly* 80:2 (June 1999), pp. 213ff.

Sandage, Allan. "A Scientist Reflects on Religious Belief." *Truth Journal*. Retrieved from http://www.leaderu.com/truth/1truth15.html.

Schlafly, Phyllis. *Feminist Fantasies*. Dallas: Spence Publishing, 2003.

Schmid, Randolph E. "Scientists Confirm Mistake: 'New' Dinosaur a Combination of 2 Mismatched Fossils." Associated Press. April 7, 2000. Retrieved from http://abcnews.go.com/sections/science/DailyNews/dino_mistke000407.html.

Scruton, Roger. "Why I Became a Conservative." *The New Criterion*. Retrieved from http://www.newcriterion.com/archive/21/feb03/burke.htm.

Shalit, Wendy. "A Ladies' Room of One's Own." *Commentary* 100:2 (August 1995), pp. 33-37.

Singer, Charles. *A History of Scientific Ideas*. 1959. Rpt., New York: Dorset, 1990.

Sloan, Christopher P. "Feathers for T. Rex? New Birdlike Fossils Are Missing Links in Dinosaur Evolution." *National Geographic*. November 1999, pp. 98-107.

Sokal, Alan and Jean Bricmont. *Fashionable Nonsense: Postmodern Intellectuals' Abuse of Science*. New York: Picador USA, 1998.

Solzhenitsyn, Alexander. "A World Split Apart," June 8, 1978. Retrieved from http://www.Columbia.edu/cu/Augustine/arch/Solzhenitsyn/harvard1978.html.

Sommers, Christina Hoff. *The War Against Boys: How Misguided Feminism Is Harming Our Young Men*. New York: Simon & Schuster, 2000.

————. *Who Stole Feminism?* New York: Simon and Schuster, 1994.

Sowell, Thomas. "Cultural Diversity: A World View." Retrieved from http://www.tsowell.com/spcultur.html.

————. "Morality Vs. Sanctimoniousness." Retrieved from http://www.tsowell.com/spmorali.html.

Stark, Rodney "False Conflict," *The American Enterprise* 14:7 (Oct./Nov. 2003), pp. 27-33.

Stein, Harry. *How I Accidentally Joined the Vast Right-Wing Conspiracy (And Found Inner Peace)*. New York: Delacorte, 2000.

Stolba, Christine. "Lying in a Room of One's Own: How Women's Studies Textbooks Miseducate Students." *Independent Women's Forum*, 2002. Retrieved from http://www.iwf.org/pdf/roomononesown.pdf.

Stoll, David. *Rigoberta Menchu and the Story of All Poor Guatemalans*. Boulder, CO: Westview, 1999.

Stroll, Avrum. "Twentieth-Century Analytic Philosophy." In Richard H. Popkin, ed. *The Columbia History of Western Philosophy*. New York: MJF Books, 1999.

Sykes, Charles J. *The Hollow Men: Politics and Corruption in Higher Education*. Washington, D.C: Regnery, 1990.

Torrey, E. Fuller. *Freudian Fraud: The Malignant Effect of Freud's Theory on American Thought and Culture*. 1992. Rpt. New York: Harper, 1993.

Varghese, Roy Abraham. *The Intellectuals Speak Out About God*. Chicago: Regnery Gateway, 1984.

Veith, Gene Edward Jr. *Postmodern Times: A Christian Guide to Contemporary Thought and Culture*. Wheaton, IL: Crossway Books, 1994.

Vitz, Paul C. *Faith of the Fatherless: The Psychology of Atheism*. Dallas: Spence Publishing, 1999.

Wells, Jonathan. "Catch-23." *Center for Science and Culture*. July 1, 2002. Retrieved from http://www.discovery.org.

Wells, Jonathan. "Critics Rave Over Icons of Evolution: A Response to Published Reviews." Center for Science and Culture, June 12, 2002. Retrieved from http://www.discovery.org.

—————. *Icons of Evolution: Science or Myth? Why Much of What We Teach About Evolution Is Wrong*. Washington, D. C.: Regnery, 2000.

West, John G. "The Death of Materialism and the Renewal of Culture." *Intercollegiate Review* 31:2 (Spring 1996), pp. 3-5.

Whalen, David M. "'A Little More than Kin and Less than Kind': The Affinity of Literature and Politics. *Intercollegiate Review* 37:1 (Fall 2001), pp. 22-30.

Wieland, Carl. "National Geographic Backs Down—Sort Of." *Answers in Genesis*. Retrieved from http://www.answersingenesis.org/docs2/4273news4-11-2999.asp?vPrint=1.

Wolterstorff, Nicholas. "The Mission of the Christian College at the End of the 20th Century." *Reformed Journal* 33:6 (June 1983), pp. 14-18.

——————. *Reason Within the Bounds of Religion.* 2nd ed. Grand Rapids: Eerdmans, 1984.

Xu Xing. "Feathers for T. Rex?" *National Geographic*, March 2000, n.p.

Zacharias, Ravi. *Jesus Among Other Gods: The Absolute Claims of the Christian Message.* Nashville: Word, 2000.

Zinsmeister, Karl. "The Shame of America's One-Party Campuses." *The American Enterprise*, Sept. 2002, 18-25.